D0964820

Her Own Words

To The Nuclear Age

The Memoirs of Sr. Lucia

With Comments
by
John M. Haffert

Let us remember that God performed a formidable unprecedented miracle *"so that everyone may believe"* this message.

Nihil Obstat: Rev. William Collins, OFM

Permission to print this book with the Nihil Obstat was granted by the Archdiocese of Miami, February, 18, 1992. This permission implies nothing more than that this book has been read by an Ecclesiastical examiner and that nothing was found herein contrary to faith and morals.

Published in the U.S., 1993

The 101 Foundation, Inc.
P.O. Box 151
Asbury, New Jersey 08802-0151
U.S.A.

Above: Pope Paul VI and Lucia. With arms still outstretched, His Holiness stepped back as though presenting Lucia to the almost one million pilgrims in the Cova, May 16, 1967. Left is Most. Rev. John Venancio, second Bishop of Fatima, one of the three great persons in the story of Fatima to whom this book is dedicated.

```
```

To Bishop John P. Venancio, D. D. — 1904 - 1985:

Before becoming the second Bishop of Fatima, The Most Rev. John P. Venancio was the head of the Episcopal Commission which investigated the events of Fatima. In 1967, after Pope Paul VI had visited Fatima on May 13 of that same year (50th anniversary of the apparitions), he accepted the position of International President of the World Apostolate of Fatima (The Blue Army). *It was the wish of this saintly bishop that the memoirs of Lucia should have the widest possible distribution* without monetary consideration. In his honor all proceeds of this work are offered as a gift to Our Lady. A dear friend on earth, he has become even dearer since (See SOUL, Nov. 1985, p. 8).

Above: Bishop Jose Correia da Silva, to whom Lucia addressed her memoirs, is shown inspecting the work during construction of the Basilica of Fatima in 1933. Speaking to the Bishop is Canon Galamba de Oliveira who is frequently mentioned in the memoirs and who made them available to John Haffert. Bishop da Silva gave Haffert permission to speak to Lucia in 1946 with a note to the effect that the American writer was to be received as though he (the Bishop) had come.

To Msgr. Canon Galamba De Oliveira — 1905 - 1984:

Over forty years before the publication of this book, Canon Oliveira (often mentioned in Lucia's memoirs) offered us the use of the Memoirs of Lucia. He was not only one of the closest advisors to the Bishop, but also a member of the Episcopal Commission for the investigation of the Fatima events and President of the World Apostolate of Fatima (The Blue Army) for Portugal. His help has been invaluable.

To Dr. Joachim Maria Alonso, C.M.F. — 1905 - 1981:

This Claretian from Spain was chosen by the Bishop of Fatima as the official documentarian of the Fatima events. Father Alonso suggested the division of Lucia's Memoirs followed in this book and wrote many of the notes. These notes are more important than mere references and *should be read along with the text.* Just before he died in 1981, Fr. Alonso was writing a book on the spirituality of The Blue Army. His documentation on Fatima fills 18 volumes. His popular books covered such subjects as the Third Secret of Fatima and the importance of the Fatima apparitions which took place in Spain, especially those at Pontevedra. He was a great and holy man to whom future generations will owe a debt greater than may ever be known.

Above: An unretouched photo of the three children at the time of the apparitions in 1917. Their lives had been threatened so they seem not only camera-shy but apprehensive. We can only imagine their usually frank, childlike and bright expressions.

iii.

O povo ora ajoelhado e olhando o alto

manifestações sobrenaturaes, sem temer que a invernia as prejudicasse, diminuindo-lhes o esp'endor e a imponencia... Vi que o desalento não invadiu as almas, que a confiança se conservou viva e ardente, a despeito das inesperadas contrariedades, que a compostura da multidão em que superabundavam os camponios foi perfeita e que as crianças, no seu entender privilegiadas, tiveram a acolhel-as as demonstrações do mais intenso carinho por parte d'aquele povo que ajoelhou, se descobriu e rezou a seu mandado ao aproximar-se a hora do «milagre», a hora do «sinal sensivel», a hora mistica e suspirada do contacto entre o céu e a terra...

E, quando já não imaginava que via alguma coisa mais impressionante do que essa rumorosa mas pacifica multidão animada pela mesma obcessiva idéa e movida pelo mesmo poderoso anceio, que vi eu ainda de verdadeiramente estranho na charneca de Fátima? A chuva, á hora prenunciada, deixar de cair; a densa massa de nuvens romper-se e o astro-rei—disco de prata fosca—em pleno zenith aparecer e começar dançando n'um bailado violento e convulso, que grande numero de pessoas imaginava ser uma dança serpentina, tão belas e rutilantes côres revestiu sucessivamente a superficie solar...

Milagre, como gritava o povo; fenomeno natural, como dizem sabios? Não curo agora de sabel-o, mas apenas de te afirmar o que vi... O resto é com a Ciencia e com a Egreja...

Avelino de Almeida.

As tres crianças que dizem ter a Virgem falado com elas.

May the angels be with you
as you read this book,
and may God grant you
the grace of finding
at least one word which
will inspire you to
a greater love for God
and an increased
personal holiness.

At Left: Portuguese magazine in October, 1917, reports the Miracle, concluding with the words: "I affirm only what I saw. The rest is with science and the Chruch." See other photo from the same article on page 8.

TABLE OF CONTENTS:

The English translation of the memoirs used in this book was made by the author. When compared to one French and two English translations, only minor differences in idioms and phrasing appeared.

viii.

FOREWORD

After interviewing Lucia in 1946 I was offered the use of her memoirs. It was expected that I would write a book on the story of the children and their apparitions at Fatima as told graphically and often poignantly by Lucia herself.

But I was taken up with the "March of Pledges" (later the Blue Army). Then other books based on the memoirs appeared and it no longer seemed necessary.

But the story grew in facts and in importance. More and more came to light and a new sense of urgency developed. This was heightened after the collegial consecration in 1984 and the subsequent changes in Russia.

As I had information from interviews with Lucia and had read almost every book on the subject in several different languages (some of which had never been translated into English), I saw an ever increasing need for this present book. When Dr. Joachim Alonso, the greatest of all experts on Fatima, came to me some years ago and offered me his complete notes on the memoirs and rights to publish them, I began this work which continued over several years.

Now in my 77th year, I had thought it might be published after my death. However, as 1992 ushered in the 75th anniversary of Fatima and the Communist revolution in Russia, we saw the world gaping in hope before the sudden dissolution of the Soviet Union and in shock at the loss of a central control of its 30,000 nuclear weapons.

Could any moment in history call more urgently for a factual review of this most important message of our time? May it be eagerly received by the millions who respond to the appeal of Pope John Paul II to enter the 21st century "in advent with Mary."

John M. Haffert

Chapter I.

Comments On

FATIMA IN THE NUCLEAR AGE

I was only five years younger than little Jacinta on August 13, 1917, when the three children of Fatima were taken to jail and threatened *to be fried in boiling oil if they would not reveal a "secret"* told to them by Our Lady of Fatima. The oldest of the three children who faced this threat of death on August 13, 1917, was Lucia, only ten years old.

Two of the children (Francisco and Jacinta) expected to die because two months before Our Lady had told them She would "come soon" to take them to Heaven. But Lucia had been told by Our Lady that she was to remain on earth. Therefore, among the first questions which came to my mind when I interviewed her thirty-nine years later were:

...how did *she personally* feel (after Francisco and Jacinta had been taken out to be *boiled* alive in oil) and then, at last, they came to take her to the same painful death?

...and why would atheists place such emphasis upon the *secret* of Fatima?

Francisco and Jacinta faced the ultimatum of either death in *boiling oil* or telling the "secret" with the consolation that now Our Lady was going to come for them. They assured each other that it would be painful only for a short time. Then they would be able to see Her all the time, and not just on the 13th of the month when She had been appearing to them.

So what did Lucia think at that moment, considering that Our Lady had said:

"*You are to remain on earth. God wishes to establish devotion in the world to my Immaculate Heart.*" Lucia was to learn to read and write! As you are about to read this book, stop and think of that for a moment:

Even though Francisco and Jacinta were soon going to Heaven, Lucia had something very important to write down so that in the years to come a desire of God would be fulfilled: Devotion to the Immaculate Heart of Mary would be made known to the world.

So I asked her, "Sister, what did you think when Francisco and Jacinta had been taken out, expecting to die in a vat of boiling oil?"

Her answer surprised me. She said:

"*At that moment I thought Francisco and Jacinta were already dead* and I thought that perhaps I had misunderstood Our Lady. *I thought that I too was about to die.*"

When she had said this, there was a long moment of silence while I grasped the awesome fact that these three little children had really been dry *martyrs.*

The ultimate power of the tyrant over life and death had failed, not only against the children's faith in having seen an apparition of the Mother of The Savior, but also against their fidelity to the "secret" She had imparted to them.

Importance of Her Words

Since it was only a few years later (when indeed Francisco and Jacinta had been taken to Heaven) Lucia *actually did reveal a great part of that "secret,"* one wonders why it might not have been revealed to those atheists. Oh, how precious to the world must be every word that Lucia finally put to paper after she had learned not only to read, but had been able to ponder in her heart the great and stunning message which God chose to reveal to the world through her as mankind teetered on the brink of nuclear war.

The Terrible Secret

In that "secret" Our Lady foretold the rise of militant atheism which would spread "from an atheist Russia throughout the entire world fomenting further wars... and several entire nations will be annihilated."

I was tempted to call this book *Fatima And Nuclear War*, but greater than the terrible prophecy of "annihilation of several entire nations" is the secret's fantastic promise: If men listen to this message from Heaven, not only would the atheist leadership in Russia *be converted*, but there would be *"an era of peace."*

Think of it! Depending on the world's response to this message, the nuclear age could be one of destruction in which "the living will envy the dead," or of that peace of which the angels sang over Bethlehem.

Our Lady, gentle Mother who stood beneath the Cross on Calvary, has brought from Heaven from Her Divine Son a message of *change.* When we ponder the fullness of Her message, we see that the conversion of militant atheists can mean also a conversion of the atomic age... from the annihilation of entire nations to an era of peace and prosperity perhaps *never before seen in the history of the world.*

Thousands of Nuclear Bombs

Less than twelve months after an atomic bomb (dropped by my own government) destroyed the city of Hiroshima, I first interviewed Lucia. Like every other man, woman, and child of the world at that moment, I was in awe of the destructive power man had discovered.

I felt a certain hope because this power rested in the hands of the United States of America which I felt sure would never use it except to maintain peace and freedom. But now after the breakup of the Soviet

Union in the decade before the year 2000, some 30,000 of these incredibly destructive weapons were without any central control... and several smaller nations had already acquired them. So, the likelihood of a nuclear holocaust was not lessened by the changes in Russia.

Before those changes there was a "nuclear peace" in a frightful balance of superpowers. And as we shall see later, Lucia herself commented that the changes in Russia were "too late" to make the era of peace possible without a greater response to the urgent message of Fatima.[1] The warning of Our Lady of Akita, given on the anniversary of the miracle of Fatima and made known to the world just before the changes in Russia, sounded the ultimate alarm.

Earth-shaking Importance

In this light, what you are about to read in these pages is of earth-shaking importance.

And even after we finally come into the era of peace... the era of the triumph of the Immaculate Heart of Mary... the message will continue to be urgent because we cannot expect all men and women and children on earth to enter that glorious era of Christian triumph as a single body. The formula of holiness given to us by our Heavenly Mother at Fatima will have to be taken by each one, one by one, to bring each into the era of Divine Love... the era of the triumph of the Heart of our Heavenly Mother.

Before that triumph, it seems that all the world must tremble before a threat of death not unlike that which those three children faced on the morning of August 15, 1917.

What gave them their heroic courage? I was invited to discover their secret back in 1946. I was invited to read the *Memoirs of Sister Lucia,* written by her under obedience.

5.

At that time, just as it was perhaps too early to appreciate the full meaning of the atomic bomb, so it was too early for me to appreciate the full meaning of these writings for which Lucia was "to remain on earth." The sublime messenger from Heaven, the Mother of Jesus Himself, had told her that she was to learn *to read and to write,* and as far as we then knew, *everything* she had written was in these Memoirs.

In them is an incredible lesson of courage and an enormous challenge. But there was much more to be learned, as I myself came to realize during my interviews with Lucia in 1946 and when I talked to eyewitnesses of the Fatima miracle.

On the same day after the children had been released from the jail in Ourem, Our Lady reassured them that the miracle She had promised to perform on October 13 *(so that everyone may believe)* would indeed take place. But She added that because of what those evil men had done to them, *the miracle would not be as great* as Heaven had intended.

One must wonder what the miracle *would* have been, when indeed *it turned out to be the greatest miracle in two thousand years!* Over 100,000 people gathered on the mountain of Fatima were terrified by what seemed to be the sun falling upon the earth. Many thought it was the end of the world. It was seen up to 32 miles away!

After I wrote a book about that miracle in 1960 (based on interviews with over 200 living witnesses)[2] I came to the conclusion that it is impossible for *anyone* really to understand its impact without having actually witnessed it.

It was the first miracle in the history of the world at a predicted time and place "so that everyone might believe."

Never before, *never,* had God permitted any prophet or seer to announce to the world that witnesses should be at a certain place, at a certain time, to see something beyond the laws of nature... attributable only to God Himself, and performed for the sole purpose of *confirming belief* in a message from Heaven!

Yet what a few atheists did to three children resulted in God's decision to make that miracle less than had been intended. Let us stop and think of that for a moment.

What *Might* Have Been!

Our Lady had foretold that error would spread from "an atheist Russia" throughout the entire world, but that finally Her Immaculate Heart would triumph and an era of peace would come. Content with the promise, *many of us have done little to stop that avalanche of evil* which little by little began to engulf the world and to turn it more and more from God. And with what consequences? *What blessings might we have had* if we had responded to the message of Fatima with *timely* faith? How much sooner we would have seen changes in Eastern Europe! How much sooner would we see a world truly free of the fear of war?

Reason For This Book:
Not Everything Contained in Memoirs

The actual Memoirs of Lucia, which contained what Our Lady left her on earth to write, were for many years available only to a select few... mostly writers like myself. Even though we were free to quote from them at length, the Memoirs were never made available to the general public until a Portuguese Jesuit, Father Antonio Martins, obtained them from the Sanctuary at Fatima and published them in their entirety in an enormous book with a photocopy of the actual writings of Lucia in her own hand on one side of the page, and a translation into three languages on the facing page.

The impact on readers of Lucia's own complete words was nothing less than stunning. Subsequently the Sanctuary at Fatima published the entire Memoirs, edited by Father Joachim Alonso, C.M.F. (official documentarian of Fatima) in a small popular paperback edition.[3] A few years before his death, Father Alonso gave me "exclusive rights" to his edition in the English language. Most of the footnotes in this book were prepared by him.

Since the Memoirs were already available in English exactly as Lucia wrote them, what seemed most needed now was a presentation *in the context of other statements of Lucia* and of the historical events. For example, the Memoirs have no description of the great miracle because the three children were seeing a series of Heavenly visions and were only aware of the miracle from the shouts of the people.

In a four-hour interview with Lucia in 1946, I myself asked some pertinent questions to which I had not found the answers in the Memoirs themselves. For example, she had not thought to mention how *she felt* when Francisco and Jacinta were taken out to be fried in boiling oil. From her Memoirs we would never have known that she, too, on that day was truly a dry martyr.

Nuclear Connections

But most important is the clarification by Lucia, during interviews, of the Fatima message... *exactly what must be done in order to avoid the annihilation of nations* and to bring about the era of peace. The "Nuclear Connection" in the Fatima Message was not evident in 1917.

It was unknown when Lucia wrote the Memoirs. She was merely telling frankly and honestly what

O MILAGRE DE FÁTIMA

Varios aspectos do povo ajoelhado e orando no momento de descobrir o sol e de se
dar o fenomeno que tanto impressionou a multidão.

no vagalhão colossal d'aquele povo que ali se juntou a 13 de outubro. O teu racionalismo sofreu um formidavel embate e quer s estabelecer uma opinião segura socorrendo-te de depoimentos ins eitos com o meu, pois que estive lá apenas no desempenho de uma missã bem di icil, tal a de relatar imparcia mente para um grande diario, O Seculo, os fact s que diante de mim se desenrolassem e tud quanto de curioso e d elucidativo a eles se prendesse. Não ficará por satisfazer o teu desejo, mas decerto que os nossos olhos e os nossos ouvidos não viram nem ouviram coisas diversas, e que raros foram os que ficaram insensiveis á grandeza de semelhante espectaculo, unico entre nós e de todo o ponto digno de meditação e de estudo...

(Carta a alguem que pede um testemunho insuspeito).

Quebrando um silencio de mais de vinte anos e com a invocação dos longinquos e saudosos tempos em que convivemos n'uma fraternal camaradagem, ilumi nada então p la fé comum e fortalecida por identicos propositos, escreves-me para que te diga, sincera e minuciosamente, o que vi e ouvi na ch rneca de Fátima, quando a fama de celestes aparições congregou n'aquele desolado ermo dezenas de milhares de pessoas mais sedentas, segundo creio, de sobrenatural do que impelidas por mera curiosidade ou receosas de um l gro... Estão os catolicos em desacordo sobre a importancia e a significação do que presenciaram. Uns convenceram-se de que se tinham cumprido prometimentos do Alto; outros acham-se ainda longe de acreditar na incontroversa realidade de um milagre. Foste um crente na tua juventude e deixaste de sel-o. Pessoas de familia arrastaram-te a Fátima,

O que ouvi e me levou a Fátima? Que a Virgem Mar a, depois da festa da Ascensão, aparecera a tres crianças que apascentavam gado, duas mocinhas e um zagalete, recomendando-lhes que orassem e prometendo-lhes aparecer ali, sobr uma azinheira, no dia 13 de cada mez, até que em outubro lhes daria qualquer si nal do poder de Deus e faria revelações. Espalhou-se a nova p r muitas leguas em redondez voou, de terra em terra, até os con ins de Portugal, e a roma-

she and her cousins experienced... exactly what they heard as the "message from Heaven."

The most dramatic connection, the so-called "miracle of the sun," was for her eclipsed by the visions she saw during the phenomenon which we now know was something like an atomic fireball plunging upon the world.

Only a month before the Communist coup in Russia, Our Lady of Fatima foretold that "error would spread from an atheist Russia through the entire world, fomenting further wars"... and this was to be *after a war worse than World War I,* which was at its peak at the very time of the Fatima apparitions!

No one could have foreseen that Russia would lead the world into a nuclear armament race creating enough weapons to destroy life on earth. Yet well in advance, Our Lady of Fatima foretold the ultimate outcome (if men ignored this message):

"Several entire nations will be annihilated."

Seeming End of the World

Who in 1917 would have believed that any weapons might be developed which could *annihilate* entire nations... today a reality? And even one or two small nations could set it off.

Now we know there are two "nuclear connections" in the Fatima Message. After the "sun miracle" performed at Fatima, October 13, 1917 "so that all may believe," Our Lady also predicted the "great sign" of January 25-26, 1938... which Lucia herself witnessed and mentions in the Memoirs.

To write a book about the "sun miracle" of 1917, as said before, I interrogated dozens upon dozens of living witnesses to recreate *what actually happened.* This event, unprecedented in the history of the world, was at once so awesome and terrible that it is virtually impossible for anyone who was not there to *realize* how terrifying it was. A *fireball,* which the crowd thought was actually the sun, plunged towards the earth over the mountain of Fatima. It was *objectively* real. It was not something created in the imagination of those tens of thousands of witnesses. *Everyone* saw it! Furthermore, it was seen over a radius of 32 miles. *Everyone* who saw it, at least within a six-mile radius, *thought it was the end of the world... and they felt the heat.*

The Great Sign

But then came a second miracle, even more significant to our nuclear age: The *"great sign"* which Our Lady said would indicate that all *the prophecies She had made were about to unfold upon the world* (another, more terrible war, followed by the spread of error from an atheist Russia throughout the world fomenting still further wars, and leading eventually to *the annihilation of several entire nations).*

When that "great sign" appeared in 1938, *there were not merely tens of thousands who thought the world was about to end, but millions.* Over all of Europe (eastward to the Urals, westward to Bermuda and beyond, northward to the Arctic and southward into North Africa) the *world seemed to be on fire* on the night of January 25-26, 1938.

All trans-Atlantic cable communication was interrupted from 8 o'clock that night until 11 o'clock the following morning. For that reason the amazing descriptions in U.S. papers (e.g., *The New York Times*) appeared only the day after.

The newspapers opined it was probably an extraordinary aurora borealis. But Lucia, who had been left on earth not only to write the Memoirs but also to be a continuing link of communication between heaven and earth, said *if scientists would investigate,* they would find that it *could not have been an aurora bo-*

realis... that it was indeed "the great sign" Our Lady had predicted.

False Aurora of Nuclear Blast

It was not until 1980 that a nuclear physicist in communication with other scientists discovered that the phenomenon of 1938 was not like a natural aurora, *but like the false aurora created by atomic explosion only recently discovered!*

Perhaps nothing underlines the *timeliness* of the Message of Fatima as much as the fact that the "great sign" was not "discovered" to be a great sign *until the 1980s!* Then the World Apostolate of Fatima sponsored a major motion picture (*A State of Emergency*) based upon the true life experience of the nuclear physicist who had discovered the connection between the "great sign" of 1938 and the aurora created by a nuclear explosion. The film was produced to give "the great sign" its meaning because *a sign is not a sign unless it is recognized as such.*

If I am driving down a road and there is a sign with a "Bridge Out" warning... and if the sign is so obscured by trees that I do not see it... I will probably plunge ahead into the chasm. The "great sign" of 1938 was indeed obscured to almost all the world until the nuclear armament race had gone so far that scientists from both Russia and America were talking of the "nuclear winter."

Is this all quite unbelievable? Yet somehow, as we read the simple words of Lucia, their candor and absolute honesty bring us into the reality which she and her cousins experienced. And in that realm a hope begins to dawn. What you are now about to read in the next chapter is Lucia's own explanation of how she came to write the memoirs, and her own description of her heroic little cousin Jacinta. So that you may properly esteem these words, let us remember constantly as we read them that Lucia was chosen from among the three children to *remain on earth specifically so that these words could be written.*

"So That Everyone May Believe"

Let us remember also that God performed a formidable, unprecedented miracle *"so that everyone may believe"* what is contained in these words. Furthermore, Lucia has told us that she could feel the Divine Presence when writing... that she was "helped" by God.

The readers will be surprised at the absolute candor and simplicity of this writing. Father Alonso, the official documentarian of the Fatima events, remarked: "She appears to be seeing rather than remembering. And the ease of her remembering is indeed so great that she seems only to have to read, as it were, from her own soul."

This firsthand account of Lucia (or rather the first long document from her hand) was begun in the second week of December 1935, and completed on Christmas Day... *a period of less than three weeks.*

On the previous September 12, the body of Jacinta had been taken from the cemetery in Ourem to Fatima and when the tomb was opened the body was found intact. Some photographs were sent to Lucia by the Bishop of Fatima. At that time she was in the convent of the Dorothean Sisters in Spain. (This convent is now administered by the World Apostolate of Fatima and has become a world center of devotion to the Immaculate Heart of Mary.)

On November 17, when Lucia wrote to the Bishop to thank him for the photographs, she said:

"I can never express how much I value them, especially those of Jacinta. I felt like removing the wrappings (from the body) in order to see all of her... I was so enraptured! My joy of seeing the friend of my childhood was again so great... she was a child only in years. As to the rest, she already knew how to be virtuous, and to show God and the Most Holy Virgin her love through sacrifice..."

These recollections caused the Bishop to request Lucia to *write down everything she could remember about Jacinta.* These first writings opened the door to all the other innocent and yet profound revelations you are about to read.

✝✝✝

[1.] In a letter to her confessor dated May 18, 1936, (from the convent in Pontevedra), Lucia wrote that the collegial consecration and the conversion of Russia were delayed because of the sins of the world and the lack of response to the message of Fatima. She said: "Pray very much for the Holy Father. He will do it (the collegial consecration), but it will be too late. Nevertheless the Immaculate Heart of Mary will save Russia. It has been entrusted to Her."

In an interview on May 14, 1981, after the Pope made the consecration at Fatima, Lucia made a similar statement and said that if the triumph of the Immaculate Heart of Mary was to be obtained without the great chastisement there would have to be a much greater response to the urgent message of Fatima (see p. 307).

[2.] *Meet the Witnesses,* 1961, A.M.I. Press, Washington, New Jersey 07882

[3.] Rev. Dr. Joachim Maria Alonso, C.M.F. was chosen by the Bishop of Leiria/Fatima to gather together and evaluate all the documents of the Apparitions and he worked at Fatima over a period of many years. His total work fills eighteen volumes.

Chapter II.

In the First Memoir —
Lucia Remembers

JACINTA

In her first Memoir, Lucia writes to her bishop mentioning some of her thoughts regarding Jacinta.

✝✝✝

Having implored the protection of the most holy Hearts of Jesus and of Mary, our tender Mother, and having sought light and grace at the foot of the tabernacle, so as not to write anything which would not be exclusively for the glory of Jesus and of the most Blessed Virgin, I now take up this work in spite of the repugnance I feel since I can say almost nothing about Jacinta without speaking either directly or indirectly about my miserable self.

Nevertheless I obey the will of Your Excellency[1] which, for me, is the expression of the Will of our good God, and I begin this task asking the most holy Hearts of Jesus and Mary to deign to bless it, and to make use of this act of obedience to obtain the conversion of poor sinners, for whom Jacinta so generously sacrificed herself.

I know Your Excellency does not expect a well-written account from me, for you know my inadequacy.

I am going to tell you, then, what I can remember about this soul for, by God's grace, I was her most intimate confidante and have most tender memories and esteem for her great holiness.

Keeping Secrets

In spite of my good will to be obedient, I trust Your Excellency will permit me to withhold certain matters concerning myself as well as Jacinta that I would not wish to be read before I enter eternity. Your Excellency will not find it strange that I should reserve for eternity certain secrets and other matters. After all, is it not the Blessed Virgin Herself who sets me the example? Does not the Holy Gospel tell us that Mary kept all things in Her heart?[2] And who better than this Immaculate Heart could have revealed to us the secrets of Divine Mercy? Nonetheless, She kept them to Herself as in a garden enclosed, and took them with Her to the palace of the Divine King.

I remember yet another saying I heard from a venerable priest when I was only eleven years old. Like so many others, he came to question me. He asked among other things about a matter of which I did not wish to speak. After he had exhausted his whole repertoire of questions on this subject without succeeding in obtaining a satisfactory answer, realizing that he was perhaps touching on too delicate a matter, the good priest gave me his blessing and said:

"You are right, my child. The secret of the King's Daughter should remain hidden in the depths of Her Heart."

At the time I did not understand the meaning of what he said, but I realized that he approved of my manner of acting. I did not forget his words, and now I understand them.

This venerable priest was at that time Vicar of Torres Novas.[3] Little does he know all the good that these few words did for my soul. That is why I remember him with such gratitude. One day, how-

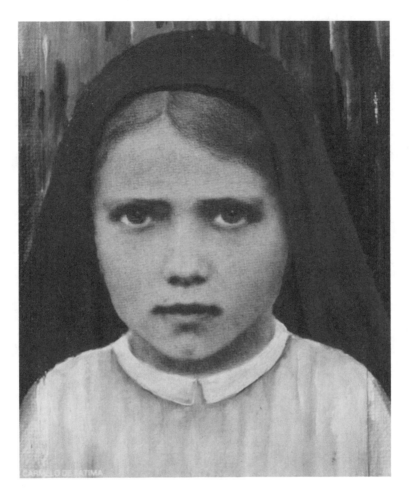

ever, I sought the advice of a holy priest regarding my reserve in such a matter because I did not know how to answer when they asked me if the most Blessed Virgin had not told me anything else as well. This priest, who was then Vicar of Olival,[4] said to us:

"You do well, my little ones, to keep for God and yourselves the secret of your souls. When they put that question to you, just answer: 'Yes, She did say more, but it is a secret.' If they question you further

on this subject, think of the secret that this Lady made
known to you, and say: 'Our Lady told us not to say
anything to anyone; for this reason, we are saying
nothing.' In this way, you can keep your secret under
Our Lady's shelter."

How well I understood the explanation and guid-
ance of this venerable old priest!

I am already taking too much time with these
preliminaries. Your Excellency will be wondering
what is the purpose of it all. I must see if I can make
a start with my account of what I can remember of
Jacinta's life. As I have no free time at my disposal,
I must make the most of the hours when we work in
silence, to recall and jot down on a bit of paper with
a pencil which I keep hidden under my sewing, all that
the most holy Hearts of Jesus and Mary want me to
remember.

TO JACINTA

Oh dear one from earth
Gone quick as in flight!
Jacinta my dear,
Who won the great fight
For love of Our Lord!
Forget not my plea
Be ever my friend
Before the bright throne
Of Heaven's great Queen.
O Lily so pure
O pearl shining bright
While there up above
Triumphant in light,
(That angel of love,
Your brother, there too)
Remember me now
To Jesus with you.[5]

Jacinta's Natural Characteristics

Before the events of 1917, apart from the family relationship that united us, no other particular affection led me to prefer the companionship of Jacinta and Francisco to that of any other child. On the contrary, I sometimes preferred to avoid Jacinta's company on account of her over-sensitive temperament.

The slightest quarrel which arose among the children when at play was enough to send her pouting into a corner, "to tie the donkey" as we used to say. The coaxing and caressing children know so well how to give on such occasions were not enough. She herself had to be allowed to choose the game, and her partner as well. Her heart, however, was well disposed. God had endowed her with a sweet and gentle character which made her at once lovable and attractive.

I don't know why, but Jacinta and her brother Francisco almost always came in search of me when they wanted to play. They did not enjoy the company of the other children, and they used to ask me to go with them to the well belonging to my parents.

Once we arrived there, Jacinta chose which games we were to play. The ones she liked best were usually "pebbles" and "buttons," which we played as we sat on the stone slabs covering the well in the shade of an olive tree and two plum trees. Playing "buttons" often left me in great distress, because when they called us into meals I used to find myself minus my buttons.

More often than not, Jacinta had won them all and this was enough to make my mother scold me. I had to sew them on again in a hurry. But how could I persuade Jacinta to give them back to me, since beside her pouty ways she had another little defect... she was possessive!

Ti Marto (in cap) poses with some children visiting the well where his little Francisco and Jacinta, together with Lucia, went so often.

She wanted to keep all the buttons for the next game so as to avoid taking off her own! It was only by threatening never to play with her again that I succeeded in getting them back!

Not a few times, I found myself unable to do what my little friend wanted. One of my older sisters was a weaver and the other a seamstress, and both were home all day. The neighbors, therefore, used to ask my mother if they could leave their children in my parents' yard, while they themselves went out to work in the fields. The children stayed with me and played while my sisters kept an eye on us.

My mother was always willing to do this, although it meant a great loss of time for my sisters. I was therefore charged with amusing the children, and watching to see that they did not fall into the well in the yard.

Three large fig trees sheltered the children from the scorching sun. We used their branches for swings, and an old threshing floor for a dining room. On days like these, when Jacinta came with her brother to invite me to go with them to our favorite retreat, I used to tell them I could not go because my mother had ordered me to stay where I was. Then, disappointed but resigned, the two little ones joined in our games. At siesta time, my mother used to give her children their catechism lessons, especially when Lent was drawing near, for as she said:

"I don't want to be ashamed of you when the priest questions you on your catechism at Easter time."

All the other children were present at our catechism lessons and Jacinta was there as well.

Her Sensitiveness

One day one of these children accused another of improper talk. My mother reproved him very severely, pointing out that one does not say such ugly things because they are sinful and displease the Child Jesus, and that those who commit such sins and don't confess them go to hell. Little Jacinta did not forget the lesson. The very next time the children came, she said:

"Will your mother let you come away with us today?"

"No."

"Then I'm going with Francisco over to our yard."

"And why won't you stay here?"

"My mother doesn't want us to stay when those other children are here. She told us to go and play in our own yard. She does not want me to learn these ugly things which are sins and which the Child Jesus doesn't like." Then she whispered in my ear:

"If your mother lets you, will you come to my house?"

"Yes."

"Then go and ask her." And taking her brother by the hand, she went home.

Speaking of Jacinta's favorite games, one of them was "Forfeits." The loser has to do whatever the winner tells him. Jacinta loved to send the loser chasing after butterflies, to catch one and bring it to her. At other times, she demanded some flower of her own choosing.

Her Love for the Crucified Savior

One day, we were playing forfeits at my home and I won... so this time it was I who told her what to do. My brother was sitting at a table, writing. I told her to give him a hug and a kiss, but she protested:

"That, no! Tell me to do some other thing. Why don't you tell me to go and kiss Our Lord over there?"

There was a crucifix hanging on the wall.

"All right," I answered, "get up on a chair, bring the crucifix over here, kneel down and give Him three hugs and three kisses: one for Francisco, for me, and the other for yourself."

"To Our Lord, yes, I'll give as many as you like," and she ran to get the crucifix. She kissed it and hugged it with such devotion that I have never forgotten it. Then, looking attentively at the figure of Our Lord, she asked:

"Why is Our Lord nailed to a cross like that?"

"Because He died for us."

"Tell me how it happened," she said.

In the evenings my mother used to tell stories. My father and my older sisters told us fairy stories about magic spells and princesses robed in gold and royal little doves. Then my mother would bring in stories of the Passion, St. John the Baptist, and so on. That is how I came to know the story of Our Lord's Passion.

As it was enough for me to have heard a story once

to be able to repeat it in all its details, I began to tell my companions, word for word, what I used to call Our Lord's Story. Just then, my sister[6] passed by and noticed that we had the crucifix[7] in our hands. She took it from us and scolded us, saying that she did not want us to touch such holy things. Jacinta got up and approached my sister saying:

"Maria, don't scold her! I did it. But I won't do it again."

My sister caressed her, and told us to go and play outside, because we left nothing in its proper place. Off we went to continue our story down at the well which I have already mentioned. As it was hidden behind some chestnut trees and a heap of stones and bushes, we chose this spot some years later for our more intimate talks, our fervent prayers, and (to tell all) our tears as well... and sometimes very bitter tears they were. We mingled our tears with the waters of the same well from which we drank. Would this well not be an image of Mary, in whose Heart we dried our tears and drank of the purest consolation?

But let us come back to our story. When the little one heard me telling of the sufferings of Our Lord, she was moved to tears. From then on she often asked me to tell it to her all over again. She would weep and grieve, saying:

"Our poor dear Lord! I'll never sin again! I don't want Our Lord to suffer anymore!"

Her Delicate Sensibility

Jacinta also loved going out at nightfall to the threshing floor situated close to the house. There she watched the beautiful sunsets and contemplated the starry skies.

She was enraptured with the lovely moonlit nights. We vied with each other to see who could count the most stars. We called the stars Angels' lamps, the moon Our Lady's lamp and the sun Our Lord's. This led Jacinta to remark sometimes:

"You know, I like Our Lady's lamp better; it doesn't burn us up or blind us, the way Our Lord's does."

Indeed the sun can be very strong there on summer days and Jacinta, a delicate child, suffered greatly from the heat.

As my sister[8] belonged to the Sodality of the Sacred Heart of Jesus, every time a children's solemn Communion came round she took me along to renew my own. On one occasion my aunt took her little daughter to see the ceremony and Jacinta was fascinated by the "angels" strewing flowers.

From that day on she sometimes left us when we were playing to gather an apron full of flowers. Then she came back and strewed them over me, one by one.

"Jacinta, why on earth are you doing that?"

"I'm doing what the little angels do. I'm strewing you with flowers."

Every year on a big feast, probably Corpus Christi, my sister used to prepare the dresses for the children chosen to represent the angels in the procession. They walked beside the canopy strewing flowers. I was always among the ones chosen. One day after my sister had tried on my dress, I told Jacinta all about the coming feast and how I was going to strew flowers before Jesus.

Will We See Him?

The little one begged me to ask my sister to let her go as well. The two of us went along to make our request. My sister said she could go, and tried a dress on Jacinta. At the rehearsals she explained how we were to strew the flowers before the Child Jesus.

"Will we see Him?" asked Jacinta.

"Yes," replied my sister, "the parish priest will be carrying Him."

Jacinta jumped for joy and kept on asking how much longer we had to wait for the feast. The longed-for day arrived at last. Jacinta was beside herself with excitement. The two of us took our places near the altar.

Later in the procession, we walked beside the canopy, each of us with a basket of flowers. Wherever my sister told us to strew flowers, I strewed mine before Jesus, but in spite of all the signs I made to Jacinta, I couldn't get her to strew a single one. She kept her eyes fixed on the priest, and that was all. When the ceremony was over my sister took us outside the church and asked:

"Jacinta, why didn't you strew your flowers before Jesus?"

"Because I didn't see Him."

Jacinta then asked me: "But did you see the Child Jesus?"

"Of course not. Don't you know that the Child Jesus in the Host can't be seen? He's hidden! He's the one we receive in Communion!"

"And you, when you go to Communion, do you talk to Him?"

"Yes, I do."

"Then, why don't you see Him? I'm going to ask my mother to let me go to Communion too."

"The parish priest won't let you go until you're ten years old."[9]

"But you're not ten yet, and you go to Communion!"

"Because I know the whole catechism, and you don't."

After this, my two companions asked me to teach them the catechism so I became their catechist, and they learned with exceptional enthusiasm. But though I could always answer any questions put to me, when it came to teaching, I could only remember a few things here and there. This led Jacinta to say to me one day:

"Teach us some more things; we know all those."

I had to admit that I could remember things only when people questioned me on them, and I added:

"Ask your mother to let you go to the church to learn your catechism."

The two children, who so ardently desired to receive the "hidden Jesus," as they called Him, went to ask their mother. My aunt agreed but she rarely let them go there, for she said:

"The church is a good way from here (about a mile) and you are very small. In any case, the priest won't give you Holy Communion before you're ten years old."

Jacinta never stopped asking me questions about the Hidden Jesus and I remember how, one day, she asked me:

"How is it that so many people receive the little Hidden Jesus at the same time? Is there one small piece for each person?"

"Not at all! Don't you see that there are many hosts, and that there is a Child Jesus in every one of them?"

What a lot of nonsense I must have told her!

Jacinta, the Little Shepherdess

By now I had reached the customary age to be sent out to mind our sheep. My sister Carolina was thirteen. It was time for her to go out to work so my mother put me in charge of our flock. I passed on the news to my two companions that I would not be playing with them any more. They could not bring themselves to accept such a separation and went at once to ask their mother to let them come with me, but she refused.

Nearly every day after that they came to meet me on my way home at dusk. Then we made for the threshing floor and ran about for a while, waiting for Our Lady and the Angels to light their lamps — or put them, as we used to say, at the window to give us light. On moonless nights, we used to say that there was no oil for Our Lady's lamp!

Jacinta and Francisco found it very hard to get used to the absence of their former companion. For this reason, they pleaded with their mother over and over again to let them, also, look after their sheep. Finally my aunt, hoping perhaps to be rid of such persistent requests even though she knew the children were too small, handed over to them the care of their own flock.

Radiant with joy they ran to give me the news and talk over how we could put our flocks together every day. Each one was to open the pen, whenever their mother decided, and whoever reached the Barreiro first was to await the arrival of the other flock. Barreiro was the name of a pond at the bottom of the hill. As soon as we met at the pond we decided where we would pasture the flock that day. Then off we'd go, as happy as if we were going to a party.

And now we see Jacinta in her new life as a shepherdess. We won over the sheep by sharing our lunch with them. This meant that having reached the pasture we could play at our ease, quite sure that they would not stray far away from us.

Jacinta loved to hear her voice echoing down in the valleys. For this reason, one of our favorite amusements was to climb to the top of the hills, sit down on the biggest rock we could find, and call out different names at the top of our voices. The name that echoed back most clearly was "Maria." Sometimes Jacinta used to say the whole Hail Mary this way, only calling out the following word when the preceding one had stopped reechoing.

We loved to sing, too. Interspersed among the popular songs — of which, alas! we knew quite a number — were Jacinta's favorite hymns: "Salve Nobre Padroeira" (Hail Noble Patroness), "Virgem

Pura" (Virgin Pure), "Anjos, Cantai Comigo" (Angels, Sing with Me). We were very fond of dancing and any instrument we heard being played by the other shepherds was enough to set us off. Jacinta, tiny as she was, had a special aptitude for dancing.

We had been told to say the Rosary after our lunch, but as the whole day seemed too short for our play we worked out a fine way of getting through it quickly. We simply passed the beads through our fingers, saying nothing but "Hail Mary, Hail Mary, Hail Mary..." At the end of each mystery, we paused awhile, then simply said "Our Father." And so, in the twinkling of an eye, as they say, we had our Rosary finished!

Jacinta also loved to hold the little white lambs tightly in her arms, sitting with them on her lap, fondling them, kissing them, and carrying them home at night on her shoulders so that they wouldn't get tired. One day on her way back, she walked along in the middle of the flock.

"Jacinta, what are you doing there," I asked her, "in the middle of the sheep?"

"I want to do the same as Our Lord in that holy picture they gave me. He's just like this, right in the middle of them, and He's holding one of them in His arms."

The First Apparition

And now, Your Excellency, you know more or less how Jacinta spent the first seven years of her life right up to that 13th day of May 1917, which dawned bright and fair like so many others before it. That day, by chance — as if in the designs of Providence there can be such a thing as chance — we chose to pasture our flock on some land belonging to my parents, called Cova da Iria.

We chose the pasture at the Barreiro I have already mentioned. This meant we had to cross a barren stretch of land which made the journey doubly long. Since we had to go slowly to give the sheep a chance to graze along the way, it was almost noon when we arrived.

I will not delay here to tell you what happened that day... Your Excellency knows it well already.

(Lucia, because of this, would be asked by the Bishop to "tell all" as we shall see late in these pages, but she continues to speak... as she was asked... only about Jacinta.)

Before beginning to tell what I remember of this new period of Jacinta's life, I must first admit that there were certain aspects of Our Lady's apparitions which we had agreed not to make known to anyone. But now I may have to speak about them in order to explain whence Jacinta imbibed such great love for Jesus, for suffering and for sinners, for whose salvation she sacrificed herself so generously.

She was the one who, unable to contain herself for joy, broke our agreement to keep the whole matter to ourselves. That very afternoon, while we remained thoughtful and rapt in wonder, Jacinta kept breaking into enthusiastic exclamations:

"Oh what a beautiful Lady!"

"I can see what's going to happen," I said, "you'll end up saying that to somebody else."

"No I won't," she answered, "don't worry." Next day, Francisco came running to tell me how she had told them everything at home the night before. Jacinta listened to the accusation without a word.

"You see, that's just what I thought would happen," I told her.

"There was something within me that wouldn't let me keep quiet," she said, with tears in her eyes.

"Well, don't cry now, and don't tell anything else to anybody about what the Lady said to us."

"But I've already told them."

"And what did you say?"

"I said that the Lady promised to take us to Heaven."

"To think you told them that!"

"Forgive me. I won't tell anybody anything ever again!"

That day, when we reached the pasture, Jacinta sat thoughtfully on a rock.

"Jacinta, come and play."

"I don't want to."

"Why not?"

"Because I'm thinking. The Lady told us to pray the Rosary and to make sacrifices for the conversion of sinners. So from now on, when we pray the Rosary we must say the whole Hail Mary and the whole Our Father! And the sacrifices, how are we going to make them?"

Right away Francisco thought of a good sacrifice: "Let's give our lunch to the sheep and make the sacrifice of doing without it."

In a couple of minutes the contents of our lunch bag had been divided among the sheep so that day we fasted as strictly as the most austere Carthusian!

Reflecting on Hell

Jacinta remained sitting on her rock, looking very thoughtful, and asked:

"That Lady also said that many souls go to hell! What is hell, then?"

"It's like a deep pit of wild beasts, with an enormous fire in it — that's how my mother used to explain it to me — and that's where people go who commit sins and don't confess them. They stay there and burn forever!"

"And they never get out of there again?"

"No!"

"Not even after many, many years?"

"No! Hell never ends."

"And Heaven never ends, either?"

"Whoever goes to Heaven, never leaves it again!"

"And whoever goes to hell, never leaves it either?"

"They're eternal, don't you see? They never end."

That was how, for the first time, we made a meditation on hell and eternity. What made the biggest impression on Jacinta was the idea of eternity. Even in the middle of a game, she would stop and ask:

"But listen! Doesn't hell end after many, many years?" Or again:

"Those people burning in hell, don't they ever die? And don't they turn into ashes? And if people pray very much for sinners, won't Our Lord get them out of there? And if they make sacrifices as well? Poor sinners! We have to pray and make many sacrifices for them!"

Then she went on:

"How good the Lady is! She has already promised to take us to Heaven!"

Conversion of Sinners

Jacinta took this matter of making sacrifices for the conversion of sinners so much to heart that she never let a single opportunity escape her. There were two families in Moita[10] whose children used to go around begging from door to door. We met them one day as we were going along with our sheep. As soon as she saw them, Jacinta said to us:

"Let's give our lunch to these poor children, for the conversion of sinners!" And she ran to take it to them.

That afternoon she told me she was hungry. There were holm oaks and oak trees nearby. The acorns were still quite green. However, I told her we could eat them. Francisco climbed up a holm oak to fill his pockets but Jacinta remembered that we could eat the ones on the oak trees instead and thus make a sacrifice by eating the bitter kind. So it was there, that

afternoon, that we enjoyed this delicious repast!
Jacinta made this one of her usual sacrifices and
often picked the acorns of the oaks or the olives off the
trees.

One day I said to her: "Jacinta, don't eat that, it's
too bitter!"

"But it's because it's bitter that I'm eating it, for the
conversion of sinners."

These were not the only times we fasted. We had
agreed that whenever we met any poor children like
these, we would give them our lunch. They were only
too happy to receive such an alms and they took good
care to meet us; they used to wait for us along the
road. We no sooner saw them than Jacinta ran to give
them all the food we had for that day, as happy as if
she had no need of it herself.

On days like that, our only nourishment consisted
of pine nuts and little berries about the size of an olive
which grow on the roots of yellow bell-flowers, as well
as blackberries, mushrooms, and some other things
we found on the roots of pine trees — I can't remember
now what these were called. If there was fruit available on the land belonging to our parents, we used to
eat that.

Jacinta's thirst for making sacrifices seemed insa-
tiable. One day a neighbor offered my mother a good
pasture for our sheep. Though it was quite far away
and we were at the height of summer, my mother
accepted the offer made so generously and sent me
there. She told me that we should take our siesta in
the shade of the trees, as there was a pond nearby
where the flock could go and drink. On the way we
met our dear poor children and Jacinta ran to give
them our usual alms.

It was a lovely day but the sun was blazing, and in
that arid, stony wasteland, it seemed as though it
would burn everything up. We were parched with
thirst, and there wasn't a single drop of water for us

to drink! At first, we offered this sacrifice generously for the conversion of sinners, but after midday, we could hold out no longer.

As there was a house quite near, I suggested to my companions that I should go and ask for a little water. They agreed so I went and knocked on the door. A little old woman gave me not only a pitcher of water but also some bread, which I accepted gratefully. I ran to share it with my little companions and then offered the pitcher to Francisco and told him to take a drink.

"I don't want to," he replied.

"Why?"

"I want to suffer for the conversion of sinners."

"You have a drink, Jacinta!"

"But I want to offer this sacrifice for sinners, too."

Then I poured the water into a little hollow in the rock so that the sheep could drink it and went to return the pitcher to its owner. The heat was getting more and more intense. The shrill singing of the crickets and grasshoppers coupled with the croaking of the frogs in the neighboring pond made an uproar that was almost unbearable. Jacinta, frail as she was and weakened still more by the lack of food and drink, said to me with the simplicity which was natural to her:

"Tell the crickets and frogs to keep quiet! I have such a terrible headache."

Then Francisco asked her: "Don't you want to suffer this for sinners?"

The poor child, clasping her head between her two little hands, replied: "Yes, I do! Let them sing!"

In the meantime, news of what had happened was spreading. My mother was getting worried and wanted at all costs to make me deny what I had said. One day before I went out with the flock, she was determined to make me confess that I was telling lies, and to this end she spared neither caresses nor threats, nor even the broomstick. To all this she received nothing but a mute silence or the confirmation of all that I had already said.

Family Opposition

She told me to go and let out the sheep and during the day to consider well that she had never tolerated a single lie among her children, and much less would she allow a lie of this kind. She warned me that she would force me, that very evening, to go to those people whom I had deceived, confess that I had lied and ask their pardon.

I went off with my sheep and that day my little companions were already waiting for me. When they saw me crying they ran up and asked me what was the matter. I told them all that had happened, and added:

"Tell me now, what am I to do? My mother is determined at all costs to make me say that I was lying. But how can I?"

Then Francisco said to Jacinta:

"You see! It's all your fault. Why did you have to tell them?"

The poor child, in tears, knelt down, joined her hands, and asked our forgiveness:

"I did wrong," she said through her tears, "but I will never tell anything to anybody again."

Your Excellency will probably be wondering who taught Jacinta to make such an act of humility? I don't know. Perhaps she had seen her brothers and sisters asking their parents' forgiveness before going to Communion... or else, as I think myself, Jacinta was the one who received from Our Lady a greater abundance of grace, and a better knowledge of God and of virtue.

When the parish priest sent for us some time later to question us, Jacinta put her head down, and only with difficulty did he succeed in getting a word or two out of her. Once outside I asked her:

"Why didn't you answer the priest?"[11]

"Because I promised you never to tell anything to anybody again!" One day she asked:

"Why can't we say that the Lady told us to make sacrifices for sinners?"

"So they won't be asking what kind of sacrifices we are making." My mother became more and more upset at the way things were progressing. This led her to make yet another attempt to force me to confess that I had lied. One morning early, she called me and told me she was taking me to see the parish priest, saying:

"When you get there, go down on your knees, tell him that you've lied, and ask his pardon." As we were going past my aunt's house, my mother went inside for a few minutes. This gave me a chance to tell Jacinta what was happening. Seeing me so upset, she shed some tears and said:

"I'm going to get up and call Francisco. We'll go and pray for you at the well. When you get back, come and find us there." On my return, I ran to the well, and there were the two of them on their knees, praying. As soon as they saw me, Jacinta ran to hug me, and then she said:

"You see! We must never be afraid of anything! The Lady will help us always. She's such a good friend of ours." Ever since that day Our Lady taught us to offer our sacrifices to Jesus and any time we had something to suffer, or agreed to make a sacrifice, Jacinta asked:

"Did you tell Jesus that it's for love of Him?" If I said I hadn't, she answered: "Then I'll tell Him," and joining her hands, she raised her eyes to Heaven and said:

"Oh Jesus, it is for love of You, and for the conversion of sinners!"

Two priests who had come to question us recommended that we pray for the Holy Father. Jacinta asked who the Holy Father was. The good priests explained who he was and how much he needed prayers. This gave Jacinta such love for the Holy Father that every time she offered her sacrifices to Jesus, she added: "... and for the Holy Father."

Love For The Holy Father

At the end of the Rosary she always said three Hail Marys for the Holy Father and sometimes she would remark:

"How I'd love to see the Holy Father! So many people come here, but the Holy Father never does!"[12] In her childish simplicity, she supposed that the Holy Father could make this journey just like anybody else!

One day my father and my uncle[13] were summoned to appear next morning with the three of us before the Administrator.[14]

"I'm not going to take my children," announced my uncle, "nor present them before any tribunal. Why, they're not old enough to be responsible for their actions, and besides all that, they could never stand the long journey on foot to Vila Nova de Ourem. I'll go myself and see what they want."

My father thought differently:

"As for my girl, I'm taking her! Let her answer for herself; I don't understand a thing about this."

They all took advantage of this occasion to frighten us in every way they could. Next day as we were passing by my uncle's house my father had to wait a few minutes for my uncle. I ran to say goodbye to Jacinta, who was still in bed. Doubtful as to whether we would ever see one another again, I threw my arms around her. Bursting into tears the poor child sobbed:

"If they kill you, tell them that Francisco and I are just the same as you, and that we want to die too. I'm going right now to the well with Francisco, and we'll pray hard for you."

In Prison at Ourem

When I got back at nightfall, I ran to the well, and there were the pair of them, on their knees, leaning over the side of the well, their heads buried in their hands, weeping bitterly. As soon as they saw me, they cried out in astonishment:

"You've come then? Why, your sister came here to draw water and told us that they'd killed you! We've been praying and crying so much for you!"

When we were put in prison some time later, what made Jacinta suffer most was to feel that their parents had abandoned them. With tears streaming down her cheeks she would say:

"Neither your parents nor mine have come to see us. They don't care about us any more!"

"Don't cry," said Francisco, "we can offer this to Jesus for sinners." Then, raising his eyes and hands to Heaven, he made the offering:

"O my Jesus, this is for love of You, and for the conversion of sinners." Jacinta added:

"And also for the Holy Father, and in reparation for the sins committed against the Immaculate Heart of Mary."

Another Sacrifice

After being separated for awhile, we were reunited in one of the other rooms of the prison. When they told us they were coming soon to take us away to be fried alive, Jacinta went aside and stood by a window overlooking the cattle market. I thought at first that she was trying to distract her thoughts with the view but I soon realized that she was crying. I went over and drew her close to me asking her why she was crying:

"Because we are going to die," she replied, "without ever seeing our parents again, not even our mothers!"

With tears running down her cheeks, she added: "I would at least like to see my mother."

"Don't you want then, to offer this sacrifice for the conversion of sinners?"

"I do want to, I do!"

With her face bathed in tears, she joined her hands, raised her eyes to Heaven and made her offering:

"O my Jesus! This is for love of You, for the conversion of sinners, for the Holy Father, and in reparation for the sins committed against the Immaculate Heart of Mary."

The prisoners who were present at this scene sought to console us. "But all you have to do," they said, "is to tell the Administrator the secret! What does it matter whether the Lady wants you to or not?"

"Never!" was Jacinta's vigorous reply. "I'd rather die!"

The Rosary in Jail

Next, we decided to pray our Rosary. Jacinta took off a medal that she was wearing around her neck, and asked a prisoner to hang it up for her on a nail in the wall. Kneeling before this medal, we began to pray. The prisoners prayed with us, that is, if they knew how to pray, but at least they were down on their knees. Once the Rosary was over, Jacinta went over to the window, and started crying again.

"Jacinta," I asked, "don't you want to offer this sacrifice to Our Lord?"

"Yes, I do, but I keep thinking about my mother, and I can't help crying."

As the Blessed Virgin had told us to offer our prayers and sacrifices also in reparation for the sins committed against the Immaculate Heart of Mary, we agreed that each of us would choose one of these intentions. One would offer for sinners, another for the Holy Father and yet another in reparation for the sins committed against the Immaculate Heart of Mary. Having decided to do this, I told Jacinta to choose whichever intention she preferred.

"I'm making the offering for all the intentions, because I love them all."

And Finally... The Dance

Among the prisoners, there was one who played the concertina. To divert our attention, he began to play and they all started singing. They asked us if we knew how to dance. We said we knew the "fandango" and the "vira." Jacinta's partner was a poor thief who, finding her so tiny, picked her up and went on dancing with her in his arms! We only hope that Our Lady has had pity on his soul and converted him!

Now, Your Excellency will be saying:

"What fine dispositions for martyrdom!" That is true. But we were only children and we didn't think beyond this. Jacinta dearly loved dancing, and had a special aptitude for it. I remember how she was crying one day about one of her brothers who had gone to the war and was reported killed in action.[15]

To distract her, I arranged a little dance with two of her brothers. There was the poor child dancing away as she dried the tears that ran down her cheeks. Her fondness for dancing was such that the sound of some shepherd playing his instrument was enough to set her dancing all by herself. In spite of this, when Carnival time or St. John's Day festivities came round, she announced:

"I'm not going to dance any more."

"Why not?"

"Because I want to offer this sacrifice to Our Lord."

✝✝✝

39.

^{1.} Dom Jose Alves Correia da Silva, 1872-1957, first Bishop of reestablished Diocese of Leiria-Fatima.

^{2.} Lk. 2:19-51.

^{3.} Father Antonio de Oliveira Reis, died 1962, at the time Vicar of Torres Novas.

^{4.} Father Faustino Jose Jacinto Ferreira, died 1924.

^{5.} Lucia had quite a talent for poetry and wrote several poems in perfect rhythm and rhyme. Unfortunately the English translation does not do them justice.

^{6.} Maria dos Anjos, Lucia's oldest sister.

^{7.} Visitors can still see this crucifix at Lucia's old home.

^{8.} Here Lucia refers to Carolina, who was living in Casa Velha near Aljustrel when the book began. By 1992, all the brothers and sisters of the three children of Fatima had died except John, brother of Francisco and Jacinta.

^{9.} Jacinta was born on March 11, 1910.

^{10.} A small hamlet north of the Cova da Iria where the apparitions took place.

^{11.} The first interrogation by the parish priest took place at the end of May 1917.

^{12.} On May 13, 1967, Pope Paul VI went to the Sanctuary of Fatima as a pilgrim. His successor, Pope John Paul II, also went to Fatima for the ceremonies of May 12-13, 1982, to thank Our Lady for saving his life in an assassination attempt on May 13 of the previous year in Saint Peter's square in Rome. His Holiness returned on the same Feast of Our Lady of Fatima ten years later in 1991. On this occasion His Holiness said: "Fatima is the Marian Capitol of the World."

^{13.} Her father's name was Antonio dos Santos, died 1919. Her uncle, who died in 1957, was Manuel Pedro (Ti) Marto, father of Francisco and Jacinta.

¹⁴ The administrator was Arturo de Oliveira Santos, died 1955.

[15.] Portugal fought on the side of the Allies during the First World War, after Germany declared war on that country on March 8, 1916.

Above: Olympia Marto (left), mother of Francisco and Jacinta, with her sister-in-law, Maria Dos Santos, mother of Lucia.

Chapter III.

In the First Memoir —
Lucia Remembers

JACINTA'S SACRIFICES

In this chapter we continue Lucia's own words from her first memoir as she speaks about Jacinta during the time following the apparitions.

✝✝✝

Prayers and Sacrifices at the Cabeco

My aunt was worn out with having continually to send someone to fetch her children to please the people who came asking to speak to them. She therefore handed over the care of the flock to her little son John.[1] This was painful to Jacinta for two reasons: she had to speak to everyone who came looking for her, and she could no longer spend the whole day with me. She had to resign herself, however.

To escape from the unwanted visitors, she and Francisco used to go and hide in a cave hollowed out in the rock[2] on the hillside facing our hamlet. On top of the hill was a windmill. Situated as it is on the eastern slope, this hiding place is so well formed that it afforded an ideal protection from both the rain and the burning sun, especially since it is sheltered by many oak and olive trees. How many were the prayers and sacrifices Jacinta offered there to our dear Lord!

All over the slope grew innumerable varieties of flowers. Among them were many irises. Jacinta loved these especially. Every evening she was waiting for me on my way home with an iris she had picked for me. She would have some other flower if there were no irises to be found. It was a real joy for her to pluck off the petals one by one and strew them over me.

My mother was satisfied for the time being with deciding each day where I was to pasture the sheep, so that she knew where to find me when I was needed. When the place was nearby I told my little companions and they lost no time in coming to join me. Jacinta never stopped running until she caught sight of me. Then, exhausted, she sat down and kept calling to me until I answered and ran to meet her.

Troublesome Interrogators

Finally my mother, tired of seeing my sister waste her time coming to call me and taking my place, decided to sell all the sheep. She talked things over with my aunt, and they decided to send us off to school. At playtime, Jacinta loved to make a visit to the Blessed Sacrament.

"They seem to guess," she complained. "We are no sooner inside the church than a crowd of people come asking us questions! I wanted so much to be alone for a long time with the Hidden Jesus and talk to Him, but they never let us."

It was true. The simple country folk never left us alone. With the utmost simplicity they told us all about their needs and their troubles. Jacinta showed the greatest compassion, especially when it concerned some sinner, saying:

"We must pray and offer sacrifices to Our Lord, so that he will be converted and not go to hell, poor man!"

In this connection, it might be good to relate here an incident which shows to what extent Jacinta sought to escape from the people who came looking for her. We were on our way to Fatima one day.[3] Approaching the main road we noticed a group of

43.

ladies and gentlemen getting out of a car. We knew without the slightest doubt that they were looking for us. Escape was impossible. They would see us. We continued on our way, hoping to pass by without being recognized.

On reaching us, the ladies asked if we knew the little shepherds to whom Our Lady had appeared. We said we did.

"Do you know where they live?"

We gave them precise directions, and ran off to hide in the fields among the brambles. Jacinta was so delighted with the result of her little stratagem that she exclaimed:

"We must do this always when they don't know us by sight."

The Saintly Father Cruz

One day Father Cruz[4] from Lisbon came to question us. When he had finished, he asked us to show him the spot where Our Lady had appeared. On the way we walked on either side of His Reverence, who was riding a donkey so small that his feet almost touched the ground. As we went along, he taught us a litany of ejaculations, two of which Jacinta made her own and never stopped repeating ever afterwards:

"O my Jesus, I love you! Sweet Heart of Mary, be my salvation!"

One day during her illness, she told me:

"I so like to tell Jesus that I love Him! Many times, when I say it to Him, I seem to have a fire in my heart, but it doesn't burn me." Another time she said:

"I love Our Lord and Our Lady so much that I never get tired of telling Them that I love Them."

There was a woman in our neighborhood who insulted us every time we met her. We came upon her one day as she was leaving a tavern. Not in her right mind and not satisfied with mere insults, she went still further. When she had finished taking us to task, Jacinta said to me:

"Let us plead with Our Lady and offer sacrifices for the conversion of this woman. She says so many sinful things that if she doesn't go to confession, she'll go to hell."

Graces Through Jacinta

A few days later, we were running past this woman's door when Jacinta suddenly stopped. Turning around she asked:

"Listen! Is it tomorrow that we're going to see the Lady?"

"Yes, it is."

"Then let's not play anymore. We can make this sacrifice for the conversion of sinners."

Without realizing that someone might be watching her, she raised her hands and eyes to heaven and made her offering. The woman, meanwhile, was peeping through a shutter in the house. Afterwards she told my mother that Jacinta made such an impression on her that she needed no other proof to make her believe in the reality of the apparitions: henceforth, she would not only not insult us any more, but would constantly ask us to pray to Our Lady that her sins might be forgiven.

Another poor woman afflicted with a terrible disease met us one day. Weeping, she knelt before Jacinta and begged her to ask Our Lady to cure her. Jacinta was distressed to see a woman kneeling before her and caught hold of her with trembling hands to lift her up. Seeing this was beyond her strength, she knelt down and said three Hail Marys with the woman. She then asked her to get up, and assured her that Our Lady would cure her. After that Jacinta continued to pray daily for that woman until she returned later to thank Our Lady for her cure.

On another occasion there was a soldier who wept like a child. He had been ordered to leave for the front although his wife was sick in her bed and he had three small children. He pleaded that either his wife would be cured or that the order would be revoked. Jacinta invited him to say the Rosary with her, and then said to him:

"Don't cry! Our Lady is so good! She will certainly grant you the grace you are asking."

From then on, she never forgot her soldier. At the end of the Rosary, she always said one Hail Mary for him. Some months later, he appeared with his wife and his three small children to thank Our Lady for the two graces he had received. Having become ill with fever on the eve of his departure, he had been released from military service. As for his wife, he said she had been miraculously cured by Our Lady.

More and More Sacrifices

One day we were told that a priest was coming to see us who was very holy and who could tell what was going on in people's inmost hearts. This meant that he would find out whether we were telling the truth or not. Full of joy, Jacinta exclaimed:

"When is this Father coming? If he can really tell, then he'll know we are telling the truth."

We were playing one day at the well I have already mentioned. Close to it, there was a grape vine belonging to Jacinta's mother. She cut some and brought them to us to eat. But Jacinta never forgot her sinners.

"We won't eat them," she said, "we'll offer this sacrifice for sinners."

Then she ran out with the grapes and gave them to the other children playing in the road. She returned radiant with joy, for she had found our poor children and given them the grapes.

Another time my aunt called us to come and eat some figs which she had brought home... and indeed they would have given anyone an appetite. Jacinta sat down happily next to the basket with the rest of us and picked up the first fig. Just as she was about to eat it she suddenly remembered and said:

"It's true! We haven't made a single sacrifice today for sinners! We'll have to make this one."

She put the fig back in the basket for the conversion of sinners.

Jacinta made such sacrifices over and over again, but I won't stop to mention any more, or I shall never finish.

†††

[1.] John Marto, Jacinta's brother was still living in the old house in 1993.

[2.] The hill is called "Cabeco." and the cave (or rather an overhanging of rock) on its slope is known as "Loca do Cabeco."

[3.] This happened in the course of 1918-1919, one year after the apparitions.

[4.] Father Francisco Cruz, S.J., 1859-1919, Servant of God, whose Cause for Beatification has been instituted.

Below: Crowd at Miracle of the Sun, Oct. 13. 1917

Chapter IV.

In the First Memoir —
Lucia's Remembers

HER FAREWELL TO JACINTA

*Lucia describes the last illness and death of Jacinta
in this conclusion of her first Memoir.*

ttt

Jacinta's Illness

This was how Jacinta spent her days until Our Lord
sent the illness of the lungs which confined herself
and Francisco to bed.[1] The evening before she fell sick
she said:

"I have a terrible headache and I'm so thirsty! But
I won't take a drink, because I want to suffer for
sinners."

Apart from school or the small tasks I was given to
do, I spent every free moment with my little companions. One day, when I called in on my way to school,
Jacinta said to me:

"Tell the Hidden Jesus that I love Him very much,
that I really love Him very much indeed!" At other
times, she said:

"Tell Jesus that I send Him my love, and long to see
Him." Whenever I visited her room first, she used to
say:

"Now go and see Francisco. I'll make the sacrifice
of staying here alone."

On another occasion her mother brought her a cup
of milk and told her to take it. "I don't want it, mother,"

she answered, pushing the cup away with her little hand. My aunt insisted a little, and then left the room, saying:

"I don't know how to make her take anything. She has no appetite."

As soon as we were alone, I asked her:

"Jacinta, how can you disobey your mother like that and not offer this sacrifice to Our Lord?" When she heard this, she shed a few tears which I had the happiness of drying, and said:

"I forgot this time." She called her mother and asked her forgiveness. She said she would take whatever she wanted. Her mother brought back the cup of milk and Jacinta drank it down without the slightest sign of repugnance. Later, she told me:

"If you only knew how hard it was to drink that!"

Another time she said to me:

"It's becoming harder and harder for me to take milk and broth, but I don't say anything. I drink it all for the love of Our Lord and of the Immaculate Heart of Mary, our dear heavenly Mother."

Again, I asked her: "Are you better?" "You know I'm not getting better," she replied, and added:

"I have such pains in my chest! But I don't say anything. I'm suffering for the conversion of sinners."

One day when I arrived, she asked:

"Did you make many sacrifices today? I've made a lot. My mother went out, and I wanted to go and visit Francisco many times, and I didn't go."

Visit From The Blessed Virgin

However, Jacinta did improve somewhat. She was even able to get up, and could thus spend her days sitting on Francisco's bed. On one occasion she sent for me to come and see her at once. I ran right over.

"Our Lady came to see us," Jacinta said. "She told us she would come to take Francisco to Heaven very soon, and She asked me if I still wanted to convert more sinners. I said I did. She told me I would be going to a hospital where I would suffer a great deal... and that I am to suffer for the conversion of sinners, in reparation for the sins committed against the Immaculate Heart of Mary, and for the love of Jesus. I asked if you would go with me. She said you wouldn't, and that is what I find hardest. She said my mother would take me, and then I would have to stay there all alone!"

After this, Jacinta was thoughtful for awhile, and then added:

"If only you could be with me! The hardest part is to go without you. Maybe the hospital is a big, dark house, where you can't see and I'll be there suffering all alone! But never mind! I'll suffer for love of Our Lord, to make reparation to the Immaculate Heart of Mary, for the conversion of sinners and for the Holy Father."

When the moment arrived for her brother to go to Heaven, she confided to him these last messages:[2]

"Give all my love to Our Lord and Our Lady, and tell them that I'll suffer as much as They want for the conversion of sinners and in reparation to the Immaculate Heart of Mary."

Jacinta suffered a great deal when her brother died. She remained a long time buried in thought. If anyone asked her what she was thinking about, she answered:

"About Francisco... I'd give anything to see him again!" Then her eyes brimmed over with tears.

One day, I said to her:

"It won't be long now till you go to Heaven. But what about me?"

"You poor thing! Don't cry! I'll pray lots and lots for you when I'm there. As for you, that's the way Our Lady wants it. If She wanted that for me, I'd gladly stay and suffer more for sinners."

In The Hospital At Ourem

The day came for Jacinta to go to the hospital.[3] There indeed she was to suffer a great deal. When her mother went to see her, she asked if she wanted anything. She told her that she wanted to see me.

This was no easy matter for my aunt, but she took me with her at the first opportunity. As soon as Jacinta saw me she joyfully threw her arms around me and asked her mother to leave me with her while she went to do her shopping. Then I asked her if she was suffering a lot.

"Yes, I am. But I offer everything for sinners, and in reparation to the Immaculate Heart of Mary." Then with enthusiasm she spoke of Our Lord and Our Lady:

"Oh, how much I love to suffer for love of Them, just to give Them pleasure! They greatly love those who suffer for the conversion of sinners."

The time allotted for the visit passed rapidly, and my aunt arrived to take me home. She asked Jacinta if she wanted anything.

The child begged her mother to bring me with her the next time she came to see her... so my good aunt, who loved to make her little daughter happy, took me with her a second time. I found Jacinta with the same joy in suffering and offering all for the love of our Good God and of the Immaculate Heart of Mary, for sinners and the Holy Father. That was her ideal. She could speak of nothing else.

Return to Aljustrel

She returned home to her parents for a little while. She had a large open wound in her chest which had to be treated every day, but she bore this without complaint and without the least sign of irritation. What distressed her most were the frequent visits and questionings on the part of many people who wanted to see her, and whom she could no longer avoid by running off to hide.

"I am offering this sacrifice, too, for the conversion of sinners," she said resignedly. "I would give anything to be able to go up to the Cabeco and say a Rosary there in our favorite place! But I am not able to anymore. When you go to the Cova da Iria, pray for me. Just think... I'll never go there again!" The tears streamed down her cheeks.

One day my aunt made this request:

"Ask Jacinta what she is thinking when she covers her face with her hands and remains motionless for such a long while. I've already asked her, but she just smiles and does not answer." I put the question to Jacinta:

"I think of Our Lord," she replied, "and of Our Lady, of sinners, and of... (and she mentioned certain parts of the Secret). I love to think."

My aunt asked me how she answered. I just smiled. This led my aunt to tell my mother what had happened. "The life of these children is an enigma to me," she exclaimed, "I can't understand it!" And my mother added:

"Yes, and when they are alone, they talk a blue streak. Yet, however hard you listen, you can never catch a single word! And when someone approaches they bow their heads and are silent. I just can't understand this mystery."

Renewed Visits From The Blessed Virgin

Once again, the Blessed Virgin deigned to visit Jacinta, to tell her of new crosses and sacrifices awaiting her. She gave me the news saying:

"She told me that I am going to Lisbon to another hospital... that I will not see you again, nor my parents either, and after suffering a great deal, I shall die alone. But She said I must not be afraid, since She Herself is coming to take me to Heaven."

She hugged me and wept:

"I will never see you again! You won't be coming to visit me there. Oh please, pray hard for me, because I am going to die alone!"

Jacinta suffered terribly right until the day of her departure for Lisbon. She kept clinging to me and sobbing:

"I'll never see you again! Nor my mother, nor my brothers, nor my father! I'll never see anybody ever again! And then, I'll die all alone!"

"Don't think about it," I advised her one day.

"Let me think about it," she replied, "for the more I think the more I suffer, and I want to suffer for love of Our Lord and for sinners. Anyway, I don't mind! Our Lady will come to me there and take me to Heaven."

At times, she kissed and embraced a crucifix, exclaiming:

"O my Jesus! I love You, and I want to suffer very much for love of You." How often did she say:

"O Jesus! Now You can convert many sinners, because this is really a big sacrifice!"

From time to time, she asked me:

"Am I going to die without receiving the Hidden Jesus? If only Our Lady would bring Him to me when She comes to fetch me!" One day I asked her:

"What are you going to do in Heaven?"

"I'm going to love Jesus very much, and the Immaculate Heart of Mary, too. I'm going to pray a lot for you, for sinners, for the Holy Father, for my parents and my brothers and sisters, and for all the people who have asked me to pray for them..."

When her mother looked sad at seeing the child so ill, Jacinta used to say:

"Don't worry, mother. I'm going to Heaven, and there I'll be praying so much for you."

Or again: "Don't cry. I'm all right." If they asked her if she needed anything, she answered:

"No, I don't. Thank you." Then when they had left the room, she said:

"I'm so thirsty, but I don't want to take a drink. I'm offering it to Jesus for sinners."

One day, when my aunt had been asking me many questions, Jacinta called me to her and said:

"I don't want you to tell anybody that I'm suffering, not even my mother. I do not want to upset her."

On one occasion, I found her clasping a picture of Our LADY to her heart, and saying:

"O my dearest heavenly Mother, do I have to die all alone?" The poor child seemed so frightened at the thought of dying alone! I tried to comfort her saying:

"What does it matter if you die alone, so long as Our Lady is coming to fetch you?"

"It's true, it doesn't matter, really. I don't know why it is, but I sometimes forget Our Lady is coming to take me. I only remember that I'll die without having you near me."

Leaving For Lisbon

The day came[4] at last when she was to leave for Lisbon. It was a heartrending farewell. For a long time she clung to me with her arms around my neck and sobbed:

"We shall never see each other again! Pray a lot for me until I go to Heaven. Then I will pray a lot for you. Never tell the Secret to anyone, even if they kill you. Love Jesus and the Immaculate Heart of Mary very much, and make many sacrifices for sinners."

From Lisbon, she sent me word that Our Lady had come to see her there; She had told her the day and hour of her death. Finally Jacinta reminded me to be very good.

Epilogue

I have now finished telling Your Excellency what I remember about Jacinta's life. I ask our Good God to deign to accept this act of obedience, that it may kindle in souls a fire of love for the Hearts of Jesus and Mary.

I would like to ask just one favor. If Your Excellency should publish anything[5] of what I have just written, would you do it in such a way that no mention whatsoever is made of my poor and miserable self?

I must confess, moreover, that if it were to come to my knowledge that Your Excellency had burnt this account, without even reading it, I would be very glad indeed, since I wrote it only out of obedience to the Will of our Good God, as made known to me through the express will of Your Excellency.

†††

[1.] Jacinta fell ill in October 1918, and Francisco soon after.

[2.] Francisco died on April 4, 1919.

[3.] St. Augustine's Hospital in Vila Nova de Ourem. Jacinta was taken there on July 1, and left it on August 31, 1919. When visited in 1990 the room was being used as a nurse's vestry.

[4.] On January 21, 1920, Jacinta went to Lisbon. Admitted to the orphanage then run by Madre Godinho, Rua de Estrela, 17, she was taken to the Dona Estefania Hospital, on February 2, 1920, where she died at 10:30 p.m. on February, 20, 1920.

[5.] Lucia's reminiscences in the First memoir were used by Dr. Jose Galamba de Oliveira for his book *Jacinta, the Flower of Fatima* (May 1938).

Chapter V.

Comments On

LUCIA'S ROLE

It is clear from these first writings of Lucia, completed in less than three weeks, that she was guarding quite a number of things which she would probably reveal only under obedience.

In April of 1937, Father Fonseca wrote to Bishop da Silva:

"This first Memoir makes one think that there are further interesting details in the history of the apparitions which are not yet known. Would it not be possible, or would there be any difficulty in persuading Sister Lucia to write down in detail, conscientiously and with the simplicity of the Gospel, and in honor of the Blessed Virgin, *every single thing* she still remembers? This is an idea and should you find it helpful, only Your Excellency can put into effect..."

Lucia was now thirty years of age. She was born on March 30, 1907, in the village of Aljustrel, which is about a mile from the parish church of Fatima, and another mile (in the opposite direction) from the Cova which is a great natural hollow in the earth where Our Lady appeared to her and her two cousins, Francisco and Jacinta.

Her parents were Antonio and Maria Rosa Santos, residents of Aljustrel, both of whom had already died when I went to that tiny village for the first time in 1946. It was a cluster of about ten "cottages" or little stone houses, very similar to the stone cottages one would have seen quite commonly at that time in Ireland.

Lucia was the youngest of seven children (six girls and a boy) and the family favorite. She was surrounded with affection from her earliest childhood. Lucia's mother was somewhat severe, but a truly loving mother who was loved very much in turn by her children, and perhaps most especially by Lucia.

Typical of the Area

From what I have observed from my many trips (more than fifty) to Portugal, I would presume that Lucia's father and mother were typical of a married couple in any remote mountain village. The women faithfully went to church while many of the men waited outside for them until the Sunday Mass was over. However, Lucia's father was spiritually perhaps a step above the usual mountain farmer. Lucia warmly defends his memory.

At the age of six Lucia received her First Holy Communion. It is one of the first major events recorded in the next of her Memoirs which in a moment you will be privileged to read. Already, in that first moment of receiving Our Lord, we shall see that Lucia — even at the age of six — was mature to a remarkable degree. As Father Alonso remarks:

"Reading the account of her First Communion necessarily moves us to joy and wonder."

The children in these mountain villages had to work from a very early age, helping not only with work about the house, but bearing the responsibility of herding.

At first, when Lucia was eight years old, her companions in the work of tending sheep were the girls and boys of Aljustrel and its surroundings. But beginning in 1916, when she was nine, her cousins Jacinta and Francisco Marto were her sole companions. And the next year was the year in which the Blessed Virgin appeared.

Lucia's Special Mission

As we mentioned in the first chapter, Lucia had a special role during the apparitions. When all three children asked Our Lady if She would not take them back to Heaven with Her, Our Lady told Lucia that she was to remain on earth with a special mission.

God wished to establish devotion to the Immaculate Heart of Mary in the world, and Lucia was to be the one to write down the details of that message. She was also to keep the Secret, parts of which would be revealed at a time to be indicated by Our Lady, and another part to be written and confided to the Pope and to be opened by His Holiness in 1960.

After the apparitions, because of her lively intelligence and extraordinary memory, Lucia learned to read and write very quickly. Concerning her memory, one can only say that it was absolutely remarkable. As she wrote one section of the Memoirs after the other under obedience, she had *the power of total recall.* She rarely changed a single word. When she wrote the very last Memoir, as she came to a point about which she had written previously, she simply stated that she had already recorded this!

Even though writing *at different times,* never once was there *a single word of contradiction.* For this reason we would like to make a side comment here on confusion concerning the date of the apparition of Our Lady at Valinhos in August of 1917.

People of the village said they thought this occurred on August 19, four days after the children were released from the jail of Ourem. But Lucia recalls that it was *"on the same day"* that they were released from the jail, namely, August 15. *Canon Galamba de Oliveira (with whom I visited in August 1984, just before beginning this book) expressed his joy that I would clarify that the apparition of Valinhos had indeed taken place on August 15 as Lucia recalled it.*

Canon Galamba, who was himself one of the greatest experts in the history of Fatima, explains that the villagers did not have a good sense of dates or time. They recalled that the apparition of Valinhos had taken place on the day *that people were coming from church,* and therefore presumed that it was a Sunday. The closest Sunday after August 13 was the 19th. But because it was a holy day, August 15 was also "when people were coming from church." Lucia affirms this with delicacy and humility.[1]

This is important. August 15 is the great feast of the Assumption of Our Lady. After Pope Pius XII proclaimed the Assumption of the Blessed Virgin a dogma of the Church in 1950, *His Holiness saw a re-enactment of the miracle of the sun over the Vatican.*[2]

Since Father Fonseca had written one of the first and most authoritative books on the Fatima apparitions, we can imagine how he felt when he read that first Memoir. We are not surprised that he immediately asked Bishop da Silva if he would not *command* that Lucia write down "every single thing she still remembered." At this time Lucia was a member of the Congregation of the Sisters of Saint Dorothy, and before giving the necessary order, the Bishop of Leiria (often also called Leiria/Fatima) conferred with the Mother Provincial.

One of the primary interests of the Bishop after the Fatima apparitions was to preserve Lucia from the thousands of people who flocked to Fatima to see her, touch her, and interrogate her. Therefore, Bishop da Silva had asked her if she would be willing to leave her home, enter school like an orphan under an assumed name, and not speak about Fatima nor indicate in any way that she might know anything about it other than what might be commonly known.

Lucia readily agreed in humble, instant obedience. But what a difficult thing to ask of the youngest child of a family of six[3] ... so devoted to her mother and so beloved by all the other children... to become a voluntary orphan with an assumed name and to be sent to a distant "foreign" place!

Lucia Becomes an "Orphan"

On the morning of June 17, 1921, she entered the school of the Sisters of Saint Dorothy at Vilar, far to the north of Portugal. A description given of her at the time corresponds to the well-known photograph:

"High and broad forehead; large brown, lively eyes; thin eyebrows; flat nose, wide mouth, thick lips, round chin. The face radiates something supernatural. Hair light and fine; of slight build but tall for her age. Strong features, but a likable face. Lively, intelligent, but modest and without presumption. Hands of normal size, roughened by work."

At the age of fourteen years and three months, Lucia entered the school... which scarcely went beyond elementary levels. Her more thorough education was in domestic work. But with her great ability, exceptional memory and perseverance, she succeeded in acquiring a fairly complete education, including typing (although when she wrote the Memoirs she did not have access to a typewriter). About her later convent life, how revealing are those words:

"As I have *no free time* at my disposal, I must make the most of those hours when we work in silence to recall and jot down, with the aid of paper and pencil which I keep hidden under my sewing, all that the most holy Hearts of Jesus and Mary want me to remember." (Emphasis has been added.)

Since she had a mandate from the Bishop to write the Memoirs, she could have requested special time, but her superiors seemed resolved that she should be treated just like any of the other sisters... and perhaps just a little more severely. (Indeed, she was assigned some of the worst tasks, such as cleaning out the cesspool.)

Most of the Memoirs were written in what could best be described as a "cubby hole" in the convent attic. Yet the manuscript shows almost no alterations or corrections. She wrote as though every word, as Fr. Alonso remarks, was being "read" from her memory and copied down.

The necessary order for Lucia to write down "every single thing," was qualified by the Bishop because he knew of Lucia's obligation to the Secret. On November 7, 1937, she wrote to His Excellency:

"I have already begun today, for this is the Will of God." Only three weeks later, in a fluid handwriting without a single major correction... she presented the pages which follow.

Housework and community prayer allowed her hardly any free time. And yet the document of thirty-eight pages filled front and back with close handwriting, and almost without corrections, seems to flow as though it had all been written without a single interruption.

Father Alonso, himself a brilliant theologian and writer, could not help but remark when he reviewed these manuscripts:

"This writing reveals Sister Lucia's clear mind, her composure and her mental equilibrium."

In this writing of 1937 many important details of the message of Our Lady became known for the first time: the angelic apparitions, the extraordinary blessings on the occasion of Sister Lucia's First Holy Communion, the turmoil the apparitions caused in Lucia's family, and much more.

†††

1. Despite Canon Galamba's important position on the canonical commission, many did not accept the August 15 date. Even at the time of the publication of this book, the Valinhos apparition was celebrated by many on the wrong day, August 19.

Canon Barthas, after a lengthy inquiry in the late forties, established beyond doubt that August 15 was the day the children were released from the jail (which Lucia said was also the day of the Valinhos apparition).

Most compelling proof is a letter written at that time by the parish priest of Fatima for publication. In a postscript the pastor stated that on August 15 the "authorities" brought the children back from Ourem.

2. This was first made public at the closing of the Holy Year in Fatima, October 13, 1951, by the Pope's Cardinal Legate who exclaimed: "Is this Fatima transported to Rome? Is this Rome transported to Fatima?" See the full message of the Pope on this occasion in *SOUL*, Jan., 1952.

3. Actually there were seven children born in the Santos family but one died in infancy. Lucia seemed especially loved because she was the youngest.

Lucia in school at Vilar.

Chapter VI.

In the Second Memoir —
Lucia's Remembers

HER CHILDHOOD

Lucia's Second Memoir opens with an account of her own life before the apparitions of our Lady

✝✝✝

...O Will of God, You are my Paradise...[1]

Your Excellency,

Here I am, with pen in hand to do the Will of my God. Since I have no other aim but this, I begin with the maxim which my holy Foundress bequeathed to me and which, after her example, I shall repeat many times in the course of this account:

"O Will of God, You are my Paradise!"

Allow me, Your Excellency, to sound the depths contained in this maxim. Whenever repugnance or love for my Secret makes me want to keep some things hidden, this maxim will be my norm and my guide.

I had a mind to ask what use there could possibly be in my writing an account like this, since even my handwriting is scarcely presentable.[2] But I am asking nothing. I know that the perfection of obedience asks for no reasons. Your Excellency's words are enough for me, since they assure me that this is for the glory of our Blessed Mother in Heaven.

In the certainty that it is so, I implore the blessing and protection of Her Immaculate Heart and, humbly prostrate at Her feet, I use Her most holy words to speak to my God:

"I, the least of Your handmaids, O my God, now come in full submission to Your most holy Will, to lift the veil and reveal the story of Fatima just as it is. No longer will I savor the joy of sharing with You alone the Secrets of Your love. Henceforth, others too, will sing with me the greatness of Your mercy!"

Before The Apparitions:

The Lord has looked upon His "lowly handmaid"; that is why all peoples will sing the greatness of His mercy.[3]

It seems to me, Your Excellency, that our dear Lord deigned to favor me with the use of reason from my earliest childhood. I remember being conscious of my actions even in my mother's lap. I remember being rocked and lulled asleep to the sound of various songs.

As I was the youngest[4] of five girls and one boy,[5] I remember how they used to argue because all wanted to hold me in their arms and play with me. On such occasions none succeeded because my mother used to take me away from them altogether. If she was too busy to hold me herself, she would give me to my father. He also would fondle me and cover me with caresses.

The first thing I learned was the "Hail Mary" which, holding me in her arms, my mother taught to my sister Caroline, the second youngest, and five years older than myself. My mother, knowing that I repeated everything I heard like a parrot, wanted them to take me with them everywhere they went. They were the leaders of the young people. There was not a festival or a dance that they did not attend. At Carnival time, on St. John's Day and at Christmas, there was certain to be a dance.

Besides this, there was the wine harvest, followed by the olive picking, with a dance almost every day.

On the big parish feasts, such as the Sacred Heart of Jesus, Our Lady of the Rosary, St. Anthony, and so on, we always raffled cakes; after that came a dance, without fail. We were invited to almost all the weddings for miles around, for if they did not invite my mother to be matron of honor, they were sure to need her for the cooking.

At these weddings, the dancing went on from after the banquet until well into the next morning. Since my sisters had to have me always with them, they took as much trouble in dressing me up as they were wont to do for themselves.

As one of them was a dressmaker, I was always decked out in a regional costume more elegant than that of any other girl around. I wore a pleated skirt, a shiny belt, a cashmere kerchief with the corners hanging down behind, and a hat decorated with gold beads and bright colored feathers. You would have thought sometimes that they were dressing a doll rather than a small child.

Popular Entertainments

At the dances, they deposited me on the top of a wooden chest or some tall piece of furniture, to save me from being trampled underfoot. Once on my perch, I had to sing a number of songs to the music of the guitar or the concertina. My sisters had already taught me to sing, as well as to dance a few waltzes when there was a partner missing. The latter I performed with agility, thus attracting the attention and applause of everyone present. Some of them even rewarded me with gifts in the hope of pleasing my sisters.

On Sunday afternoons, all these young people used to gather in our yard, in the shade of three large fig trees in summer, and in winter in an open porch that we had where my sister Maria's house now stands.

There they spent the afternoons, playing and chatting with my sisters. It was there that we used to raffle the sugared almonds at Easter time, and most of them usually found their way into my pocket; some of the winners hoped thereby to gain our good graces.

My mother would spend these afternoons seated at the kitchen door looking out on the yard, so that she could see all that was going on. Sometimes she had a book in her hand and would read for awhile; at other times, she chatted with my aunts or neighbors who sat beside her.

She was always very serious, and everybody knew that what she said was like a word of Scripture and must be obeyed without more ado. I never knew anyone to say a disrespectful word in her presence or show her any lack of consideration. It was the general opinion among them that my mother was worth more than all her daughters put together. I often heard my mother say:

"I don't know how those people enjoy going from house to house to talk! As for me, there's nothing as good as just staying at home for a quiet reading... and the lives of the saints, how beautiful they are!"

It seems to me that I have already told Your Excellency how, during the week, I used to spend the day surrounded by a crowd of children from the neighborhood. Their mothers went to work in the fields, so they used to ask my mother if they could leave the children with me.

When I wrote to Your Excellency about my cousin, I think I also described our games and amusements, so I will not dwell on them here. Amid the warmth of such affectionate and tender caresses, I happily spent my first six years.

To tell the truth, the world was beginning to smile on me and a passion for dancing was already sinking its roots deep into my poor heart... and I must confess that the devil would have used this to bring about my ruin had not the good Lord shown His special mercy towards me.

If I am not mistaken I have also told Your Excellency in the same account, how my mother was accustomed to teach catechism to her children during the summer at siesta time. In the winter we had our lesson after supper gathered around the fireside roasting and eating chestnuts and a sweet variety of acorns.

Lucia's First Communion

The day which the parish priest had appointed for the solemn First Communion of the children of the parish was drawing near. In view of the fact that I knew my catechism and was already six years old, my mother thought that perhaps I could now make my First Communion. So she sent me with my sister Caroline to the catechism instructions which the parish priest was giving to the children in preparation for this great day. Radiant with joy I went, hoping soon to be able to receive my God for the first time. The priest gave his instructions seated up on a platform. He called me to his side. When one or other of the children was unable to answer his questions, he told me to give the answer just to shame them.

The eve of the great day arrived and the priest sent word that all the children were to go to the church in the morning so that he could make the final decision as to which ones were to receive their First Communion. What was not my disappointment when he called me up beside him, caressed me and then said I was to wait till I was seven years old! I began to cry at once. Just as I would have done with my mother, I laid my head on his knees and sobbed. It happened that another priest,[6] who had been called in to help with the confessions, entered the church just at that moment. Seeing me in this position, he asked the reason for my tears. On being informed, he took me along to the sacristy and examined me on the cat- echism and the mystery of the Eucharist. After this, he took me by the hand and brought me to the parish priest, saying:

"Father Pena, you can let this child go to Commun- ion. She understands what she's doing better than many of the others."

"But she's only six years old," objected the good priest.

"Never mind! I'll take the responsibility for that."

"All right then," the good priest told me. "Go and tell your mother that you are making your First Com- munion tomorrow."

I could never express the joy I felt. Off I went, clapping my hands with delight, and running all the way home to give the good news to my mother. She at once set about preparing me for the confession I was to make that afternoon.

My mother took me to the church, and when we arrived, I told her that I wanted to confess to the other priest... so we went to the sacristy where he was sitting in a chair hearing confessions. My mother knelt down in front of high altar near the sacristy door, together with the other mothers who were waiting for their children to confess in turn. Right there before the Blessed Sacrament, my mother gave me her last recommendations.

Our Lady of the Rosary Smiles at Lucia

When my turn came, I went and knelt at the feet of our dear Lord, represented there in the person of His minister, imploring forgiveness for my sins. When I had finished, I noticed that everyone was laughing.

My mother called me to her and said:

"My child, don't you know that confession is a secret matter and that it is made in a low voice?

Everyone heard you! There was only one thing nobody heard... that is what you said at the end."

On the way home, my mother made several attempts to discover what she called the secret of my confession. But the only answer she obtained was complete silence. Now however, I am going to reveal the secret of my first confession. After listening to me, the good priest said these few words:

"My child, your soul is the temple of the Holy Spirit. Keep it always pure, so that He will be able to carry on His divine action within it."

On hearing these words I felt myself filled with respect for my soul. I asked the kind confessor what I ought to do. "Kneel down there before Our Lady and ask Her, with great confidence, to take care of your heart, to prepare it to receive Her beloved Son worthily tomorrow, and to keep it for Him alone!"

In the church, there was more than one statue of Our Lady. As my sisters took care of the altar of Our Lady of the Rosary,[7] I usually went there to pray. That is why I went there on this occasion also to ask Her, with all the ardor of my soul, to keep my poor heart for God alone. As I repeated this humble prayer over and over again, with my eyes fixed on the statue, it seemed to me that She smiled and, with a loving look and kindly gesture, assured me that She would do so. My heart was overflowing with joy. I could scarcely utter a single word.

Eager Expectancy

My sisters stayed up that night making me a white dress and a wreath of flowers. As for me, I was so happy that I could not sleep. It seemed as if the hours would never pass! I kept on getting up to ask them if the day had come, or if they wanted me to try on my dress, or my wreath, and so forth.

The happy day dawned at last; but nine o'clock —

69.

Above: Side altar in the parish church of Fatima with statue of Our Lady of the Rosary. Lucia came here to "visit" Our Lady on the eve of her first Communion. Her confessor had told her to ask Our Lady to prepare her heart to receive Our Lord.

Above: Closer view of the old statue which came alive and smiled at Lucia. It remains in the same place in the parish church to this day. This photo was taken in May, 1992, 75th anniversary of the apparitions of Fatima

how long it was in coming! I put on my white dress, and then my sister Maria took me into the kitchen to ask pardon of my parents, to kiss their hands and ask their blessing. After this little ceremony, my mother gave me her last recommendations. She told me what she wanted me to ask Our Lord when I had received Him into my heart. She said goodbye to me in these words:

"Above all, ask Him to make you a saint."

Her words made such an indelible impression on my heart, that they were the very first I said to Our Lord when I received Him.

Even today, I seem to hear the echo of my mother's voice repeating these words to me. I set out for the church with my sisters, and my brother carried me all the way in his arms so that not a speck of dust from the road would touch me.

Remembering Her Smile

As soon as I arrived at the church, I ran to kneel before the altar of Our Lady to renew my petition. There I remained in contemplation of Our Lady's smile of the previous day until my sisters came in search of me and took me to my appointed place. There was a large number of children, arranged in four lines — two of boys and two of girls — from the back of the church right up to the altar rails. Being the smallest, it happened I was the one nearest to the "angels" on the step by the altar rails.

Once the Missa Cantata began and the great moment drew near, my heart beat faster and faster in expectation of the visit of the great God who was about to descend from heaven, to unite Himself to my poor soul. The parish priest came down and passed among the rows of children, distributing the Bread of Angels. I had the good fortune to be the first one to receive. As the priest was coming down the steps, I felt as though my heart would leap from my breast. But he had no sooner placed the Divine Host on my tongue than I felt an unalterable serenity and peace. I felt myself bathed in such a supernatural atmosphere that the presence of our dear Lord became as clearly perceptible to me as if I had seen and heard Him with my bodily senses. I then addressed my prayer to Him:

"O Lord, make me a saint. Keep my heart always pure for You alone."

Then it seemed that in the depths of my heart, our dear Lord distinctly spoke these words to me:

"The grace granted to you this day will remain living in your soul, producing fruits of eternal life." I felt as though transformed in God.

It was almost one o'clock before the ceremonies were over because of the late arrival of priests coming from a distance, and because of the sermon and the renewal of baptismal promises. My mother came looking for me, quite distressed, thinking I might faint from weakness. But filled to overflowing with the Bread of Angels, I found it impossible to take any food whatsoever. After this, I lost the taste and attraction for the things of the world, and felt at home only in some solitary place where, all alone, I could recall the delights of my First Communion.

Lucia's Family

Such moments of seclusion were rare indeed. As Your Excellency already knows, I had to look after the children whom the neighbors entrusted to our care. Besides this, my mother was in much demand thereabouts as a nurse. In cases of minor ills, people came to our house to seek her advice, but when the sick person was unable to go out, they asked my mother to go to their homes. She often spent entire days there, and even nights. If the illness was prolonged, or the sick person's condition required it, she occasionally sent my sisters to stay by the patient's bedside at night, to give the family a chance to get some rest.

Whenever the sick person was the mother of a young family, or someone who could not stand the noise of children, my mother brought the little ones to our house and I had to keep them occupied. I kept them amused by teaching them how to wind the yarn into balls, roll it into spools, make it into skeins, and guide the balls of yarn as the warp was prepared on the frame.

In this way, we always had plenty to do. There were usually several girls working in our house who had come to learn weaving and dressmaking. Normally, these girls showed great affection for our family and used to say that the best days of their lives were those spent in our house.

At certain times of the year my sisters had to go out working in the fields during the daytime so they did their weaving and sewing at night. Supper was followed by prayers led by my father.[8] Then the work began.

Everyone had something to do: My sister Maria went to the loom; my father filled the spools; Teresa and Gloria went to their sewing; my mother took up her spinning; Caroline and I, after tidying up the kitchen, had to help with the sewing, taking out basting, sewing on buttons, and so forth; to keep drowsiness away, my brother played the concertina and we joined in singing all kinds of songs.

The neighbors often dropped in to keep us company. Although it meant losing their sleep, they used to tell us that the very sound of our gaiety banished all their worries and filled them with happiness. I heard different women sometimes say to my mother:

"How fortunate you are! What lovely children God has given you!"

When the time came to harvest the corn, we removed the husks by moonlight. There was I sitting on a heap of corn and chosen to give a hug to everyone whenever a dark-colored corn cob appeared.

In Retrospect

As Your Excellency has told me to give an account of all the sufferings that Our Lord has sent me, and all the graces which He has deigned in His mercy to grant me, I think it best to tell them just as they actually happened.[9] Moreover, I feel quite at peace about it because I know Your Excellency will put into the fire whatever you see does not further the glory of God and Mary most Holy.

I don't know whether the facts I have related about my First Communion were a reality or a little child's illusion. What I do know is that they always had, and still have today, a great influence in uniting me to God. What I do not know either, is why I am telling Your Excellency all this about our family life, but it is God who inspires me to do so, and He knows the reason for it. Perhaps it is to let you see how, after having had so much affection lavished upon me, I would feel all the more deeply the suffering our dear Lord was going to ask of me.

ttt

[1.] This was said by the Foundress of the congregation of Saint Dorothy, Saint Paula Frassinetti.

[2.] We have remarked on the orderly style of Lucia's manuscripts which are legible and clear, perhaps remarkably so. If given the opportunity, Lucia might have preferred to type them.

[3.] Lk. 1:48

[4.] Lucia was born on March 22, 1907.

5. The names of her brother and sisters are: Maria dos Anjos, Teresa, Manuel, Gloria, Caroline, and another girl who died in infancy.

6. He was identified later as the saintly Father Cruz, S.J., who died in 1948.

7. This beautiful statue still stands in the parish church.

8. This shows that despite his faults Lucia's father always possessed strong religious convictions.

9. This truly reveals Lucia's simplicity, and still more, her candor and honesty in all her writing.

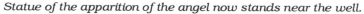

Statue of the apparition of the angel now stands near the well.

Chapter VII.

In the Second Memoir —
Lucia Remembers

THE ANGELS

The second Memoir continues in this chapter with Lucia relating her reactions and those of her companions to the apparitions of Angels prior to the visits of the Blessed Virgin.

✝✝✝

Lucia the Shepherdess

When I was seven years old, mother decided that I should take over the care of our sheep. My father did not agree, nor did my sisters. They were so fond of me that they wanted an exception made in my case. My mother would not give in. "She's just like the rest," she said. "Caroline is twelve years old so she can now begin to work in the fields, or learn to be a weaver or a seamstress if she prefers."

The care of our flock was then given to me.[1] News that I was beginning my life as shepherdess spread rapidly among the other shepherds; almost all of them came and offered to be my companions. I said "Yes" to everybody, and arranged with each one to meet me on the slopes of the serra.

The next day, the serra was a solid mass of sheep with their shepherds, as though a cloud had descended upon it. But I felt ill at ease in the midst of so much noise. I therefore chose three companions from among the shepherds and, without saying a word to anyone, we arranged to pasture our sheep on the opposite slopes. The three I chose were Teresa Matias, her sister Maria Rosa, and Maria Justino.[2] On the following day we set out in the direction of a hill known as the Cabeco. We went up the northern slope. Valinhos, a place that Your Excellency already knows by name, is on the southern slope of the same hill. On the eastern slope is the cave which I have already spoken about in my account of Jacinta.

Together with our flocks, we climbed almost to the top of the hill. At our feet lay a wide expanse of trees — olives, oaks, pines, holm oaks, and so on, stretching away down towards the valley below.

A Mysterious Presage in 1915

About midday we ate our lunch. After this I invited my companions to pray the Rosary with me, to which they eagerly agreed. We had hardly begun when, there before our eyes, we saw a figure poised in the air above the trees; it looked like a statue made of snow, rendered almost transparent by the rays of the sun.

"What is that?" asked my companions, quite frightened.

"I don't know."

We went on praying with our eyes fixed on the figure before us. As we finished our prayer, the figure disappeared. As was usual with me, I resolved to say nothing, but my companions told their families what had happened the very moment they reached home. The news soon spread and one day when I arrived home my mother questioned me:

"Look here! They say you've seen I don't know what, up there. What was it you saw?"

"I don't know," and as I could not explain it myself, I went on:

"It looked like a person wrapped up in a sheet!" As I meant to say that I couldn't discern its features, I added: "You couldn't make out any eyes or hands on it."

My mother put an end to the whole matter with a gesture of disgust: "Childish nonsense!"[3]

After some time, we returned with our flocks to the same place, and the very same thing happened again. My companions once more told the whole story. After a brief interval, the same thing was repeated. It was the third time that my mother heard all these things being talked about outside without my having said a single word about them at home. She called me, quite displeased, and demanded:

"Now, let us see! What is it that you girls say you saw over there?"

"I don't know, Mother. I don't know what it is!"

Some people started making fun of us. My sisters, recalling that for some time after my First Communion I had been quite abstracted, used to ask me rather scornfully:

"Do you see someone wrapped in a sheet?"

I felt these contemptuous words and gestures very keenly because up till now I had been accustomed only to caresses. But this was nothing, really. You see, I did not know what the good Lord had in store for me in the future.

Apparitions of the Angel in 1916

Around this time, as I have already related to Your Excellency, Francisco and Jacinta sought and obtained permission from their parents to start taking care of their own flock, so I left my good companions and instead joined my cousins Francisco and Jacinta. To avoid going to the serra with all the other shepherds, we arranged to pasture our flocks on properties belonging to my uncle and aunt and my parents.

One fine day we set out with our sheep for some land that my parents owned at the foot of the eastern slope of the hill that I have already mentioned. This property was called Chousa Velha. Soon after our arrival, about midmorning, a fine drizzle began to fall... so fine that it seemed like a mist. We went up the hillside, followed by our flocks, looking for any overhanging boulder where we could take shelter. Thus it was for the first time that we entered this blessed hollow among the rocks. It stood in the middle of an olive grove belonging to my godfather Anastacio.

From there, one could see the little village where I was born, my parents' home, and the hamlets of Casa Velha and Eira da Pedra. The olive grove, owned by several people, extended to the hamlets themselves. We spent the day there among the rocks even though the rain was ended and the sun was shining bright and clear.

We ate our lunch and prayed our Rosary. I'm not sure, but perhaps we said it in the way I have already described to Your Excellency, just saying the words Hail Mary and Our Father on each bead, so great was our eagerness to get out to our play! Our prayer finished, we started to play "pebbles."

We had enjoyed our game for only a few moments when a strong wind began to shake the trees. Startled, we looked up to see what was happening because the day was unusually calm. Then we saw coming toward us, above the olive trees, the figure of which I have already spoken.

Jacinta and Francisco had never seen it before, nor had I ever mentioned it to them. As it drew closer we were able to distinguish its features. It was a young man, about fourteen or fifteen years old, whiter than snow, transparent as crystal when the sun shines through it, and of great beauty. On reaching us, he said:

"Do not be afraid! I am the Angel of Peace. Pray with me."[4]

Kneeling on the ground, he bowed down until his forehead touched the ground, and made us repeat these words three times:

"My God, I believe, I adore, I trust and I love You! I ask pardon for those who do not believe, do not adore, do not trust, and do not love You."

Then, rising, he said:

"Pray thus. The Hearts of Jesus and Mary are attentive to the voice of your supplications."

His words engraved themselves so deeply on our minds that we could never forget them. From then on we used to spend long periods of time, prostrate like the Angel, and repeating his words until sometimes we fell exhausted. I warned my companions right away that this must be kept secret and, thank God, they did.

Some time passed. When summer came we had to go home for siesta. One day, we were playing on the stone slabs of the well down at the bottom of the garden belonging to my parents, which we called the Arneiro (I have already mentioned this well to Your Excellency in my account of Jacinta). Suddenly, we saw beside us the same figure, or rather Angel as it seemed to me.[5]

"What are you doing? Pray... pray very much. The most holy Hearts of Jesus and Mary have designs of mercy on you. Offer prayers and sacrifices constantly to the Most High."

"How are we to make sacrifices?" I asked.

"Make everything you do a sacrifice, and offer it to God as an act of reparation for the sins by which He is offended, and in supplication for the conversion of sinners. You will thus draw down peace upon your country. I am its Angel Guardian, the Angel of Portugal. Above all, accept and bear with submission the suffering which the Lord will send you."

A considerable time elapsed. Then one day we went to pasture our sheep on a property belonging to my parents on the slopes of the hill I have mentioned, a little higher up than Valinhos. It is an olive grove called Pregueria. After our lunch we decided to go and pray in the hollow among the rocks on the opposite side of the hill. To get there, we went around the slope, and had to climb over some rocks above the Pregueira. The sheep could only scramble over these rocks with great difficulty.

As soon as we arrived there we knelt down, our foreheads touching the ground, and began to repeat the prayer of the Angel:

"My God, I believe, I adore, I trust and I love You..."
I don't know how many times we had repeated this prayer, when an extraordinary light shone upon us. We sprang up to see what was happening and beheld the Angel. He was holding a chalice in his left hand with the Host suspended above it, from which some drops of Blood fell into the chalice.[6] Leaving the chalice suspended in the air, the Angel knelt down beside us and made us repeat three times:

"O Most Holy Trinity, Father, Son and Holy Spirit, I adore Thee profoundly. I offer Thee the most precious Body, Blood, Soul and Divinity of Jesus Christ, present in all the tabernacles of the world, in reparation for the outrages, sacrileges and indifference by which He is offended. By the infinite merits of the Sacred Heart of Jesus and the Immaculate Heart of Mary, I beg the conversion of poor sinners."[7]

Then, rising he took the chalice and the Host in his hands. He gave the Sacred Host to me, and shared the Blood from the chalice between Jacinta and Francisco.[8] As he did so he said:

"Take and drink the Body and Blood of Jesus Christ, horribly outraged by ungrateful men! Make reparation for their crimes and console your God."

Once again, he prostrated himself on the ground and repeated with us, three times more, the same prayer "Most Holy Trinity...," and then disappeared.

Trouble at Home

Here I am, Your Excellency, at the end of my three years as a shepherdess, from the time I was seven until I was ten years old. During these three years our home, and I would venture to say our parish as well, underwent an almost total change.

Reverend Father Pena was no longer our parish priest, and had been replaced by Reverend Father Boicinha. When this most zealous priest learned that such a pagan custom as endless dancing was only too common in the parish, he promptly began to preach against it from the pulpit in his Sunday sermons. In public and in private, he lost no opportunity of attacking this bad custom. As soon as my mother heard the good priest speak in this fashion, she forbade my sisters to attend such amusements.

As my sisters' example led others also to refrain from attending, this custom gradually died out. The same thing happened among the children, who used to get up their little dances apart, as I have already explained to Your Excellency when writing about my cousin Jacinta. Somebody remarked one day to my mother:

"Up to now, it was no sin to go to dances, but just because we have a new parish priest, it is a sin. How could that be?"

"I don't know," replied my mother. "All I know is my daughters are not going to such gatherings any more. At most, I would let them dance a bit within the family, because the priest says there is no harm in that."

During this period, my two eldest sisters left home after receiving the sacrament of matrimony. My father had fallen into bad company, and let his weakness get the better of him; this meant the loss of some of our property.[9] When my mother realized that our means of livelihood were diminishing, she resolved to send my two sisters, Gloria and Caroline, out to work as servants.

At home there remained only my brother to look after our few remaining fields, my mother to take care of the house, and myself to take our sheep out to pasture. My poor mother seemed just drowned in the depths of distress. When we gathered about the fire at night time waiting for my father to come in to supper, my mother would look at her daughters' empty places and exclaim with profound sadness:

"My God, where has all the joy of our home gone?" Then, resting her head on a little table beside her, she would burst into bitter tears. My brother and I wept with her. It was one of the saddest scenes I have ever witnessed. What with longing for my sisters, and seeing my mother so miserable, I felt my heart was just breaking. Although I was only a child, I understood perfectly the situation we were in.

Then I remembered the Angel's words:

"Above all, accept submissively the sacrifices that the Lord will send you." At such times, I used to withdraw to a solitary place so as not to add to my mother's suffering by letting her see my own. This place usually was our well. There, on my knees, leaning over the edge of the stone slabs that covered the well, my tears mingled with the waters below and I offered my suffering to God.

Sometimes, Jacinta and Francisco would come and find me like this, in bitter grief. As my voice was choked with sobs and I couldn't say a word, they shared my suffering to such a degree that they also wept copious tears. Then Jacinta made our offering aloud:

"My God, it is as an act of reparation, and for the conversion of sinners, that we offer You all these sufferings and sacrifices." The formula of the offering was not always exact, but the meaning was always the same.

So much suffering began to undermine my mother's health. She was no longer able to work so she sent for my sister Gloria to come and take care of her and look after the house as well. All the surgeons and doctors around were consulted. We had recourse to every kind of remedy but there was no improvement whatsoever.

The good parish priest kindly offered to take my mother to Leiria in his mule cart, to consult the doctors there. Accompanied by my sister Teresa, she went to Leiria, but she arrived home half dead from such a journey, worn out after so many consultations and having obtained no beneficial results of any kind. Finally, a surgeon in S. Mamede was consulted. He declared that my mother had a cardiac lesion, a dislocated spinal vertebra, and fallen kidneys. He prescribed for her a rigorous treatment of red-hot needles and various kinds of medicines which brought about some improvement in her condition.

This is how things were with us when the 13th of May 1917 arrived. It was also around this time that my brother reached the age for enlistment in the army. As his health was excellent, there was every reason to expect that he would be accepted. There was a war on, and it would be difficult to obtain his exemption from military service. My mother, afraid of being left alone and with no one to look after the land, sent also for my sister Caroline to come home. Meanwhile, my brother's godfather promised to obtain his exemption. He put in a word with the doctor responsible for his medical examination. Thus the good Lord deigned to grant my mother this relief.

†††

1. This was in 1915.

2. The two first-mentioned persons were still living when Lucia's Memoirs were first published in 1978

3. Father Alonso comments that these indistinct apparitions of the Angel were probably meant to prepare Lucia for the future.

4. This was the first apparition of the Angel, who appeared three times in 1916.

5. The second apparition of the same Angel.

6. The third and last apparition of the same Angel.

7. A theologian who had difficulty with this prayer protested to Lucia that it could not be correct from a theological point of view. Sister Lucia quietly affirmed that nevertheless, these were the exact words spoken by the Angel. In reply to two difficulties which might suggest themselves in the Angel's prayer, it might be observed:

 a) When we are offering the Body, Blood, Soul and Divinity of Jesus Christ to the Most Holy Trinity, this is essentially what is done in the sacrifice of the Mass;

 b) The "infinite merits of the Sacred Heart of Jesus and the Immaculate Heart of Mary" may mean to apply the word "infinite" only to the merits of Jesus, together with which we also offer the merits of the Immaculate Heart of Mary.

 But we might also consider the word "infinite" in the meaning of "inexhaustible," in which sense it might also apply to the merits of the Immaculate Heart of Mary in the light of words spoken to Saint Catherine Laboure at the time of the revelation of the "Miraculous Medal."

8. Francisco and Jacinta had not yet received their First Communion. However, they never regarded this as their "official" First Communion.

9. One should not exaggerate her father's conduct. Even if it is true that he liked his wine, he must not be regarded as an alcoholic. As to his religious duties, it is certain that he did not fulfill them in the parish of Fatima for some years, as he did not get along with the priest. However, he did fulfill his Easter duties in Vila Nova de Ourem.

At Right: Family picture taken at funeral of Lucia's father in 1919. Left to right: Manuel, Maria dos Anjos, Carolina and Gloria. Seated is Lucia's mother with Lucia standing at her side. (Missing is Teresa.)

*Above: Archbishop of Evora blesses the cornerstone
of the Basilica on May 13, 1922, the year
after Lucia entered school in far away Vilar.*

Chapter VIII.

In the Second Memoir —
Lucia Remembers

THE APPARITIONS OF OUR LADY

*Lucia continues her Second Memoir with an account
of the apparitions and the reaction of her own family to
the events taking place at the Cova da Iria.*

†††

I will not delay now by describing the Apparition of
May 13. It is well known to Your Excellency, and it
would therefore be a waste of time for me to repeat it
here. You also know how my mother came to be aware
of what happened, and how she spared no efforts to
make me admit that I had lied.

We agreed never to reveal to any one the words that
Our Lady spoke to us that day. After having promised
to take us to Heaven, she asked:

*"Are you willing to offer yourselves to God and to
bear all the sufferings He wills to send you, as an act
of reparation for the sins by which He is offended, and
in supplication for the conversion of sinners?"*

"Yes, we are willing," was our reply.
*"Then you are going to have much to suffer, but the
Grace of God will be your comfort."*

The Following Month

Every year the 13th of June, feast of St. Anthony,
was a day of great festivities in our parish. On that

special day we usually took the flocks out very early in the morning and at nine o'clock shut them up in their pens again so we could go off to the festival. My mother and my sisters, who knew how much I loved a festival, kept saying to me:

"We've yet to see if you'll leave the festival just to go to the Cova da Iria to talk to that Lady!"

On that day itself nobody said a single word to me. They acted as if they were saying:

"Leave her alone. We'll soon see what she'll do!"

I took out my flock at daybreak, intending to put them back in the pen at nine, go to Mass at ten, and after that, go to the Cova da Iria. The sun was no sooner up than my brother came and told me to go back home because there were several people there waiting to speak to me. He himself stayed with the flock and I went to see what they wanted. I found some women, and men too, who had come from such places as Minde, from around Tomar, Carrascos, Boleiros, etc.[1]

They wished to accompany me to the Cova da Iria. I told them that it was early and invited them to go with me to the 8 o'clock Mass. When I returned home they were waiting for me out in the yard, in the shade of our fig tree.

My mother and my sisters persisted in their contemptuous attitude. This cut me to the heart and was more painful to me than an insult.

Around 11 o'clock I left home and called at my uncle's house where Jacinta and Francisco were waiting. We set off together for the Cova da Iria in expectation of the longed-for moment. All those people followed us, asking a thousand questions.

On that day I was overwhelmed with bitterness. I could see that my mother was deeply distressed. She wanted at all costs to compel me, as she put it, to admit that I had lied. I wanted so much to do as she wished, but the only way I could do so was to tell a lie.

From the cradle, she had instilled into her children a great horror of lying, She used to chastise severely any one of us who told an untruth.

"I've seen to it," she often said, "that my children always told the truth, and am I now to let the youngest get away with a thing like this? If it were just a small thing...! But such a big lie, deceiving so many people and bringing them all the way here!" After these bitter complaints, she would turn to me, saying:

"Whatever it costs, undo this deception by telling these people that you've lied, or I'll lock you up in a dark room where you won't even see the light of the sun. After all the trouble I've been through, and now a thing like this to happen!" My sisters sided with my mother. All around me the atmosphere was one of utter scorn and contempt. Then I would remember the old days, and ask myself:

"Where now is all that affection my family had for me just such a short while ago?" My one relief was to weep before the Lord, as I offered Him my sacrifice. It was on this very day that, in addition to what I have already narrated, Our Lady said to me:

"Are you suffering a great deal? Do not be discouraged. I will never forsake you.

"My Immaculate Heart will be your refuge and the way that will lead you to God."

When Jacinta saw me in tears, she tried to console me: "Don't cry. Surely, these are the sacrifices which the Angel said that God was going to send us. That's why you are suffering, so that you can make reparation to Him and convert sinners."

Around that time our parish priest learned what was happening and sent word to my mother to take me to his house. My mother felt she could breathe again thinking the priest was going to take responsibility for these events on himself. She said to me:

"Tomorrow, we're going to Mass the first thing in the morning. Then you are going to the Reverend

Pastor's house. Just let him compel you to tell the truth, no matter how he does it; let him punish you; let him do whatever he likes with you; just so long as he forces you to admit that you have lied. Then I'll be satisfied."

My sisters also took my mother's part and invented endless threats, just to frighten me about the interview with the parish priest. I told Jacinta and her brother all about it.

"We're going also," they replied. "The Reverend Father told our mother to take us there too, but she didn't say any of those things to us. Never mind! If they beat us, we'll suffer for love of Our Lord and for sinners."

Lucia's Doubts and Temptations

The next day[2] I walked along behind my mother. She did not address one single word to me the whole way. I must admit that I was trembling at the thought of what was going to happen. During Mass I offered my suffering to God.[3] Afterwards, I followed my mother out of the church over to the priest's house.

I started up the stairs leading to the veranda. We had climbed only a few steps when my mother turned around and exclaimed:

"Don't annoy me any more! Tell the Reverend Father now that you lied, so that on Sunday he can say in the church that it was all a lie, and that will be the end of the whole affair. A nice business, this is! All this crowd running to the Cova da Iria, to pray in front of a holm oak bush!"

Without more ado, she knocked on the door. The good priest's sister opened the door and invited us to sit down on a bench and wait a while. At last the parish priest appeared. He took us into his study, motioned my mother to a seat, and beckoned me over to his desk. When I found that His Reverence was questioning me quite calmly, and with such a kindly manner, I was amazed.

I was still fearful, however, of what was yet to come. The interrogation was very minute and, I would even venture to say, tiresome. His Reverence concluded with this brief observation:

"It doesn't seem to me to be a revelation from Heaven. It is usual in such cases for Our Lord to tell the souls to whom He makes such communications to give their confessor or parish priest an account of what has happened.

"But this child, on the contrary, keeps it to herself as far as she can. This may also be a deceit from the devil. We shall see. The future will give us the answer."

Encouragement of Jacinta and Francisco

How much this reflection made me suffer only God knows, for He alone can penetrate our inmost heart. I began then to have doubts as to whether these manifestations might be from the devil seeking to make me lose my soul. As I heard people say that the devil always brings conflict and disorder, I began to think that, truly, ever since I had started seeing these things our home was no longer the same because joy and peace had fled. What anguish I felt! I made known my doubts to my cousins.

"No, it's not the devil!" replied Jacinta. "Not at all! They say that the devil is very ugly and that he's down under the ground in hell! But the Lady is so beautiful, and we saw Her go up to Heaven!"

Our Lord made use of this to allay somewhat the doubts I had. But during the course of that month, I lost all enthusiasm for making sacrifices and acts of mortification. I ended up hesitating as to whether it wouldn't be better to say that I had been lying, and so put an end to the whole thing.

"Don't do that!" exclaimed Jacinta and Francisco. "Don't you see that now you are going to tell a lie, and to tell lies is a sin?"

While in this state of mind I had a dream which only increased the darkness of my spirit. I saw the devil laughing at having deceived me as he tried to drag me down to hell. On finding myself in his clutches I began to scream so loudly, calling on Our Lady for help, that I awakened my mother. She called out to me in alarm and asked what was the matter. I can't recall what I told her, but I remember that I was so paralyzed with fear that I couldn't sleep any more that night.

This dream left my soul clouded over with real fear and anguish. My one relief was to go off by myself to some solitary place, there to weep. Even the company of my cousins began to seem burdensome. I began to hide from them as well. The poor children! At times they would search for me calling out my name and receiving no answer, but I was there all the while, hidden right close to them in some corner where they never thought of looking.

The 13th of July was close at hand. I was still doubtful as to whether I should go. I thought to myself, "If it's the devil, why should I go to see him? If they ask me why I'm not going, I'll say that I'm afraid it might be the devil who is appearing to us, and for that reason I'm not going. Let Francisco and Jacinta do as they like; I'm not going back to the Cova da Iria any more." My decision made, I was firmly resolved to act on it.

By the evening of the 12th, the people were already gathering in anticipation of the events of the following day. I called Jacinta and Francisco and told them of my resolution.

"We're going," they answered. "The Lady said we were to go." Jacinta volunteered to speak to the Lady, but she was so upset over my not going that she started to cry. I asked the reason for her tears.

"Because you don't want to go!"

"No, I'm not going. Listen! If the Lady asks for me, tell Her I'm not going, because I'm afraid it might be the devil."

I left them then to go and hide and so avoid having to speak to all the people who came looking for me to ask questions. My mother thought I was playing with the children of the village while all the time I was hidden behind the bushes in a neighbor's property adjoining the Arneiro, a little to the east of the well which I have mentioned so many times already. She scolded me as soon as I got home that night.

"A fine little plaster saint you are, to be sure! All the time you have left from minding the sheep you do nothing but play, and what's more you have to do it in such a way that nobody can find you!"

On the following day, when it was nearly time to leave, I suddenly felt I had to go. I was impelled by a strange force that I could hardly resist. I called at my uncle's house to see if Jacinta was still there. I found her in her room with her little brother. She was kneeling at the foot of the bed, crying.

"Well, aren't you going?" I asked.

"Not without you! We don't dare. Do come!"

"Yes, I'm going," I replied.

Their faces alight with joy, they set out with me. Crowds of people were waiting for us along the road. Only with difficulty did we finally get to the Cova. This was the day which Our Lady deigned to reveal to us the Secret. After that, to revive my flagging fervor, She said to us:

"Sacrifice yourself for sinners, and say many times to Jesus, especially when you make some sacrifice:

'O Jesus, it is for love of You, for the conversion of sinners, and in reparation for the sins committed against the Immaculate Heart of Mary.'"

Thanks to our good Lord, this apparition dispelled the doubts from my soul and my peace was restored.

Lucia's Mother Has Her Doubts

My poor mother worried more and more, as she saw the crowds who came flocking from all parts.

"These poor people," she said, "come here because of your trickery, you can be sure of that, and I really don't know what I can do to undeceive them."

A poor man who boasted of making fun of us, of insulting and of even going so far as to beat us, asked my mother one day:

"Well, ma'am, what have you got to say about your daughter's visions?"

"I don't know," she answered. "It seems to me that she's nothing but a fake, who is leading half the world astray."

"Don't say that out loud, or somebody's likely to kill her. I think there are people around here who would be only too glad to do so."

"Oh, I don't care, just so long as they force her to confess the truth. As for me, I always tell the truth, whether against my children, or anybody else, or even against myself." One day, she resolved to make a fresh attempt to compel me to retract all that I had said, as she put it. She made up her mind to take me back the very next day to the parish priest's house.

Once there, I was to confess that I had lied, to ask his pardon, and to perform whatever penance His Reverence thought fit or desired to impose on me. This time the attack was so strong that I did not know what to do. On the way, as I passed my uncle's house, I ran inside to tell Jacinta, who was still in bed, what was taking place. Then I hurried out and followed my mother. In my account about Jacinta, I have already told Your Excellency about the part played by her and her brother in this trial which the Lord had sent us, and how they prayed as they waited for me at the well, and so on.

As we walked along, my mother preached me a fine sermon. At a certain point, I said to her, trembling:

"But, mother, how can I say that I did not see, when I did see?"

My mother was silent. As we drew near the priest's house, she declared:

"Just you listen to me! What I want is that you should tell the truth. If you saw, say so! But if you didn't see, admit that you lied."

Without another word, we climbed the stairs. The good priest received us in his study with the greatest kindness and even, I might almost say, with affection. He questioned me seriously but courteously, and resorted to various stratagems to see if I would contradict myself, or be inconsistent in my statements. Finally he dismissed us, shrugging his shoulders as if to imply:

"I don't know what to make of all this!"

The Administrator's Threats

Not many days later, our parents were notified to the effect that all three of us, Jacinta, Francisco and myself, together with our fathers, were to appear at a given hour of the following day before the Administration in Vila Nova de Ourem. This meant that we had to make a journey of about nine miles, a considerable distance for three children, as small as we were. The only means of transport in those days was either one's own two feet or on a donkey. My uncle sent word right away to say that he would appear himself, but he would not bring his children.

"They'd never stand the trip on foot," he said, "and not being used to riding, they could never manage to stay on the donkey. Anyway, there's no sense in bringing two children like that before a court."

My parents thought the very opposite. "My daughter is going. Let her answer for herself. As for me, I understand nothing of these things. If she's lying, it's a good thing that she should be punished for it."

Very early the next morning they put me on a donkey and off I went, accompanied by my father and uncle. I fell off the donkey three times along the way. I think I have already told Your Excellency how much Jacinta and Francisco suffered that day, thinking that I was going to be killed.

As for me, what hurt me most was the indifference shown me by my parents. This was all the more obvious since I could see how affectionately my aunt and uncle treated their children. I remember thinking to myself as we went along:

"How different my parents are from my uncle and aunt. They risk themselves to defend their children while my parents hand me over with the greatest indifference, and let them do what they like with me! But I must be patient," I reminded myself in my inmost heart, "since by this means I have the happiness of suffering more for love of You, O my God, and for the conversion of sinners." This reflection never failed to bring me consolation.

At the Administration office, I was interrogated by the Administrator in the presence of my father, my uncle and several other gentlemen who were strangers to me. The Administrator was determined to force me to reveal the Secret and to promise him never again to return to the Cova da Iria.

To attain his end, he spared neither promises nor threats. Seeing that he was getting nowhere, he dismissed me, protesting however that he would achieve his end, even if this meant that he had to take my life.

He then gave a strong reprimand to my uncle for not having carried out his orders, and finally let us go home.

In the intimacy of my own family there was fresh trouble, and the blame was thrown on me. The Cova da Iria was a piece of land belonging to my parents. The hollow was fertile and there we cultivated maize, greens, peas and other vegetables. Now, ever since the people began to go there, we had been unable to cultivate anything at all. Everything was trampled down.

As the majority came mounted, their animals ate up all they could find and wrecked the whole place. My mother bewailed the loss:

"You, now," she said to me, "when you want something to eat, go and ask the Lady for it!" My sisters chimed in with:

"Yes, you can have what grows in the Cova da Iria!"

These remarks cut me to the heart, so much so that I hardly dared to take a piece of bread to eat. To force me to tell the truth, as she said, my mother, more often than not, beat me soundly with the broom-handle or a stick from the woodpile near the fireplace. But in spite of this, mother that she was, she then tried to revive my failing strength.

She was full of concern when she saw me so thin and pale, and feared I might get sick. Poor mother! Now, indeed, that I understand what her situation was, how sorry I feel for her!

Truly, she was right to judge me unworthy of such a favor, and therefore to think I was lying. By a special grace from God, I never experienced the slightest thought or feeling of resentment regarding her manner of acting towards me.

As the Angel had announced that God would send me sufferings, I always saw the hand of God in it all. The love, esteem and respect which I owed her went on increasing, just as though I were her most dearly cherished.

And now, I am more grateful to her for having treated me like this than if she had constantly continued to surround me with endearments and caresses.

Lucia's First Spiritual Director

It seems to me that it was in the course of this month that Rev. Dr. Formigao came for the first time to question me. His interrogation was serious and detailed. I liked him very much because he spoke a great deal to me about the practice of virtue and taught me various ways of exercising myself in it. He showed me a holy picture of St. Agnes, told me about her martyrdom and encouraged me to imitate her. His Reverence continued to come every month for an interrogation,[4] and always ended up by giving me some good advice which was of help to me spiritually. One day he said to me:

"My child, you must love Our Lord very much in return for so many favors and graces that He is granting you."

These words made such an impression on my soul that, from then on, I acquired the habit of constantly saying to Our Lord:

"My God, I love You, in thanksgiving for the graces which You have granted me." I so loved this ejaculation that I passed it on to Jacinta and her brother, who took it so much to heart that, in the middle of the most exciting games, Jacinta would ask:

"Have you been forgetting to tell Our Lord how much you love Him for the graces He has given us?"

Meanwhile the 13th day of August had dawned. Ever since the previous evening, crowds had been pouring in from all parts. They wanted to see and question us, and recommend their petitions to us, so that we could transmit them to the most Holy Virgin. In the midst of all those people we were like a ball in the hands of children.

We were pulled here and there, everyone asking us questions without giving us a chance to answer. Amid all this commotion, an order came from the

Administrator telling me to go to my aunt's house where he was awaiting me. My father got the notification and took me there. When I arrived, he was in a room with my cousins.

Imprisonment at Ourem

He interrogated us there and made fresh attempts to force us to reveal the secret and to promise that we would not go back to the Cova da Iria. As he achieved nothing, he gave orders to my father and my uncle to take us up to the parish priest's house.

I will not delay now to tell Your Excellency about everything else that happened during our imprisonment, for you already know it all. As I have previously explained to Your Excellency, what I felt most deeply and what caused me the most suffering on that occasion was my being completely abandoned by my family... and it was the same for my little cousins.

After this journey or imprisonment, for I really don't know what to call it, I returned home, as far as I can remember, on the 15th of August. To celebrate my arrival they sent me right away to let out the sheep and take them off to pasture. My uncle and aunt wanted their children to stay with them at home and their brother John went with me in their place. As it was already late, we stayed in the vicinity of our little hamlet at a place called Valinhos.

Penances and Sufferings

What happened next is also known to Your Excellency so I will not delay here to describe it. Once again, the most Blessed Virgin recommended to us the practice of mortification, and ended by saying:

"Pray, pray much, and make sacrifices for sinners; so many souls go to hell because they have no one to pray and to make sacrifices for them."

Some days later, as we were walking along the road with our sheep, I found a piece of rope that had fallen off a cart. I picked it up and, just for fun, I tied it around my arm. Before long I noticed that the rope was hurting me.

"Look, this hurts!" I said to my cousins. "We could tie it round our waists and offer this sacrifice to God."

The poor children fell in with my suggestion. We then set about dividing it among the three of us by placing it across a stone and striking it with the sharp edge of another one that served as a knife. Either because of the thickness or roughness of the rope, or because we sometimes tied it too tightly, this instrument of penance often caused us terrible suffering. Now and then, Jacinta could not keep back her tears, so great was the discomfort this caused her. Whenever I urged her to remove it, she replied:

"No! I want to offer this sacrifice to Our Lord in reparation, and for the conversion of sinners."

Another day we were playing, picking little plants off the walls and pressing them in our hands to hear them crack. When Jacinta was plucking these plants, she happened to catch hold of some nettles and stung herself.

She no sooner felt the pain than she squeezed them more tightly in her hands, and said to us:

"Look! Look! Here is something else with which we can mortify ourselves!" From that time on, we used to hit our legs occasionally with nettles, so as to offer to God yet another sacrifice.

If I am not mistaken, it was also during this month that we acquired the habit of giving our lunch to our poor little children, as I have already described to Your Excellency in the account about Jacinta. It was during this month too, that my mother began to feel a little more peace. She would say:

"If there were even just one more person who had seen something... why then, I might believe! But among all those people, they're the only ones who saw anything!"

Now, during this past month, various people were saying that they had seen different things. Some had seen Our Lady; others, various signs in the sun, and so on. My mother declared:

"I used to think before that if there were just one other person who saw anything, then I'd believe. And I still don't believe!" My father also began, about then, to come to my defense and to silence those who started scolding me. He used to say:

"We don't know if it's true, but neither do we know if it's a lie."

Then it was that my uncle and aunt, wearied by the troublesome demands of all these outsiders who were continually wanting to see us and speak to us, began to send their son John out to pasture the flock. They themselves remained at home with Jacinta and Francisco.

Shortly afterwards, they ended by selling the sheep altogether. As I did not enjoy any other company, I started to go out alone with my sheep.

As I have already told Your Excellency, whenever I happened to be nearby, Jacinta and her brother would come to join me; and when the pasture was at a distance they would be waiting for me on my way home.

I can truly say that these were really happy days. Alone, in the midst of my sheep, whether on the tops of the hills or in the depths of the valleys below, I contemplated the beauty of the heavens and thanked the good God for all the graces He had bestowed on me.

When the voice of one of my sisters broke in on my solitude, calling for me to go back home to talk to some person or other who had come looking for me, I felt a keen displeasure. My only consolation was to be able to offer up to our dear Lord yet another sacrifice.

On a certain day, three gentlemen came to speak to us. After their questioning, which was anything but pleasant, they took their leave with this remark:

"See that you decide to tell that secret of yours. If you don't the Administrator has every intention of taking your lives!" Jacinta, her face light up with a joy that she made no effort to hide, said:

"How wonderful! I so love Our Lord and Our Lady, and this way we'll be seeing them soon!"

The rumor got around that the Administrator did really intend to kill us. This led my aunt, who was married and living in Casais, to come to our house with the express purpose of taking us home with her, for, as she explained:

"I live in another district and this Administrator cannot lay hands on you there." But her plan was never carried out because we were unwilling to go. We said:

"If they kill us, it's all the same! We'll go to heaven!"

September 13th

Now the 13th of September was drawing near. In addition to what I have already related, Our Lady said to us on this day:

"God is pleased with your sacrifices, but He does not wish you to sleep with the rope on; wear it only during the day."

Needless to say, we promptly obeyed His orders. Since it seems Our Lord had, a month before, wished to give some visible sign out of the ordinary, my mother eagerly hoped that on this day such signs would be still more clear and evident. The good Lord, however, perhaps to give us the opportunity to offer Him yet another sacrifice... permitted that no ray of His glory should appear on this day. My mother lost heart once more... and the persecution at home began all over again.

She had indeed many reasons for being so upset. The Cova da Iria was now a total loss, not only as a fine pasture for our flock but even more because of the vegetables we had grown there. Added to this was my mother's almost certain conviction, as she expressed it, that the events themselves were nothing but foolish fancies and mere childish imaginings. One of my sisters did scarcely anything else but go and call me and take my place with the flock, while I went to speak to the people who were asking to see and talk to me.

Lucia's Spirit of Sacrifice

This waste of time would have meant nothing to a wealthy family... but for ourselves, who had to live by our work, it meant a great deal. After some time my mother found herself obliged to sell our flock, and this made no small difference to the support of the family. I was blamed for the whole thing, and at critical moments it was all flung in my face. I hope our dear Lord has accepted it all from me for I offered it to Him, always happy to be able to sacrifice myself for Him and for sinners.

On her part, my mother endured everything with heroic patience and resignation. If she reprimanded me and punished me, it was because she really thought that I was lying. She was completely resigned to the crosses which Our Lord was sending her. At times she would say:

"Could it be that all this is God's work in punishment for my sins? If so, then blessed be God!"

A neighbor took it upon herself one day (why, I don't know) to remark that some gentleman had given me some money. I cannot remember how much.

Without more ado, my mother called me and asked for it. When I told her I hadn't received any, to force me to hand it over to her she had recourse to the broom handle.

When the dust had been well beaten out of my clothes, Caroline, one of my sisters, intervened along with a girl from our neighborhood called Virginia. They said they had been present at the interrogation and they had seen that the gentleman had actually given me nothing at all. Thanks to their defending me, I was able to slip away to my beloved well and there offer yet another sacrifice to our good Lord.

A Tall Visitor

If I am not mistaken, it was also during this month that a young man made his appearance at our home.[5] He was of such tall stature that I trembled with fear. When I saw he had to bend down in order to come through the doorway in search of me, I thought I must be in the presence of a German. At that time we were at war, and grown-ups would try to frighten children by saying:

"Here comes a German to kill you."

I thought that my last hour had come. My fright did not pass unnoticed by the young man, who sought to calm me. He made me sit on his knee and questioned me with great kindness. His interrogation over, he asked my mother to let me go and show him the site of the apparitions and to pray with him there.

All along the way I trembled with fear at finding myself alone in the company of this stranger. Then I began to feel tranquil again at the thought that if he killed me I would go to see Our Lord and Our Lady.

On arriving at the place, he knelt down and asked me to pray the Rosary with him to obtain a special grace from Our Lady that he greatly desired... that a certain young woman would consent to receive with him the sacrament of Matrimony. I wondered at such a request and thought to myself:

"If she has as much fear of him as I, she will never say 'Yes'!"

When the Rosary was over the good young man accompanied me most of the way home and then he bade me a friendly farewell, recommending his request to me again. I ran off helter skelter to my aunt's house still afraid he might turn around and come back!

What was my surprise then, on the 13th of October, when I suddenly found myself, after the apparitions, in the arms of this same person sailing along over the heads of the people. It actually served to satisfy the curiosity of everyone who wanted to see me!

After a little while, unable to see where he was going, he stumbled and fell. I did not fall because I was caught in the crush of people who pressed around me. Right away others took hold of me and this gentleman disappeared.

It was not until some time later that he appeared again, this time accompanied by the aforesaid girl, now his wife! He came to thank the Blessed Virgin for the grace received and to ask Her copious blessings on their future. This young man is today Dr. Carlos Mendes of Torres Novas.

October 13th

Now, Your Excellency, here we are at the 13th of October. You already know all that happened on that day. Of all the words spoken at this Apparition, the ones most deeply engraved upon my heart were those of the request made by our heavenly Mother:

"Do not offend Our Lord and God any more, because He is already much offended!"

How loving a complaint... how tender a request! Who will grant me to make it echo through the whole world, so that all the children of our Mother in Heaven may hear the sound of Her voice!

The rumor had spread that the authorities intended to explode a bomb quite close to us at the very moment of the Apparition. This did not frighten me in the least. I spoke of it to my cousins.

"How wonderful," we exclaimed, "if we were granted the grace of going up to Heaven from there, together with Our Lady!"

My parents, however, were very much afraid and for the first time they wished to accompany me, saying that if their daughter was going to die, they wanted to die by her side. My father took me by the hand to the place of the Apparitions. From the moment of the Apparition itself I did not set eyes on him again until I was back home with the family that night.

I spent the afternoon of that day with my cousins. We were like some curious creatures that the multitudes wanted to see and observe. By night time I was really exhausted after so many questions and interrogations. These did not even end with nightfall. Several people who had been unable to question me remained over till the following day awaiting their turn. Some of them even tried to talk to me that night, but overcome by weariness I just dropped down and fell asleep. Thank God, human respect and self-love were, at that time, unknown to me. For that reason

I was as much at ease with any person at all as I was with my parents.

On the following day, or rather, to be accurate, on the following days, the questionings continued. Almost every day from then on people went to the Cova da Iria to implore the protection of our heavenly Mother. Everybody wanted to see the seers, to put questions to them, and to recite the Rosary with them.

At times, I was so tired of saying the same thing over and over again, and also of praying, that I looked for any pretext for excusing myself and making my escape. But those poor people were so insistent that I had to make an effort, and indeed no small effort, in order to satisfy them. I then repeated my usual prayer deep down in my heart:

"O my God, it is for love of You, in reparation for the sins committed against the Immaculate Heart of Mary, for the conversion of sinners, and for the Holy Father!"

Questioned by Priests

In the account I have written about my cousin, I have already told Your Excellency how two holy priests came and spoke to us about the Holy Father (the Pope), and told us of his great need of prayers. From that time on, there was not a prayer or sacrifice that we offered to God which did not include an invocation for His Holiness. We grew to love the Holy Father so deeply that when the parish priest told my mother that I probably would have to go to Rome to be interrogated by His Holiness, I clapped my hands with joy and said to my cousins:

"Won't it be wonderful if I can go and see the Holy Father?"

They burst into tears and said:

"We can't go, but we can offer this sacrifice for him."

The parish priest questioned me for the last time.

The events had duly come to an end at the appointed time, and still His Reverence did not know what to say about the whole affair.[6] He was also beginning to show his displeasure:

"Why are all those people going to prostrate themselves in prayer in a deserted spot like that, while here the Living God of our altars is left all alone in the Blessed Sacrament, abandoned in the tabernacle? What's all the money for, the money they leave for no purpose whatsoever under the holm oak, while the church, which is under repairs, cannot be completed for lack of funds?"[7]

I understood perfectly why he spoke like that, but what could I do? If I had been given authority over the hearts of those people, I would certainly have led them to the parish church, but as I had not, I offered to God another sacrifice.

As Jacinta was in the habit of putting her head down, keeping her eyes fixed on the ground and scarcely uttering a word during the interrogations, I was usually called upon to satisfy the curiosity of the pilgrims. For that reason, I was continually being summoned to the house of the parish priest.

On one occasion, a priest from Torres Novas came to question me.[8] When he did so, he went into such minute details, and tried so hard to trip me up, that afterwards I felt some scruples about having concealed certain things from him. I consulted my cousins on the matter.

"I don't know," I asked them, "if we are doing wrong by not telling when they ask us if Our Lady told us anything else. When we just say that She told us a secret, I don't know whether we are lying or not by saying nothing about the rest."

"I don't know," replied Jacinta, "that's up to you! You're the one who does not want us to say anything!"

"Of course I don't want you to say anything," I answered. "Why, they'll start asking us what sort of mortifications we are practicing! And that would be the last straw.

"Listen! If you had kept quiet, and not said a word nobody would have known by now that we saw Our Lady, or spoke to Her, or to the Angel; and nobody needed to know it anyway!"

The poor child had no sooner heard my arguments than she started to cry. Just as she did in May, she asked my forgiveness in the way I have already described in my account of her life. So I was left with my scruple, and had no idea as to how I was to resolve my doubt.

A little while later, another priest appeared. He was from Santarem. He looked like a brother of the first I've just spoken of, or at least they seemed to have rehearsed the same attempts to trip me up, laughing and making fun of me in the same way; in fact, their height and features were almost identical.

After this interrogation, my doubt was stronger than ever. I really did not know what course of action to follow. I constantly pleaded with Our Lord and Our Lady to tell me what to do.

"O my God, and my dearest Mother in Heaven, You know that I do not want to offend You by telling lies; but You are well aware that it would not be right to tell them all You told me!"

In the midst of this perplexity, I had the happiness of speaking to the Vicar of Olival.[9] — I do not know why, but His Reverence inspired me with confidence, and I confided my doubt to him. I have already explained, in my account of Jacinta, how he taught us to keep our secret. He also gave us some further instructions on spiritual life. Above all, he taught us to give pleasure to Our Lord in everything, and how to offer Him countless little sacrifices.

"If you feel like eating something, my children," he would say, "leave it, and eat something else instead and thus offer a sacrifice to God. If you feel inclined to play, do not do so, and offer to God another sacrifice. If people question you, and you cannot avoid answering them, it is God who wills it so offer Him this sacrifice too."

This holy priest spoke a language that I could really understand, and I loved him dearly. From then on he never lost sight of my soul. Now and then, he called in to see me, or kept in touch with me through a pious widow, Senhora Emilia, who lived in a little hamlet[10] near Olival. Very devout, she often went to pray at the Cova da Iria. Afterwards she used to come to our house and ask to have me go and spend a few days with her. Then we paid a visit to the Reverend Vicar who was kind enough to invite me to remain for two or three days as company for one of his sisters.

At such times he was patient enough to spend whole hours alone with me, teaching me the practice of virtue and guiding me with his own wise counsels. Even though at that time I did not understand anything about spiritual direction, I can truly say that he was my first spiritual director. I cherish grateful and holy memories of this saintly priest.

†††

[1.] These places are situated in the vicinity of Fatima. The farthest is fifteen miles away.

[2.] The day mentioned as the "next day" was August 11, 1917.

[3.] One should note that this was a state of confusion and helplessness, rather than actual doubts, and it was caused by the difficulties in her family in addition to the cautious attitude of the priest.

[4.] Dr. Manuel Nunes Formigao Jr., later the great apostle of Fatima, went first to the Cova where the Apparitions took place on September 13.

5. This refers to the visit of Dr. Carlos de Azevedo Mendes on September 8, 1917. While his great size frightened Lucia at the time, he became a staunch witness to the Fatima miracle and was so dedicated to the apparitions that he built a house near the Cova and spent the last years of his life there. See *Meet the Witnesses*.

6. The Postulation Office in Fatima has in its possession the parish priest's valuable report; the same questions were brought up during every interrogation.

7. The documents of the period show that one reason for the priest's departure was the difficulty he had to face in connection with the restoration of the church building.

8. Canon Ferreira, priest of Torres Novas at that time, once confessed that he was one of those troublesome interrogators.

9. This was Father Faustino.

10. The place is called Soutaria. Senhora Emilia's house was rebuilt as a chapel.

Lucia's House

Chapter IX.

Comments On

THE SACRIFICE OF MEETING PRIESTS

Lucia's sufferings would probably have been unbearable in a child of her age were it not, as she says, that she always remembered the words of the angel and saw their fulfillment in the incredible deluge of suffering that now engulfed her. And on top of it all, Satan came and tempted her to believe that there had been no angel... there had been no vision of Our Lady... there had been only he, the great deceiver using her to deceive.

The severe beatings from her mother were less painful by far than the change in her mother's attitude... and that she was *commanded* by her mother to say that she lied!

One would think (at least before reading the memoirs) that the children went to see Our Lady on June 13 with great joy and anticipation because seeing Her was such a joy for them. But Lucia says:

"On that day I was *overwhelmed* with bitterness."

It must be remembered that Lucia's mother was ill. Shortly afterwards, as we shall see, she almost died. Also the family was very, very poor. While they refused any money (one of Lucia's worst beatings was because her mother thought she had taken money) they had to sell the sheep because the children were always being called and their truck garden in the Cova was destroyed. Lucia's mother's rebuke, because of this alone, "Cut me to the heart so much that I hardly dared take a piece of bread to eat."

But even all this suffering was not the greatest. The greatest suffering came from priests. When the children saw priests coming, Lucia said, "We prepared to make our greatest sacrifices." However, some priests brought consolation and direction, and the children had only the greatest respect for ALL priests.

There is a very important message here, but before going into it there is a subsequent story about Dr. Carlos Mendes very worth remembering.

Dr. Mendes seemed truly, especially in Portugal where at the time most people were of small stature, a giant. I am six feet tall and the many times I met him in the Cova where, year after year, he came on the 13th of the month to assist the sick, he seemed to tower over me.

It makes one smile now to think that when Lucia first saw him she thought she was about to die and that Dr. Mendes had much to do to calm her fears, because he was truly a gentle giant and became one of the greatest devotees of Fatima we have ever known. More of his personal story and his testimony about the miracle of Fatima will be found in *Meet the Witnesses.* But the story I want to record here has never been told before.

In his last years he had moved from Torres Novas to a house very close to the Cova and one day, only a short time before he died, I told him that a large group of Americans meeting at the Blue Army International center would like to meet this man who knew the children and witnessed the miracle of the sun... and indeed many other miracles at Fatima.

"Dr. Mendes," I said in presenting him to the group, "you saw the miracle of the sun and you have seen several great miracles in the Cova during the many years you have served the sick. What, of all that you have seen and experienced at Fatima, impressed you most?"

I thought certainly it would be the miracle of the sun... "the greatest, most colossal miracle in history." Or at least it would be one of the miracles such as two I personally witnessed on days he was in the Cova... instantaneous cures of persons close to death... and he had certainly seen many more such miracles than I. But what HAD impressed him most?

"The second time I came back to Fatima," he said, "I was walking with the children as they returned from the Cova. They were saying the Rosary and nothing I have seen and heard in all these years impressed me more than those children praying the Rosary together."

I have no comment. Neither did he. Just his telling this gave me such a feeling about the Rosary... what it CAN be... that I can recall my standing beside him and my surprise and awe at the tone of his voice as though it were yesterday.

Why Were priests So Negative?

We know that the parish priest was negative and very harsh with Lucia because he feared, as did Lucia's mother, that the child was deceived... and he had the grave responsibility of judging.

We presume that most of the other priests had the same motive.

It must be remembered that this was a terrible time for the Church in Portugal. Only a short time before the apparitions of Fatima the government had proclaimed Lisbon "the atheist capital of the world" and had vowed to wipe out all religion. Little more than eighty years before, all religious orders had been expelled from the country and the persecution of the secular clergy which remained had escalated ever since.

In the last chapter Lucia mentions Dr. Formigao, who asked the children many questions... but with kindness. He was actually the priest sent by the Archbishop of Lisbon to report on the matter. His notes and testimony are among the most important documents on Fatima after Lucia's own memoirs and letters. His sincerity was evident to the children.

However, all the above taken into consideration, then and now, there seems to be a generally negative attitude towards events like Fatima among much of the clergy. The most frequent complaint of those who want to start prayer cells or First Saturday devotions in parishes is that the pastor will not allow it... or that when he does allow it, he does not participate.

The reaction of the laity must be always like that of the children of Fatima. Bishop Venancio, one of the four to whom this book is dedicated, used to say: "Always respect and obey the pastor." And then he would add: "But never take 'no' for an answer. Keep asking."

Two Different Views of Fatima

The usual view of Fatima held by the clergy is that we are speaking of only a private revelation. It is of value in that it reaffirms the Gospel, but is not to be taken too seriously in itself but only in the context of public revelation. Those who hold this view will add, often with unnecessary emphasis, that "we do not have to believe in Fatima."

Another view, usually of persons not unlike the children of Fatima, is that this is the most important event perhaps since the time of Our Lord. As Jean Guitton puts it: An intervention of God *"At the hinge of history, before and after Hiroshima, dividing history forever."*[1]

Those who hold the first view either oppose the Fatima Apostolate or accept it in degrees varying from toleration to reluctant support. Those who hold the second view usually become active in the Fatima

Apostolate in degrees which range from just making the pledge to making the First Friday-Saturday Vigils and even parish and diocesan leaders. And a few... usually very few, but quite vocal... become what some seem to delight in calling "fanatics."

As is usually the case, *Virtus stat in medio:* Virtue is in the middle.

Fatima is not JUST another private revelation. And even though it is not what we call *de fide,* it is a credible revelation from God approved by the Church. When we know this, we are bound to give it human belief. We cannot deny what we know is true.

Lack of Knowledge

The negative attitude of much of the clergy is certainly attributable to lack of knowledge... which may seem curious to say about priests because of their years of training. However, it is unlikely that seminarians, in all their years of study, would have even three or four classroom hours on Fatima... if any at all.

This may change, but it should not be such a surprise. Medical doctors, in all their years of study, get on the average only four classroom hours on nutrition which some would say is as important to health as medicine.

Yet the study of the miracle of Fatima in itself could be a major work. Dr. Alonso, one of the great Mariologists of our time (again one of the four to whom this book is dedicated) was documentarian of Fatima and his findings fill *eighteen volumes.* This event needs to be studied, not only by priests but by everyone. It marks a *turning point in history.*

To this day Jews refer over and over, as also do we, to the miracle of the Red Sea. It recurs again and again in our liturgy, in our worship, and in our acknowledgment of what God has done for His people.

Yet the miracle of Fatima could be considered even greater than the miracle of the Red Sea for at least five reasons:

1) It was intended to deliver the world not from Egypt but from Communism, and from a tide of evil which merited that "several entire nations be annihilated";

2) Just ONE element of the miracle of Fatima was essentially the same as the miracle of the Red Sea: The Cova, which had become a sea of water and mud, dried instantly;

3) More than this similarity to the Red Sea Miracle, the miracle of Fatima was also essentially the same as the miracle performed by Elias "That all may know that God is God," when the prophet called down fire from Heaven;

4) It is furthermore essentially the same as the miracle of Joshua causing the light of the sun to shine independently of the sun;

5) But over and beyond all the reasons above, it was the FIRST miracle in history permitted by God *at a predicted time and place* "so that all may believe."

Certainly all the Popes since Fatima have taken it very, very seriously as a Divine intervention at a most critical moment in the history of man. It is not only a reaffirmation of the Gospel. It is a new Sinai.

As we continue to read the words Lucia was left on earth to write for us, may our minds be illuminated to see, even between the lines, the beautiful message which God's Merciful Love conveys through her to our atomic age.

†††

[1.] Portrait de Marthe Robin, 1986, p. 248.

Chapter X.

In the Second Memoir —
Lucia Remembers

SUFFERING AND A CURE

After the apparitions, Lucia began to go to school to learn to read and write as Our Lady had directed. In this Memoir she recalls continued attempts by the government officials to keep people away from the Cova da Iria, the serious illness of her mother and the sudden and unexpected death of her father.

†††

Lucia Goes to School

Oh dear, here I am writing without rhyme or reason, as the saying goes, and already leaving out various things that I should have said! But I am doing as Your Excellency told me... writing just what I remember and in all simplicity. That is what I want to do, without worrying about order or style. In that way I think my obedience is more perfect... and therefore more pleasing to Our Lord and to the Immaculate Heart of Mary.

I will go back, then, to my parents' home. I have told Your Excellency that my mother had to sell our flock. We kept only three sheep, which we took along with us when we went to the fields. Whenever we stayed at home, we kept them in the corral and fed them there. My mother then sent me to school and in my free time she wanted me to learn weaving and sewing. In this way she had me safe in the house and did not have to waste time looking for me.

One fine day my sisters were asked to go with some other girls to help with the grape harvest on the property of a wealthy man of Pe de Cao.[1] My mother decided to let them go, as long as I could go too, as I have already said earlier my mother never allowed them to go anywhere unless they took me with them.

Lucia and the Parish priest

It was at this time that the parish priest began preparing the children for a solemn Communion. Since the age of six I had repeated my solemn Communion every year, but this year my mother decided I would not do so. For this reason I did not attend the Catechism classes. After school the other children went to the parish priest's verandah while I went home to get on with my sewing or weaving.

The good priest did not take kindly to my absence from the catechism class. One day on my way home from school his sister sent another child after me. She caught up with me on the road to Aljustrel near the house of a poor man who was nicknamed "Snail." She told me that the parish priest's sister wanted me and that I was to go straight back.

Thinking that I was just wanted for questioning, I excused myself. I explained that my mother had told me to go home right after school. Without further word I took to my heels across the fields like a mad thing in search of a hiding place where no one could find me, but this time the prank cost me dearly. Some days later there was a big feast in the parish and several priests came from all around to sing the Mass.

When it was over the parish priest sent for me and in front of all those priests he scolded me severely for not attending the Catechism lessons and for not running back to his sister when she had sent for me. In short, all my faults and failings were brought to light and the sermon went on for quite a long while.

At last, though I don't know how, a holy priest appeared on the scene and sought to plead my case. He suggested that perhaps my mother had not given me permission. But the pastor replied:

"Her mother! Why, she's a saint! But as for this one, it remains to be seen what she'll turn out to be!"

The good priest, who later became the Vicar of Torres Novas, then asked me very kindly why I had not been to the Catechism classes. I therefore told him of my mother's decision. The pastor did not seem to believe me. He sent for my sister Gloria, who was over by the church, to find out the truth of the matter. Having found that indeed things were just as I had said, he came to the conclusion:

"Well, then! Either the child is going to attend the Catechism classes for the days still remaining, and afterwards come to me for Confession and then make her solemn Communion with all the rest of the children, or she's never going to receive Communion again in the parish!"

When my sister heard this she told the pastor that I was due to leave with my sisters five days before, and that such an arrangement would be most inconvenient. She added that, if His Reverence so desired, I could go to Confession and Communion some other day before our scheduled departure. He ignored her request and stood firm by his decision.

When we reached home, we told my mother all about it. She also went to the pastor to ask him to hear my Confession and give me Holy Communion on another day. But it was all in vain. My mother then decided that after the solemn Communion day, my brother would make the journey with me in spite of the long distance and the difficulties caused by the extremely bad roads winding up and down the hills and highlands. I think I must have sweated ink at the mere idea of having to go to Confession to the parish priest! How much I feared him! I cried with anguish.

On the day before the solemn Communion, the pastor sent for all the children to go to church in the afternoon to make their Confession. As I went, fear gripped my heart as in a vise, but as I entered the church I saw that there were several priests hearing Confessions.

There at the end of the church was Reverend Father Cruz from Lisbon. I had spoken to His Reverence before and I liked him very much indeed. Without noticing that the parish priest was in an open confessional halfway up the church, I thought to myself:

"First I'll go and make my Confession to Father Cruz and ask him what I am to do, and then I'll go to the parish priest." Fr. Cruz received me with great kindness.

After hearing my Confession he advised me that if I did not want to go to the parish priest I should not do so, and that he could not refuse me Communion for a reason such as that. I was radiant with joy on hearing this advice and said my penance. Then I made good my escape from the church for fear lest somebody might call me back.

The next day when I went to the church all dressed in white, I was still afraid that I might be refused Communion. After the feast was over the pastor contented himself with letting me know that my lack of obedience in going to Confession to another priest had not passed unnoticed. The good priest grew more and more displeased and perplexed concerning these events until one day he left the parish.

Word circulated that His Reverence had left on account of me and because he did not want to assume responsibility for these events.[2] He was a zealous pastor and much beloved among the people so I had much to suffer. Several pious women, whenever they met me, gave vent to their displeasure by insulting me. Sometimes they sent me on my way with blows or kicks.

Companions in Sympathy and Suffering

These Heaven-sent "caresses" were rarely meted out to Jacinta and Francisco, for their parents would not allow anyone to lay hands on them, but they suffered when they saw me suffering. Many times tears ran down their cheeks when they saw me distressed or humiliated. One time Jacinta said to me:

"If only my parents were like yours, so that those people would beat me too, then I'd have more sacrifices to offer Our Lord." However, she well knew how to make the most of countless opportunities for mortifying herself.

Now and then we were also in the habit of offering to God the sacrifice of spending nine days or a month without taking a drink. Once we made this sacrifice even in the month of August when the heat was suffocating.

As we were returning from the Cova da Iria where we had been praying our Rosary, we came to a dirty pond beside the road and Jacinta said to me:

"Oh, I'm so thirsty and my head aches so! I'm going to drink a little drop of this water."

"Not that water," I answered. "My mother doesn't want us to drink it, because it's not good for us. We'll go and ask Maria dos Anjos for some." (She was a neighbor of ours, who had recently married and was living near there in a small house.)

"No! I don't want good water. I'd rather drink this because instead of offering Our Lord our thirst, I could offer Him the sacrifice of drinking this dirty water."

This water was filthy. People washed their clothes in it, and the animals came there to drink and waded right into it. That was why my mother warned her children not to drink this water. At other times, Jacinta would say:

"Our Lord must be pleased with our sacrifices, because I am so thirsty, so thirsty! Yet I do not want to take a drink. I want to suffer for love of Him."

One day, we were sitting in the doorway of my uncle's house when we noticed several people approaching. Not having time to do anything, Francisco and I ran inside to hide under the beds, he in one room, and I in another. Jacinta said:

"I'm not going to hide. I'm going to offer this sacrifice to Our Lord." These people came up and talked to her, waiting around quite a long time until I could be found. Finally they went away. I slipped out of my hiding place and asked Jacinta:

"What did you answer when they asked you if you knew where we were?"

"I said nothing at all... I just put my head down, kept my eyes fixed on the ground and said nothing. I always do that when I don't want to tell the truth and I don't want to tell a lie either, because lying is a sin."

She was indeed accustomed to do just this and it was useless to question her. Those who did so obtained no response whatever. However, if escape were at all possible we normally felt little inclined to offer this kind of sacrifice.

Another day we were sitting in the shade of two fig trees overhanging the road that runs by my cousin's house. Francisco began to play a little way off. He saw several ladies coming toward us and ran back to warn us. We promptly climbed up the fig trees.

In those days it was the fashion to wear hats with very wide brims and we were sure that, with such headgear, those people would never catch sight of us up there. As soon as the ladies had gone by, we came down as fast as we could, took to our heels and hid in a corn field.

This habit we had of making good our escape whenever possible was yet another cause for complaint on the part of the parish priest. He bitterly complained of the way we tried to avoid priests in particular. This was true and His Reverence was certainly right. It was priests especially who put us through the most rigorous cross-examinations and then returned to question us all over again. Whenever we found ourselves in the presence of a priest, we prepared to offer to God one of our greatest sacrifices!

Government Opposition

Meanwhile, the government showed disapproval of the way affairs were progressing. At the place of the Apparitions some people had erected poles to form an arch hung with lanterns which they were careful to keep always burning. One night some men were sent in a car to pull down the arch and to cut down the holm oak on which the Apparitions had taken place, and drag it away with them behind the car.

In the morning news of what had happened spread quickly. I ran to see if it was true. What was my delight to find that the poor men had made a mistake. Instead of cutting down the holm oak they had carried off one of the others growing nearby! I then asked Our Lady to forgive these poor men and prayed for their conversion.

Some time later on the 13th of May, I don't remember whether it was in 1918 or 1919,[3] word came to us at dawn that cavalrymen were in Fatima to prevent the people from going to the Cova da Iria. Everyone was alarmed. They came to give me the news, assuring me that without any doubt this was to be the last day of my life. Without taking this too seriously I set out for the church.

When I reached Fatima I passed through the horses which were all over the church grounds and went into the church. I heard a Mass celebrated by a priest I did not know, received Holy Communion, made my thanksgiving and went back home without anyone saying a single word to me. I don't know whether it was because they did not see me or that they did not think me worthy of notice.

News kept coming in that the troops were trying in vain to keep people away from the Cova da Iria. In spite of this I went there, too, to recite the Rosary. On the way I was joined by a group of women who had come from a distance. As we drew near the place two cavalrymen gave their horses a smart crack of the whip and advanced at full speed toward the group. They pulled up beside us and asked where we were going. The women boldly replied that "it was none of their business."

They whipped the horses again as though they meant to charge forward and trample us all underfoot. The women ran in all directions and a moment later I found myself alone with the two cavalrymen. When they asked me my name I gave it without hesitation.

They then asked me if I were the seer and I said I was. They ordered me to step out onto the middle of the road between the two horses and proceed in the direction of Fatima.

As we reached the pond I spoke of earlier, a poor woman who lived there and whom I have also mentioned, seeing me coming in the distance between the two horses ran out into the middle of the road like another Veronica.

The soldiers lost no time in getting her out of the way. The poor woman burst into a flood of tears, loudly bewailing my misfortune. A few paces farther on they stopped and asked me if the woman was my mother, I said she was not. They did not believe me. They asked if that house was my home. I again said "No." Still apparently not believing me, they ordered me to walk a little ahead until I arrived at my parents' house. When we reached a plot of ground that lies on the outskirts of Aljustrel where there was a small spring and some trenches dug for planting vines, they called a halt and one said to another, probably to frighten me:

"Here are some open trenches. Let's cut off her head with one of our swords and leave her here dead and buried. Then we'll be finished with this business once and for all."

I thought that my last moment had really come. But I was as much at peace as if it did not concern me at all. After a minute or two, during which they seemed to be thinking it over, the other replied:

"No, we have no authority to do such a thing."

They ordered me to keep on going so I went straight through our little village until I arrived at my parents' house. All the neighbors were at the windows and doors of their houses to see what was going on. Some were laughing and making fun of me, others lamenting my sorry plight.

When we reached my home they ordered me to call my parents but they were not at home. One of them dismounted and went to see if my parents were hiding inside. After he searched the house and found no one he gave orders for me to stay indoors the rest of the day. Then he mounted his horse and they both rode off. Late in the afternoon we heard that the troops had withdrawn, defeated by the people.

At sunset I was praying my Rosary in the Cova da Iria accompanied by hundreds of people. According to what I heard later, while I was under arrest some persons went to tell my mother what was happening and she replied:

"If it's true that she saw Our Lady, Our Lady will defend her; and if she's lying, it will serve her right to be punished." And she remained as unperturbed as before.

Now someone asked me:

"And where were your little companions while this was going on?" I don't know. I can recall nothing at all of their whereabouts at that time. Perhaps in view of the news that spread abroad, their parents did not allow them to leave the house all that day.

Lucia's Mother Falls Seriously Ill

Such suffering on my part must have been pleasing to Our Lord because He was about to prepare a most bitter chalice which He was soon to give me to drink. My mother fell so seriously ill that we thought she was dying. All her children gathered around her bed to receive her last blessing and to kiss the hand of our dying mother. As I was the youngest my turn came last. When my poor mother saw me she brightened a little, flung her arms around my neck and, with a deep sigh exclaimed:

"My poor daughter, what will become of you without your mother! I am dying with my heart pierced through because of you!" Then bursting into tears and sobbing bitterly she clasped me more and more tightly in her arms.

My eldest sister forcibly pulled me away from my mother, took me to the kitchen and forbade me to go back to the sick room, saying:

"Mother is going to die of grief because of all the trouble you've given her!" I knelt down, put my head on a bench, and in a distress more bitter than any I had ever known before, I made the offering of my sacrifice to our dear Lord.

A few minutes later my two older sisters, thinking the case was hopeless, came to me and said:

"Lucia! If it is true that you saw Our Lady go right now to the Cova da Iria and ask Her to cure our mother. Promise Her whatever you wish and we'll do it, and then we'll believe."

Without losing a moment I set out. In order not to be seen, reciting the Rosary all the way I made my way across the fields along some by-path. Finally at the Cova I placed my request before Our Lady and unburdened myself of all my sorrow, shedding copious tears. Then I went home comforted by the hope that my beloved Mother in Heaven would hear my prayer and restore health to my mother on earth. When I reached home my mother was already feeling somewhat better. Three days later she was able to resume her work around the house.

I had promised the most Blessed Virgin that if She granted me what I asked, I would go there for nine days in succession, together with my sisters, to pray the Rosary and go on our knees from the roadway to the holm oak tree... and on the next day we would take nine poor children with us and afterwards give them a meal. We went, then, to fulfill my promise and my mother came with us.[4]

"How strange!" she said. "Our Lady cured me and somehow I still don't believe! I don't know how this can be!"[5]

Lucia's Father Dies

Our good Lord gave me this consolation but once again He came knocking on my door to ask yet another sacrifice, and not a small one either. My father was a healthy man, and robust; he said he had never known what it was to have a headache. In less than twenty-four hours an attack of double pneumonia carried him off into eternity.[6] My sorrow was so great that I thought I would die as well. He was the only one who never failed to show himself to be my friend, the only one who defended me when disputes arose at home on account of me.

"My God! My God!" I exclaimed in the privacy of my room. "I never thought You had so much suffering in store for me! But I suffer for love of You, in reparation for the sins committed against the Immaculate Heart of Mary, for the Holy Father and for the conversion of sinners."

†††

1. This property near Torres Novas belonged to the engineer, Mario Godinho. On July 13, 1917, he himself took the first known photograph of the children. The testimony of Godinho appears in the book *Meet the Witnesses.*

2. This was certainly not the reason. It was rather the difficulties the priest had with the members of his parish on account of the rebuilding of the church.

3. The date in question is May 13, 1920.

4. The cure of Lucia's mother was certainly an answer to prayer. She herself marveled that she had experienced a personal miracle and still could not believe. Certainly God permitted this for what became Lucia's greatest sacrifice.

5. Because of this promise of Lucia, today hundreds of pilgrims to Fatima make the same penance in fulfillment of a similar promise for a favor asked or already received. To accommodate them a path of marble has been placed from the entrance of the Cova to the place of the apparitions.

6. Lucia's father died on July 31, 1919.

Chapter XI.

In the Second Memoir —
Lucia Remembers

HER FAREWELL

*Lucia concludes her second memoir with accounts of
the illnesses and deaths of her two little companions,
her first meeting with Bishop Correia da Silva and her
farewell to all the places she had come to know and
love so well: the Cabeco, Valinhos, the well behind her
home and the Cova da Iria.*

†††

Serious Illness of Lucia's Cousins

Around that time, Jacinta and Francisco began to
grow worse.[1] Jacinta used to tell me sometimes:

"My chest hurts so much... but I'm not saying
anything to my mother! I want to suffer for Our Lord
in reparation for the sins committed against the
Immaculate Heart of Mary, for the Holy Father and for
the conversion of sinners."

One morning when I went to see her she asked me:

"How many sacrifices did you offer to Our Lord last
night?"

"Three; I got up three times to recite the Angel's
prayers."

"Well, I offered Him many, many sacrifices. I don't
know how many there were but I had much pain and
I made no complaint."

Francisco spoke very little. He usually did everything he saw us doing and rarely suggested anything himself. During his illness he suffered with heroic patience, without ever letting the slightest moan or the least complaint escape his lips. One day shortly before his death I asked him:

"Are you suffering a lot, Francisco?"

"Yes, but I suffer it all for the love of Our Lord and Our Lady." One day he gave me the rope that I have already spoken about saying:

"Take it away before my mother sees it. I don't feel able to wear it any more around my waist."

He took everything his mother offered him and she could never discover which things he disliked. He went on like this until the day came for him to go to Heaven.[2] The day before his death he said to Jacinta and myself:

"I am going to Heaven and when I'm there I will pray a great deal to Our Lord and Our Lady asking Them to bring you there, too, very soon."

I think I have already described, in my account of Jacinta, what suffering this separation caused us. For this reason I do not repeat it here. Jacinta was already very sick and was gradually growing worse.

There is no need to describe it now as I have already done so. I shall simply relate one or two acts of virtue which I saw her practice, and which I do not think I have described before. Her mother knew how hard it was for her to take milk. One day she brought her a beautiful bunch of grapes with her cup of milk saying:

"Jacinta, take this. If you can't take the milk, leave it there and eat the grapes."

"No, mother, I don't want the grapes; take them away and give me the milk instead. I'll take that." Then without the least sign of repugnance she took it. My aunt went happily away thinking her little girl's appetite was returning. She had no sooner gone than Jacinta turned to me and said:

"I had such a longing for those grapes and it was so hard to drink the milk! But I wanted to offer this sacrifice to Our Lord."

One morning I found her looking dreadful and I asked her if she felt worse.

"Last night," she answered, "I had so much pain and I wanted to offer Our Lord the sacrifice of not turning over in bed. Therefore, I didn't sleep at all."

On another occasion, she told me:

"When I'm alone, I get out of bed and recite the Angel's prayer. But now I'm not able to touch the ground any more with my head because I fall over, so I pray only on my knees."

One day I had the opportunity of speaking to the acting pastor. His Reverence asked me about Jacinta and how she was. I told him what I thought about her condition, and afterwards related what she had said to me about being unable to touch the ground when she prayed.

His Reverence sent me to tell her that she was not to get out of bed in order to pray, but that she was to pray lying down, and then only as long as she could do so without getting tired. I delivered the message at the very first opportunity.

"And will Our Lord be pleased?" she asked.

"He is pleased," I replied. "Our Lord wants us to do whatever the Reverend Vicar says."

"That's all right then. I won't get up any more."

Whenever I could I loved to go to the Cabeco to pray in our favorite cave. Jacinta was very fond of flowers and coming down the hillside on the way home I used to pick a bunch of irises and peonies, when there were any to be found, and take them to her saying:

"Look! These are from the Cabeco!" She would take them eagerly and sometimes, with tears running down her cheeks, she would say:

"To think I'll never go there again! Nor to Valinhos, nor Cova da Iria. I miss them all so much!"

"But what does it matter if you're going to Heaven to see Our Lord and Our Lady?"

"That's true," she replied. Then she lay there contentedly, plucking off the petals and counting them one by one.

A few days after falling ill, she gave me the rope she had been wearing, and said:

"Keep it for me. I'm afraid my mother may see it. If I get better I want it back again!" This cord had three knots and was somewhat stained with blood. I kept it hidden until I finally left my mother's home. Then not knowing what to do with it, I burned it, and Francisco's as well.

Lucia in Poor health

Several people who came from a distance to see us remarked that I looked very pale and anemic. They asked my mother to let me go and spend a few days in their homes, saying the change of air would do me good. With this end in view my mother gave her consent and they took me with them, some to one place, some to another.

When away from home like this, I did not always meet with esteem and affection. While there were some who admired me and considered me a saint, there were always others who heaped abuse upon me and called me a hypocrite, a visionary and a sorceress. This was the good Lord's way of throwing salt into the water to prevent it from going bad.

Thanks to this Divine Providence I went through the fire without being burned or without becoming acquainted with the little worm of vanity, which has the habit of gnawing its way into everything. On such occasions I used to think to myself:

"They are all mistaken... I'm not a saint as some say, and I'm not a liar either as others say. Only God knows what I am."

When I got home I would run to see Jacinta, who said:

"Listen! Don't go away again. I've been so lonely for you! Since you went away I have not spoken to anyone. I don't know how to talk to other people."

The time finally came for Jacinta to leave for Lisbon. I have already described our leave-taking and therefore I won't repeat it here. How sad I was to find myself alone! In such a short space of time our dear Lord had taken to Heaven my beloved father and then Francisco, and now He was taking Jacinta whom I was never to see again in this world.

As soon as I could I slipped away to the Cabeco and hid within our cave among the rocks. There alone with God, I poured forth my grief and shed tears in abundance. Coming back down the slope everything reminded me of my dear companions: the flowers I no longer picked, not having anyone to take them to... Valinhos, where the three of us had enjoyed the delights of paradise!

As though I had lost all sense of reality and still half abstracted, I went into my aunt's house one day and made for Jacinta's room calling out to her. Her sister Teresa, seeing me like that, barred the way and reminded me that Jacinta was no longer there.

Shortly afterwards news arrived that she had taken flight to Heaven. Her body was then brought back to Vila Nova de Ourem.[3] My aunt took me there one day to pray beside the mortal remains of her little daughter in the hope of thus distracting me, but for a long time after my sorrow seemed only to grow ever greater.

Whenever I found the cemetery open I went and sat by Francisco's grave or beside my father's, and there I spent long hours. My mother, thank God, decided some time after this to go to Lisbon and to take me with her.[4]

Through the kindness of Dr. Fomigao, a good lady received us into her house and offered to pay for my education in a boarding school if I was to remain. My mother and I gratefully accepted the generous offer of this charitable lady, whose name was Dona Assuncao Avelar.

My mother, after consulting the doctors, found that she needed an operation for her kidneys and spinal column. The doctors could not operate because she also suffered from a cardiac lesion. She therefore went home leaving me in care of this lady.

When everything was ready and the day arranged for my entering the boarding school, word came that the government was aware that I was in Lisbon and was seeking my whereabouts. My friends took me to Santarem to Dr. Formigao's house, and for some days I remained hidden without being allowed out to Mass.

Finally His Reverence's sister arrived to take me home to my mother, promising to arrange for my admittance to a boarding school run by the Dorothean Sisters in Spain. She assured us that as soon as everything was settled she would come for me. All these happenings distracted me somewhat and the oppressive sadness began to disappear.

Lucia's First Meeting with the Bishop

It was about this time that Your Excellency was installed as Bishop of Leiria. Our dear Lord confided to your care this poor flock so many years without a shepherd.[5]

There were not wanting people who tried to frighten me about Your Excellency's arrival just as they had done before about another holy priest. They told me that Your Excellency knew everything, that you could read hearts and penetrate the depths of consciences, and that now you were going to discover all my deceptions.

Far from frightening me, it made me earnestly desire to speak to you. I thought to myself:

"If it's all true that he knows everything, he will know that I am speaking the truth." For this reason as soon as a kind lady from Leiria offered to take me to see Your Excellency I accepted her suggestion with joy. I was full of hope waiting for this happy moment. At last the day came and the lady and I went to the Palace.[6] We were invited to enter and shown to a room where we were asked to wait for a little while.

A few moments later Your Excellency's Secretary came in.[7] He spoke kindly with Dona Gilda who accompanied me. From time to time he asked me some questions. As I had already been twice to confession to His Reverence, I already knew him and it was therefore a pleasure to talk to him. A little later Rev. Dr. Marques dos Santos[8] came in wearing shoes with buckles and wrapped in a great big cloak. As it was the first time that I had seen a person dressed like this, it caught my attention.

He then embarked on a whole repertoire of questions that seemed unending. Now and again he laughed, as though making fun of my replies, and it seemed as if the moment when I could speak to Your Excellency would never come.

At last your Secretary returned to speak to the lady who was with me. He told her that when Your Excellency arrived she was to make her apologies and take her leave saying that she had to go somewhere, since Your Excellency might wish to speak to me in private. I was delighted when I heard this message. I thought to myself:

"As His Excellency knows everything he won't ask me many questions and he will be alone with me. What a blessing!" When Your Excellency arrived the good lady played her part very well and so I had the happiness of speaking with you alone. I am not going to describe now what happened during this interview because Your Excellency certainly remembers it better than I do.

To tell the truth, when I saw Your Excellency receive me with such kindness without in the least attempting to ask me any useless or curious questions, being concerned solely for the good of my soul and only too willing to take care of this poor little lamb that the Lord had just entrusted to you, then I was more convinced than ever that Your Excellency did indeed know everything.

I did not hesitate for a moment to give myself completely into your hands. Thereupon Your Excellency imposed certain conditions which, because of my nature, I found very easy: that is, to keep completely secret all that Your Excellency had said to me and to be good. I kept my secret to myself until the day when Your Excellency asked my mother's consent.

Farewell to Fatima

Finally the day of my departure was settled. The evening before, I went to bid farewell to all the familiar places so dear to us. My heart was torn with loneliness and longing for I was sure I would never set foot again on the Cabeco, the Rock, Valinhos, or in the parish where our dear Lord had begun His work of mercy, and the cemetery, where rested the mortal remains of my beloved father and of Francisco, whom I could still never forget.

I said goodbye to our well, already illumined by the pale rays of the moon, and to the old threshing floor where I had so often spent long hours contemplating the beauty of the starlit heavens and the wonders of sunrise and sunset which so enraptured me.

I loved to watch the rays of the sun reflected in the dew drops so that the mountains seemed covered with pearls in the morning sunshine... and in the evening, after a snowfall, to see the snowflakes sparkling in the pine trees was like a foretaste of the beauties of paradise.

Without saying farewell to anyone, I left the next day at two o'clock in the morning accompanied by my mother and a poor laborer named Manuel Correia, who was going to Leiria. I carried my secret with me, inviolate.

We went by way of the Cova da Iria so that I could bid it my last farewell. There for the last time I prayed my Rosary. As long as this place was still in sight I kept turning round to say a last goodbye.[9]

We arrived at Leiria at nine o'clock in the morning. There I met Dona Filomena Miranda, whom Your Excellency had asked to accompany me. This lady was later to be my godmother at Confirmation.

The train left at two o'clock in the afternoon. There at the station I gave my poor mother a last embrace, leaving her overwhelmed with sorrow and shedding abundant tears. The train moved out. With it went my poor heart plunged in an ocean of loneliness and filled with unforgettable memories.

Epilogue

I think, Your Excellency, that I have just picked the most beautiful flower and the most delicious fruit from my little garden, and I now place it in the merciful hands of the good Lord, whom you represent, praying that He will make it yield a plentiful harvest of souls for eternal life.

Since our dear Lord takes pleasure in the humble obedience of the least of His creatures, I end with the words of Her whom He, in His infinite mercy, has given me as Mother, Protectress and Model, the very same words with which I began:

"Behold the handmaid of the Lord! May He continue to make use of her, as He thinks best."

Further Memories of Jacinta

P.S. — I forgot to say that when Jacinta went to the hospital in Ourem and later to Lisbon, she knew she was not going to be cured but only to suffer. Long before anyone spoke to her of the possibility of her entering the hospital of Ourem, she said one day:

"Our Lady wants me to go to two hospitals not to be cured but to suffer more for love of Our Lord and for sinners."

I do not know Our Lady's exact words in these apparitions to Jacinta alone for I never asked her what they were. I confined myself merely to listen to what she occasionally confided to me. In this account I have tried not to repeat what I have written before so as not to make the account too long.

Consolation From Little Children

It may seem perhaps from this account that in my village no one showed me any love or tenderness. But this is not so. There was a dear chosen portion of the Lord's flock who showed me singular affection. These were the little children. They ran up to me bubbling over with joy, and when they knew I was pasturing my sheep in the neighborhood of our little village, whole groups of them used to come and spend the day with me.

My mother used to say:

"I don't know what attraction you have for children! They run after you as if they were going to a party!"

As for myself, I did not feel at ease in the midst of such merriment. For that reason I tried to keep out of their way.

The same thing happened to me with my companions in Vilar. I would almost venture to say that it is happening to me now with my Sisters in religion. A few years ago I was told by my Mother Mistress, who is now Rev. Mother Provincial:

"You have such an influence over the other Sisters that if you want to you can do them a great deal of good."[10]

And quite recently Rev. Mother Superior in Pontevedra[11] said to me:

"To a certain degree you are responsible to Our Lord for the state of fervor, or negligence of fervor, on the part of the other Sisters, because their fervor is increased or decreased at recreation. Whatever the others see you doing at that time, they do as well. Certain topics you brought up at recreation helped other Sisters to understand the Rule better and made them resolve to observe it more faithfully."

Why is this? I don't know. Perhaps it is a talent which the Lord has given me and for which He will hold me to account. Would that I knew how to trade with it that I might restore it to Him a thousandfold.

Lucia's Excellent Memory

Maybe someone will want to ask:

How can you remember all this? How? I don't know. Our dear Lord, Who distributes His gifts as He sees fit, has allotted to me this little portion — my memory. He alone knows why. And besides, as far as I can see there is this difference between natural and supernatural things:

When we are talking to a mere creature, even while we are speaking, we tend to forget what is being said whereas these supernatural things are ever more deeply engraved on the soul, even as we are seeing and hearing them, so that it is not easy to forget them.

†††

1. Francisco and Jacinta fell ill almost simultaneously toward the end of October 1918.

2. Francisco died on April 4, 1919, at 10:00 a.m.

3. Jacinta died on February 20, 1920, at 10:30 p.m.

4. Lucia was in Lisbon from July 7 to August 6. After that she went to Santarem, and from there she returned to Aljustrel on August 12.

5. The new bishop, Dom Jose' Correia da Silva, came to the diocese on August 5, 1920.

6. "Palace" hardly describes the very poor residence of the Bishop at that time. It was a square building with stores downstairs and nothing more than an unheated apartment upstairs where the Bishop lived and from which he directed the affairs of the diocese.

7. Fr. Augusto Maia, died 1959.

8. Msgr. Manuel Marques dos Santos, 1892-1971.

9. Lucia left Aljustrel in the early morning of June 16, 1921, and reached Leiria some hours later. From there she traveled to the college at Porto, where she arrived the following morning. Before she left the Cova, Our Lady appeared to her "a seventh time." Lucia does not mention this... perhaps because it was so personal and because it was like a farewell embrace rather than to give a message.

10. Mother Maria do Carmo Corte Real.

11. Madre Carmen Refojo, Mother Superior in Pontevedra, 1933-1939.

Chapter XII.

Comments On

LUCIA IN THE RELIGIOUS LIFE

As was explained before, Lucia was fourteen years and three months of age when she left Fatima (and her family) in obedience to the Bishop. She had already felt drawn to dedicate herself to God and it should not be surprising that she was invited to enter the Dorothean Community at the school she attended in Porto. However, she felt called to a contemplative life from the very beginning, and in particular to Carmel.

Was this because in the final apparition at Fatima on October 13 at the climax of the solar miracle, the Blessed Virgin appeared as "Our Lady of Mount Carmel" holding out the Brown Scapular?

Various explanations have been given. I was told when I went to see Lucia at the school in Porto in 1946, where she had already become a Dorothean nun, that her health was not strong enough for the rigors of the Carmelite life. In the opinion of Father Alonso, the example of her teachers and her gratitude toward them for her education made her decide to enter the Institute of Saint Dorothy.

The Dorothean novitiate in 1925 was across the border in Spain in the old town of Tuy. Lucia entered there on October 24, 1925, at the age of 18. From there she was sent to the house at Pontevedra, thirty miles farther north on the road to Santiago de Compostela, which is only another thirty miles beyond Pontevedra.

She stayed at Pontevedra from October 25, 1925, until July 20, 1926. Six years later on October 3, 1934, she made her final profession of vows in Tuy and a few days later was transferred back to the convent at Pontevedra where she remained until May of 1937. She did not return to Portugal until the end of May 1946... *almost twenty years outside her native land.*

Lucia's Concern

Meanwhile she was concerned that the Message of Fatima was not becoming known. Indeed the Child Jesus had appeared to her in Pontevedra on February 15, 1926, and asked:

"What is being done to establish the devotion to the Immaculate Heart of My Mother in the world?"

Lucia answered that she had given the Message to the Mother Superior but the latter said that of herself she could do nothing, and indeed it seemed that nothing much was done until 1946. Father Joaquin Guerra, a Jesuit who knew Lucia at this time, told me that she had drawn up an actual set of rules for an apostolate of Fatima and was thinking of leaving the Dorotheans to establish this apostolate.

"But it was just after this time that the Blue Army was formed," Father Guerra told me, "and when the Blue Army was established, Lucia felt that this was the instrument God had chosen to make known the Message of Our Lady of Fatima in the world, and she then went ahead with her plans to become a Carmelite in Coimbra, Portugal."

Incidentally, just a week before I decided to do this book, I had stopped at Lucia's Carmel in Coimbra and met Father Guerra at the door of the convent. I was amazed to see him because he had spent the last several years in Hong Kong working on some important Chinese translations. He had not been to see

Lucia for several years. As he was already advanced in age, it was probably the last time he was able to greet her in person.

Return to Fatima

But let us return to that historic event in 1946.

Now that Lucia was back in Portugal for the first time in almost twenty years, the Bishop gave her permission to make a visit to Fatima and to her own village which she had left almost thirty years before!

From the time Lucia left Fatima at the age of fourteen, tens of thousands of people who flocked to Fatima wondered where she had gone. The secret was well-kept. For some years most of those in Lucia's own school did not know who she was. Her classmates took her to be an orphan. However, after she became a Sister of Saint Dorothy the secret leaked out. Members of her family would occasionally travel up to see her.

Only a bridge between the towns of Valenca and Tuy separates Portugal and Spain at that point. Because these two towns are so close the inhabitants have a special privilege of shopping on either side of the bridge.

One day Lucia and another nun were crossing the bridge to Valenca to make some purchases for the convent when they met two Portuguese pilgrims. They had crossed the center of the bridge when the two Portuguese pilgrims crossing over to Tuy asked if it was true that *Lucia was now in Spain* (not knowing, of course, that one of the Dorotheans to whom they were speaking was Lucia herself). Without a moment's hesitation, but assuring herself that she had passed the center of the bridge, Lucia answered with her sparkling sense of humor:

"Oh, I am quite sure that *she is now in Portugal.*"

Disappointed, the two pilgrims turned back. They

undoubtedly spread the word, and the anonymity and "cloister" of Lucia was safeguarded still a bit longer.

But now, after twenty-nine years of separation from Fatima, Lucia was back... and how the area had changed!

Crowned "Queen of the World"

On that May 13 (1946) it seemed all of Portugal had come to Fatima because Pope Pius XII had sent a personal legate to crown the Statue of Our Lady at the spot of the apparitions as "Queen of the World." After twenty-nine years no one, except members of her family who had seen her from time to time, would have recognized Lucia. She was able to move about like any other Sister of Saint Dorothy.

It would be difficult to judge the depth of her feelings and her emotions as she retraced her steps to those special places... places where the Angel had appeared at the well behind her own house and at the Cabeco where she received the Sacred Host and where Francisco and Jacinta received their First Communion from the chalice offered to them from the Angel's hands. At Valinhos, nothing had changed.

The Bishop had not permitted any building, and there was even a little holm oak growing at the spot where, on a similar tree, Our Lady had appeared to her on that historic August 15, on the morning of which she thought Francisco and Jacinta were already dead and that she, too, was about to die.

"Continue to pray and make sacrifices," Our Lady had said to her on that spot. *"So many souls are lost because there is no one to pray and make sacrifices for them."*

And, oh, how many prayers she had offered (and how many sacrifices!) during these many years that had intervened. But if Valinhos was the same, how different was the Cova! Now a great basilica rose at the spot where she and Francisco and Jacinta had been playing at "building" with tiny stones when the first flash of light stunned them, announcing the miracles which were to follow and which were to be climaxed in the Miracle of the Sun only six months later.

Only one thing in the whole Cova seemed the same. It was the great oak tree beneath which the children had stood to protect themselves from the noonday sun as they watched for the globe of light to come from the east announcing Our Lady's visitations. From the position of the oak tree Lucia could verify that the pillar in front of the little chapel of the apparitions seemed to be indeed at the very place where the smaller tree stood upon which Our Lady had appeared to them.

But looking at the statue which had just been solemnly crowned by a legate of Pope Pius XII (for Our Lady of Fatima was proclaimed as "Queen of the World") Lucia remarked that if she were to have an image of Our Lady made:

"It would not be with a tassel, but with a golden globe hanging approximately over Our Lady's heart. And there would not be a double mantle, but only a single mantle. And it should not be with many designs but only with a simple golden line at the edge because the edge of Our Lady's robe was more brilliant. And a great star shone at the hem of her tunic."

When Bishop da Silva learned of this, he arranged that the famous Portuguese sculptor who had made the original statue should speak with Lucia and *make a new image* according to her description. This is important to remember. That new image became the famous "International Pilgrim Virgin" which Pope Pius XII was later to call "the messenger of Our Lady's royalty."

After the brief visit to Fatima, Lucia was assigned to the Dorothean Convent in a suburb of Porto where

I was able to interview her only a few weeks later. During my interview I had only one thing in mind, and I pursued it consistently during four consecutive hours:

"What must we do in order to bring about the conversion of Russia and world peace?

"What exactly does Our Lady request of us?

"What are the conditions for the fulfillment of the promise of the triumph of Her heart?"

On a mandate from my own Bishop I finally wrote it all down in 1980. I found that it was difficult to begin writing this book because much was personal, so I decided (not thinking that Lucia had written in the same manner) to make the book a sort of letter to my Bishop (hence the title, *Dear Bishop!*).[1]

The very important explanation by Sr. Lucia of the Message of Fatima is undoubtedly that book's most valuable contribution, even as the book by Father Thomas McGlynn has the special value of the best description of the actual vision of Fatima, because he repeatedly interviewed Lucia in order to sculpt the great statue of the front of the Fatima Basilica.

††††

[1] *DEAR BISHOP!*, 340 pp., published in 1981 by AMI Press, Washington, NJ 07882. By 1987 it was available also in French, Spanish and Portuguese. The bishop who mandated the book was the Most Rev. George W. Ahr, S.T.D., who became Bishop of Trenton in 1950 and retired in 1980.

Chapter XIII.

Comments On

OUR LADY'S SMILE

It is easy to overlook even important parts of *Her Own Words.*

If asked what was the first supernatural manifestation at Fatima, most might recall the apparitions of the angels. But four years before there was a very important manifestation to Lucia at her First Communion.

On the eve of her First Communion, the priest to whom she had made her first confession was somehow enlightened as to her special vocation. "My child," he said to her, "your soul is the temple of the Holy Spirit. Always keep it pure so that He can continue His Divine Action in it."

"And how can I do that?" Lucia asked.

As she tells us in her memoirs, the confessor told her to go and kneel before the statue of Our Lady. "Ask Her trustingly," he said, "to take care of your heart, to keep it always pure and to prepare it to receive Her beloved Son worthily tomorrow and to keep it for Him alone."[1]

This was the advice given by the great Doctor of the Church, St. Alphonsus Ligouri. And it was the usual practice of saints like Therese of Lisieux, who begged Our Lady to prepare her heart before every Communion. St. Alphonsus also advised *visits to Our Lady* (by going to kneel in front of Her statue) after we visit Our Lord in the Blessed Sacrament.[2]

Some Catholics in Protestant countries often feel uneasy about this counsel. The very expression of St. Alphonsus seems to suggest identification of a statue of Our Lady with Our Lady Herself. Especially when under Protestant influence, it is understandable that some have difficulty accepting statues of Our Lady as sacramentals of Her "moral" presence.

Important Difference

In her childlike simplicity, Lucia (like most Catholics) understood that in the Eucharist we have Our Lord really present, while in a statue we have only an image of Our Lady before which we seek the effect of Her presence as we pray to Her. Thus it was perfectly natural for Lucia to "visit Our Lady" by going to kneel before Her statue.

She knelt in front of the statue of Our Lady of the Rosary (because it was the statue before which her family kept fresh flowers). She repeated the prayer suggested by the confessor several times and *the statue came alive and smiled at her.*

In the memoirs she mentions only the smile, but in the letter to her confessor of May 13, 1936, she said that:

"The statue smiled... and with a kind gesture and look said, '*Yes.*'" Lucia was so filled with joy, she recalled:

"I could hardly speak. At night I could sleep little or not at all. At last the time came. After asking my father's, mother's, and older brother's pardon, off I went to the Church as happy as a queen. At the moment when Jesus came into my poor heart, I believe I felt the happiness of Paradise!"

And then for the second time in her life Lucia experienced a profound communication from Our Lady who said "in the depth of my heart and my inmost soul":

151.

"My child, the grace that has been granted to you today will always remain alive in your breast, bringing forth fruits of eternal life." And these words engraved themselves so indelibly on Lucia's mind that years later she said:

"Still now I feel them to be a bond of union of my soul with God."

Our primary intention here is to call attention to the fact that the first manifestation of Fatima was *through a statue.* But we cannot help remarking here, as in absolutely every facet of Fatima, *the Hearts of Jesus and Mary working together...* Our Lady of the Eucharist bringing the awareness of Jesus truly present to those who truly seek Him.

But consider in particular the fact that Lucia was sent to visit Our Lady (that is, to go before Her statue) and that the statue changed into the living person of Our Lady Herself.

Cause of Our Joy

Many thoughts come tumbling to mind. Such a wonder occurred "at the dawn of life" to St. Therese (the "Little Flower") who seemed to be dying when the little statue at her bedside was transformed and Our Lady smiled at her. Today the "statue of the smile" stands watch over the saint's tomb in the Carmel in Lisieux where she became a "victim of love," radiating the joy of Our Lady's smile throughout her life and throughout the world after her death.

For Lucia it was the smile of the Mother of the Eucharist filled with joy as Her child Lucia prepared for and then received the embrace of Her Child Jesus. It is the joy of Our Lady of the Rosary who rejoices to share Jesus, bead by bead, in His mysteries. It is Our Lady showing us that She does not come to ask for our fiats to cause pain but to be the cause of our joy.

And how did Our Lady say all this?

The statue smiled on the little girl who was to be Her messenger.

On October 13, 1973, anniversary of the miracle of Fatima, another statue of Our Lady in Akita, Japan, came alive and repeated the message of Fatima. The wooden statue had shed human tears, and when Our Lady appeared in place of the weeping image She said the world has not made adequate response. She spoke sadly of the chastisement by which God's Justice must purge the world if men continue to refuse His Mercy and Grace.

Our Lady said that She had been able to hold back the chastisement so far in part because of the generosity of some souls... the victim souls.

Some are frightened at the prospect of being "victims of love" like St. Therese and like the children of Fatima. Many admire the heroic sacrifices of which we read in *Her Own Words*... but how many volunteer to accept them?

As we state elsewhere, this may in part be due to a misconception about the children of Fatima based upon their renunciation of simple pleasures and also on the few photographs in which they seem dour when they were merely apprehensive about being photographed.

Despite their sacrifices they never ceased to be children... joyous, trusting, and never happier than when they felt they had been able to do something really worthwhile in order to console the hidden Jesus, to save souls from the horror they had seen, and to please Our Lady and help to withdraw the thorns that pierced Her Immaculate Heart.

My most vivid personal memory of Lucia is of joyous laughter... the kind of pure joy one rarely meets. It is the greatest of all joys: the joy of real love.

In between the smile of Our Lady's statue in the church at Fatima and of tears in Japan, by another statue Our Lady of Fatima has manifested Her message to millions around the world in a veritable flood of miracles and wonders. That statue is known as the Pilgrim Virgin.

As mentioned in the previous chapter, Lucia had been away from Fatima for twenty-nine years, until May of 1946. When she returned to Fatima, she remarked that the statue at the Chapel of the Apparitions was not quite like the apparition itself.

A "New" Statue

I spoke to Thedim who made the original statue. He explained that the first statue was one he had made *before* 1917. He happened to have it "on hand" at the time of the apparitions. And when people came to him wanting a statue immediately to place where the children were seeing Our Lady, he had simply adapted that existing statue with slight modifications.

But now, at the request of the Bishop of Fatima, he spent time with Lucia and carefully designed a new statue with a single tunic, a single mantle "brighter at the edge," a golden globe hanging on a chain near Our Lady's heart, and a star at the hem of her tunic.

Some months after the statue was finished and delivered to Bishop da Silva, an International Congress of Youth was held at Fatima on May 13, 1947. It was the first *International* meeting ever held at the place of the apparitions. The second World War had come to an end less than two years before.

"It was from this meeting of youth from all over Europe that Fatima dates as an international shrine," Bishop da Silva remarked to me. That Congress of Youth came up with an extraordinary idea: To *carry a statue of Our Lady processionally from Fatima to Russia.*

They asked the Bishop for permission to implement this resolution of their Congress. In turn Bishop da

Silva consulted Lucia, believing as he did that Lucia was guided by Our Lady and would give a proper indication as to whether such a daring idea should be carried out.

Lucia replied:

"Yes, Your Excellency, and let them take the statue which Thedim has just made."

That was *the new statue...* the first ever made according to Lucia's directions.

"We Can Hardly Believe"

That image of Our Lady of Fatima has subsequently traveled to the ends of the earth, visiting nation after nation, causing Pope Pius XII to exclaim in a radio address to Fatima on October 13, 1951:

"In 1946 We crowned Our Lady at Fatima as Queen of the World, and the following year through the Pilgrim Virgin, She set forth *as though to claim Her dominion, and the favors She performs along the way are such that We can hardly believe what We are seeing with Our eyes.*"

I myself have written somewhat at length of this extraordinary aspect of the "Miracle of Fatima" in my book *Dear Bishop!* which was written under obedience to my own bishop. When I learned of the miracles that occurred along the path of the Pilgrim Virgin statue, I cabled Bishop da Silva to suggest that because of its "miracles" and its worldwide publicity, the statue would probably never get to Russia.

I further suggested that the bishop have Thedim make two similar statues: one which might travel through the United States and the countries of America while the original statue was traveling through Europe, and a third to be kept secretly until we could find a way of getting it quietly into Russia.

Bishop da Silva agreed. In the presence of hundreds of thousands of people on October 13, 1947,

155.

Above: John Haffert and Canon Galamba carry Pilgrim Virgin from plane on arrival in the U.S. in October 1947. Below: Closeup.

just six months after the first Pilgrim Virgin statue had left the Cova, His Excellency blessed the two similar statues hastily made by Thedim which were even more beautiful and more perfectly sculptured than the original. (Thedim himself was undoubtedly deeply affected by the miraculous events which accompanied that first image.)

In his statement in 1951, *Pope Pius XII referred to all three statues as though they were one "Pilgrim Virgin"* because His Holiness mentioned each of the countries (without explicitly mentioning Russia) where the *three* statues were traveling, *referring simply to "the Pilgrim Virgin."*

Other entire books go into further detail about the Pilgrim Virgin. Suffice it to say that under truly unusual circumstances, *one of the statues entered Russia in January 1950,* and has remained to this day enshrined in a chapel which serves the personnel of foreign embassies in Moscow.

The statue which traveled throughout the Americas subsequently flew several times around the world with the Bishop of Fatima on special "world peace flights," and at Lucia's own request, the statue remained overnight in her convent at Coimbra, Portugal, on the occasion of the 1981 Eucharistic Congress in Lourdes.

She remarked afterwards that she had never seen any image which so resembled the actual apparition of Our Lady.

I do not hesitate to say that I myself have seen that image change its appearance. I was privileged to accompany the statue to America, with Canon Oliveira, in October 1947. On more than thirty occasions the statue has shed tears and once I myself wiped a tear from its cheek.

That Lucia found the image "so much like Our Lady" is remarkable. In 1946 I had shown Lucia *many* pictures of Our Lady, hoping that she would say that one was more like Our Lady than another. She looked at every one of the images with almost absolute indifference. *None...* not even the most beautiful, resembled the actual vision of Our Lady who was "more brilliant than the sun."

Indeed, Our Lady appeared to be so beautiful to all three children that after seeing Her they wanted to die, finding no beauty any longer in anything on earth!

I have never doubted that when Lucia had the Pilgrim Virgin statue in the Coimbra convent overnight, through this miraculous image Our Lady gave her again the experience of Her "presence," even as She has conveyed this sense of Her "presence" all around the world through this miraculous image.

More About Jacinta

As we have seen, the first two Memoirs were written at the suggestion of the first Bishop of Fatima (Bishop da Silva) and of Father Fonseca. From the first Memoir, the late Canon Galamba de Oliveira who had become a lifelong friend and with whom I visited just a few days before I began this book (then in his eighties and in greatly failing health) wrote a book about Jacinta which was published in 1938, only two years after he had received the first Memoir.

When the Silver Jubilee of Fatima was drawing near Canon Galamba wanted to publish a new edition and felt that Lucia could make a valuable contribution to it. He obtained permission from the Bishop to visit Lucia and ask further questions about Jacinta's life. At this time *Lucia felt that it would be necessary to disclose the first two parts of the secret given to the children in July 1917* in order to further describe the life of Jacinta.

Indeed she considered it essential to make a report of these parts of the secret before she could complete her account of Jacinta. Even as Canon Galamba had this thought, Lucia had already been considering it as early as the previous July. In reply to Canon Oliveira's request from the Bishop she completed her third Memoir on August 31, 1941, and without delay sent it to the Bishop. At this time, she wrote to her confessor (Father Goncalves):

"His Excellency the Bishop wrote to me about the forthcoming interrogation by Canon Galamba. He requested me to recall everything I could remember in connection with Jacinta, as a new edition of her life was about to be printed. This request penetrated the depths of my soul like a ray of light, *giving me to know that the time has come to reveal the first two parts of the secret,* and thus add two chapters to the new edition: one about hell, and the other about the Immaculate Heart of Mary. But I am still in doubt, since I am reluctant to reveal the secret. The account has already been completed. But I hesitate as to whether I should send it off or throw it into the fire. I do not know yet what to do."

Her confessor then instructed her to complete this third Memoir including the revelation of the first two parts of the secret.

In the same spirit in which she had written the previous Memoirs, Lucia set about her task with a strong dislike on the one hand (because she was revealing the matter which also made known her own intimacy with God and Our Lady) and yet on the other hand writing in complete obedience and with a certainty that it is "for the glory of God and for the salvation of souls."

✝✝✝

159.

1. From letter written by Lucia in Pontevedra, May 13, 1936.

2. *Glories of Mary*, Grimm ed., Vol. 7-8, p. 604. "Let us not think it too much *to visit our Queen* every day in some church or chapel... hence Mary's clients often visit Her images with great affection." The saint also published a little book on *Visits to the Blessed Sacrament and to the Blessed Virgin*.

Rev. Dr. Luis Fisher examines Jacinta's body at the first exhumation on September 12, 1935.

The exhumation of Jacinta's body.
Center is Bishop Venancio. Right is Canon Galamba.

Chapter XIV.

In the Third Memoir —
Lucia Remembers

THE SECRET

With the publication of the third Memoir, part of the "secret" which the atheists had failed to force the children to reveal was finally made known to the world. It helped to explain the children's many heroic sacrifices.

†††

In obeying the order Your Excellency gave me in your letter of July 26, 1941 (to think over and write down anything else I could remember about Jacinta) I have given thought to the matter and decided that, as God was speaking to me through you, the moment has arrived to reply to two questions often sent to me which I have put off answering until now.

In my opinion, it would be pleasing to God and to the Immaculate Heart of Mary if one chapter in the book *Jacinta* would be devoted to the subject of hell, and another to the Immaculate Heart of Mary.[1] Your Excellency may find this opinion rather surprising and strange and perhaps inopportune, but it is not my own idea. God Himself will make clear to you that this is a matter that pertains to His glory and to the good of souls.

This will require my speaking about the secret and giving answer to the first question.

What is the Secret? It seems to me that I can reveal it, since I already have permission from Heaven to do so. God's representatives on earth have repeatedly authorized me to do this in various letters, one of which I believe is in your keeping. This letter is from Rev. Fr. Jose Bernardo Goncalves,[2] in which he advises me to write to the Holy Father[3] and suggesting, among other things, that I should reveal the secret. I did say something about it... but in order not to make my letter too long (since I was told to keep it short) I confined myself to the essentials, leaving it to God to provide another more favorable opportunity.

In my second account, I have already described in detail the doubt which tormented me from June 13 until July 13, and how it disappeared completely during the Apparition on that day.

The Vision of Hell

Well, the secret is made up of three distinct parts, two of which I am now going to reveal.[4]

The first part consists of a vision of hell![5]

Our Lady showed us a great sea of fire which seemed to be under the earth. Plunged in this fire were demons and souls in human form, like transparent burning embers, all blackened or burnished bronze, floating about in the conflagration.

Sometimes they were raised into the air by the flames that issued from within themselves together with great clouds of smoke, at others falling back on every side like sparks in a great fire without weight or equilibrium, amid shrieks and groans of pain and despair which horrified us and made us tremble with fear. The demons could be distinguished by their terrifying and repellent likeness to frightful and unknown animals, all black and transparent.

This vision lasted but an instant. How can we ever be grateful enough to our kind heavenly Mother, who had already prepared us in the first Apparition by promising to take us to Heaven. Otherwise I think we would have died of fear and terror.

We then looked up at Our Lady who said to us kindly and so sadly:

"You have seen hell where the souls of poor sinners go. To save them God wishes to establish in the world devotion to my Immaculate Heart.[6] If what I say to you is done, many souls will be saved and there will be peace. The war[7] is going to end; but if people do not cease offending God, a worse one will break out during the pontificate of Pius XI.[8]

"When you see a night illumined by an unknown light, know that this is the great sign[9] given by God that He is about to punish the world for its crimes by means of war, famine and persecutions of the Church and of the Holy Father.

"To prevent this, I shall come[10] to ask for the consecration of Russia to my Immaculate Heart and the Communion of reparation on the First Saturdays. If my requests are heard, Russia will be converted and there will be peace; if not, she will spread her errors throughout the world, causing wars and persecutions of the Church. The good will be martyred; the Holy Father will have much to suffer; various nations will be annihilated.

"Finally, my Immaculate Heart will triumph. The Holy Father will consecrate Russia to me[11] and she will be converted, and a period of peace will be granted to the world."[12]

Lasting Impression on Jacinta

Your Excellency, as I already told you in the notes I sent to you after reading the book about Jacinta, some of the things revealed in the secret made a very strong impression on her. This was indeed the case. The vision of hell filled her with horror to such a degree that every penance and mortification was as nothing in her eyes if it could only prevent souls from going there.

Now I shall answer a second question which is often asked.

How is it that Jacinta, small as she was, could have such a spirit of mortification and penance and understand it so well? I think the reason is this: God willed to bestow on her a special grace, through the Immaculate Heart of Mary... furthermore, it was because she had looked upon hell, and had seen the ruin of souls who fall therein.

Some people, even the most devout, refuse to speak to children about hell in case it would frighten them. Yet God did not hesitate to show hell to three children, one of whom was only six years old, knowing well that they would be horrified to the point of, I dare to say, withering away with fear. Jacinta often sat thoughtfully on the ground or on a rock, and exclaimed:

"Oh! Hell! Hell! How sorry I am for the souls who go to hell! And the people down there, burning alive, like wood in the fire!"

Then, shuddering, she knelt down with her hands joined and recited the prayer that Our Lady had taught us:

"O my Jesus! Forgive us our sins, save us from the fires of hell. Lead all souls to Heaven, especially those most in need."

Now, Your Excellency will understand how my own impression was that the final words of this prayer refer to souls in greatest or most imminent danger of damnation. Jacinta remained on her knees like this for long periods of time, saying the same prayer over and over again. From time to time, like someone awaking from sleep, she called out to her brother or myself:

"Francisco! Francisco! Are you praying with me? We must pray very much to save souls from hell! So many go there! So many!" At other times, she asked:

"Why doesn't Our Lady show hell to sinners? If they saw it, they would not sin, so as to avoid going there! You must tell Our Lady to show hell to all the people (referring to those who were in the Cova da Iria at the times of the Apparition). You'll see how they will be converted."

Afterward, unsatisfied, she asked me:

"Why didn't you tell Our Lady to show hell to those people?" "I forgot," I answered.

"I didn't remember either!" she said, looking very sad. Sometimes, she also asked:

"What are the sins people commit, for which they go to hell?"

"I don't know! Perhaps the sin of not going to Mass on Sunday, of stealing, of saying ugly words, of cursing and of swearing."

"So just for one word, those people can go to hell?"

"Well, it's a sin!"

"It wouldn't be hard for them to keep quiet, and to go to Mass! I'm so sorry for sinners! If only I could show them hell!" Suddenly, she would seize hold of me and say:

"I'm going to Heaven, but you are staying here. If Our Lady lets you, tell everybody what hell is like, so that they won't commit sins any more and go to hell." At other times, after thinking for a while, she said:

"So many people falling into hell! So many people in hell!" To reassure her, I said:

"Don't be afraid! You're going to Heaven."

"Yes, I am," she said serenely, "but I want all those people to go there too!" When, in a spirit of mortification, she did not want to eat, I said to her:

"Listen, Jacinta! Come and eat now."

"No! I'm offering this sacrifice for sinners who eat too much."

When she was ill, and still went to Mass on a week day, I urged her:

"Jacinta, don't come! You can't, you're not able. Besides, today is not a Sunday!"

"That doesn't matter! I'm going for sinners who don't go on a Sunday."

If she happened to hear any of those expressions which people make a show of uttering, she covered her face with her hands and said:

"Oh, my God, don't those people realize that they can go to hell for saying those things? My Jesus, forgive them and convert them. They certainly don't know that they are offending God by all this! What a pity, my Jesus! I'll pray for them." There and then she repeated the prayer that Our Lady had taught us: "Oh my Jesus, forgive us..."

Lucia Looks Back

Now, Your Excellency, another thought comes to my mind. I have sometimes been asked if, in any of the Apparitions, Our Lady pointed out to us which kinds of sins offended God most. They say that Jacinta, when in Lisbon, mentioned sins of the flesh.[13] She had often questioned me on this matter. I think now that in Lisbon it perhaps occurred to her to put the question to Our Lady herself and that this was the answer she received.

Well, Your Excellency, it seems to me that I have now made known the first part of the secret.

The Immaculate Heart of Mary

The second part refers to devotion to the Immaculate Heart of Mary.

As I have already written in the second account, Our Lady told me on June 13, 1917, that She would never forsake me, and that Her Immaculate Heart would be my refuge and the way that would lead me to God. As She spoke these words, She opened Her hands and from there streamed forth a light from them which penetrated to our inmost hearts. I think that, on that day, the main purpose of this light was to infuse us with special knowledge and love for the Immaculate Heart of Mary,[14] just as on the other two occasions as it seems to me it was intended to enlighten us with regard to God and the mystery of the most Holy Trinity.

From that day onwards, our hearts were filled with a more ardent love for the Immaculate Heart of Mary.

From time to time Jacinta said to me: "The Lady said that Her Immaculate Heart will be your refuge and the way that will lead you to God. Don't you love that? Her Heart is so good! How I love It!"

As I explained earlier in the July secret, Our Lady told us that God wished to establish in the world devotion to Her Immaculate Heart; and that to prevent a future war, She would come to ask for the consecration of Russia to Her Immaculate Heart, and for Communion of Reparation on the First Saturdays. From then on, whenever we spoke of this among ourselves Jacinta said:

"I'm so grieved to be unable to receive Communion in reparation for the sins committed against the Immaculate Heart of Mary!"

I have also mentioned already how Jacinta chose from the litany of ejaculations which Father Cruz suggested to us the words:

"Sweet Heart of Mary, be my salvation!" After saying it, she used to add sometimes, with the simplicity that was natural to her:

"I so love the Immaculate Heart of Mary! It is the Heart of our dear Mother in Heaven! Don't you love saying many times over: *Sweet Heart of Mary, Immaculate Heart of Mary*? I love It so much... so very much!"

Jacinta's Visions of the Holy Father

One day we spent our siesta down by my parents' well. Francisco and I climbed up a steep bank in search of wild honey among the brambles in a nearby thicket. After a little while, Jacinta called out to me:

"Didn't you see the Holy Father?"

"No."

"I don't know how it was, but I saw the Holy Father in a very big house kneeling by a table with his head buried in his hands, and he was weeping. Outside the house there were many people. Some of them were throwing stones, other were cursing him and using bad language.[15] Poor Holy Father, we must pray very hard for him." I have already told you how, one day, two priests recommended us to pray for the Holy Father and explained to us who the Pope was. Afterwards, Jacinta asked me:

"Is he the one I saw weeping... the one Our Lady told us about in the secret?"[16]

"Yes, he is," I answered.

"The Lady must surely have shown him also to those priests. You see, I wasn't mistaken. We need to pray a lot for him." At another time, we went to the cave called Lapa do Cabeço. As soon as we got there we prostrated on the ground saying the prayers the Angel had taught us. After some time Jacinta stood up and called to me:

"Can't you see all those highways and roads and fields full of people, who are crying with hunger and have nothing to eat... and the Holy Father in a church praying before the Immaculate Heart of Mary[17]... and so many people praying with him?"

Some days later, she asked me:

"Can't I say that I saw the Holy Father and all those people?"

"No. Don't you see that that's part of the secret? If you do, they'll find out right away."

169.

She responded: "All right! Then I'll say nothing at all."

Visions of War

One day I went to Jacinta's house to spend a little time with her. I found her sitting on her bed deep in thought.

"Jacinta, what are you thinking about?"

"About the war that is coming.[18] So many people are going to die, and almost all of them are going to hell![19] Many homes will be destroyed and many priests will be killed. Look, I am going to Heaven, and as for you, when you see the light which the Lady told us would come one night before the war, you run up there, too."

"Don't you see that nobody can just run off to Heaven?"

"That's true, you cannot! But don't be afraid! In Heaven I'll be praying hard for you, for the Holy Father, for Portugal, so that the war will not come here,[20] and for all priests."

Your Excellency is not unaware that, a few years ago, God manifested that sign which astronomers chose to call an aurora borealis. I don't know for certain, but I think if they investigated the matter they would discover that in the form in which it appeared, it could not possibly have been an aurora borealis.

Be that as it may, God made use of this to make me understand that His justice was about to strike the guilty nations. For this reason I began to plead insistently for the Communion of Reparation on the First Saturdays and the consecration of Russia. My intention was to obtain mercy and pardon, not only for the whole world, but for Europe in particular.

When God in His infinite mercy made me feel that the terrible moment was drawing near, Your Excellency may recall how, whenever occasion offered, I took the opportunity of pointing it out. I still say that the prayer and penance which have been done in Portugal have not yet appeased the Divine Justice, for they have not been accompanied by either contrition or amendment.[21] I hope that Jacinta is interceding for us in Heaven.

As I said in the notes I sent you about the book called "Jacinta," she was most deeply impressed by some of the things revealed to us in the secret. Such was the case with the vision of hell and the ruin of the many souls who go there, or also by the future war with all its horrors which seemed to be always present to her mind. These made her tremble with fear. When I saw her deep in thought I asked her:

"Jacinta, what are you thinking about?"

Often the reply was the same:

"About the war which is coming and all the people who are going to die and go to hell! How dreadful! If they would only stop offending God, then there wouldn't be any war and they wouldn't go to hell!"

Sometimes, she also said to me:

"I feel so sorry for you! Francisco and I are going to Heaven, and you're going to stay here all by yourself! I asked Our Lady to take you to Heaven, too, but She wants you to stay here for a while longer. When the war comes do not be afraid. In Heaven I'll be praying for you." Shortly before she went to Lisbon, at one of those times when she felt sad at the thought of our coming separation, I said to her:

"Don't be upset because I can't go with you. You can then spend your time thinking of Our Lady and Our Lord, and saying many times over those words you love so much: 'My God, I love You! Immaculate Heart of Mary, Sweet Heart of Mary,' and so on."

"Yes, indeed," she eagerly replied. "I'll never get tired of saying those until I die! And then I can sing them many times over in Heaven!"

Lucia Explains Her Silence

It may be, Your Excellency, that some people think I should have made known all this some time ago because they consider that it would have been twice as valuable years beforehand![22]

This would have been the case if God had willed to present me to the world as a prophetess. But I believe that God had no such intention when He made known these things to me. If that had been the case, I think that in 1917, when He ordered me to keep silence (and this order was confirmed by those who represented Him) He would, on the contrary, have ordered me to speak.

I consider then, Your Excellency, that God willed only to make use of me to remind the world that it is necessary to avoid sin, and to make reparation to an offended God by means of prayer and penance.[23]

Where could I have hidden myself in order to escape from the innumerable questions they would have asked me about such a matter? Even now I am afraid, just thinking of what lies ahead of me!

I must confess that my repugnance in making this known is so great that, although I have before me the letter in which Your Excellency orders me to write everything else that I can remember (and I feel interiorly convinced that this is indeed the hour that God has chosen for my doing this) I still hesitate and experience a real inner conflict, not knowing whether to give you what I have written or to burn it. As yet I do not know what will be the outcome of the struggle. It will be as God wills.

For me, keeping silent has been a great grace. What would have happened had I described hell? Being unable to find words which exactly express the reality (for what I say is nothing and gives only a feeble idea of it all) I would therefore have said first one thing, then another, wanting to explain but not succeeding in doing so. Who knows but that I might thus have caused such a confusion of ideas as even to spoil the work of God. For this reason, I give thanks to the Lord. I know that He does all things well.

God usually accompanies His revelations with an intimate and detailed understanding of their meaning, but I do not venture to speak of this matter for fear of being led astray (as can all too easily happen) by my own imagination. Jacinta seemed to have this understanding to quite a remarkable degree. A little while before going to the hospital, Jacinta said to me:

"It will not be long now before I go to Heaven. You will remain here to make known that God wishes to establish in the world devotion to the Immaculate Heart of Mary. When you are to say this, don't go and hide.

Jacinta and the Immaculate Heart of Mary

"Tell everybody that God grants us graces through the Immaculate Heart of Mary... that people are to ask Her for them... and that the Heart of Jesus wants the Immaculate Heart of Mary to be venerated at His side. Also tell them to pray to the Immaculate Heart of Mary for peace, since God has entrusted it to Her.

"If only I could put into the hearts of all the fire that is burning within my own heart that makes me love the Hearts of Jesus and Mary so very much!"[24] One day I was given a holy picture. I took it to Jacinta, asking:

"Do you want this holy picture?" She took it, looked at it attentively, and remarked:

"It's so ugly! It doesn't look like Our Lord at all. He is so beautiful. But I want it... it is He just the same." She always carried it with her. At night and during her illness she kept it under her pillow until it fell apart. She kissed it frequently, saying:

"I kiss the Heart, because I love It most! How I would love to have a picture of the Heart of Mary! Don't you have one? I'd love to have the two together."

On another occasion I brought her a picture of a chalice with a Host. She took it, kissed it, and radiant with joy she exclaimed:

"It is the Hidden Jesus! I love Him so much! If only I could receive Him in church! Don't they receive Holy Communion in Heaven? If they do then I will go to Holy Communion every day. If only the Angel would go to the hospital to bring me Holy Communion again how happy I would be!"

Sometimes on returning from church I went in to see her and she asked me:

"Did you receive Holy Communion?"

If I answered in the affirmative, she said:

"Come over here close to me for you have the Hidden Jesus in your heart." At other times she told me:

"I don't know how it is, but I feel Our Lord within me! I understand what He says to me although I neither see Him nor hear Him... but it is so good to be with Him!"

On another occasion she remarked:

"Look, do you know this? Our Lord is sad because Our Lady told us not to offend Him any more, for He is already very much offended... yet nobody takes any notice and they continue to commit the same sins!"

Epilogue

There, Your Excellency, is everything else I can remember about Jacinta and which I don't think I have already said before.

The meaning of all I say is exact. But as regards the manner of expressing myself, I do not know if I have exchanged one word for another... as for example when we spoke of Our Lady. Sometimes we said Our

Lady, and sometimes the Lady. Now I no longer remember which of the two phrases we used at a given time. It is the same with a few other small details which I think are only of minor importance.

I offer to our good God and to the Immaculate Heart of Mary this little work, which is the fruit of my poor and humble submission to those who represent Him in my regard. I beg them to make it fruitful for Their glory and the good of souls.

(Place and date: Tuy, Spain, 31-8-41)

†††

[1] These chapters were published in the third edition of October 1942.

[2] Fr. Jose Bernardo Goncalves was one of her spiritual directors. He died in 1966.

[3] The letter to Pope Pius XII was dispatched on December 2, 1940.

[4] It should be noted that it concerns one single secret consisting of three parts. Here Lucia describes the first two parts. The third part was written at the end of 1943. This third part was not made public.

[5] Lucia describes the vision of hell with great realism. Dali painted a stylized version which is in the United States National Shrine of the Immaculate Heart of Mary (U.S. National Center of the Blue Army in Washington, NJ).

[6] In the Message of Fatima, the great promise of the salvation of souls is very often associated with the Immaculate Heart of Mary's intercession. These words of Our Lady have been called "the little secret" of Fatima. In a letter to her confessor in 1939, Lucia completed this response of Our Lady with two sentences which are omitted from the Memoirs. In the letter she states that Our Lady said: "To those who embrace this devotion I promise salvation. Their souls will be loved by God like flowers placed by me before His throne."

For further reflections on the "little secret," c.f. Barthas, *Fatima — 1917-1968*, p. 74.

[7.] This refers to the First World War, 1914-1918.

[8.] Lucia has again explicitly confirmed the name of Pope Pius XI. To the objection that the Second World War, 1939-1945, actually started during the pontificate of Pius XII, she replied that in fact the war began with the occupation of Austria in 1938.

[9.] Lucia recognized the "extraordinary" aurora borealis during the night of January 25-26, 1938 as the sign given by God to announce the imminence of war.

A recent study by a noted nuclear physicist has revealed that the "red glow" of the 1938 "aurora" is in fact very similar to the artificial aurora produced by the 1958 Johnson Island atomic test, code-named TEAK. (See *A State of Emergency*, p. 18, available from Lou Reda Productions, 44 N, Second Street, Box 68, Easton, PA 18042.)

[10.] This prediction was fulfilled by Our Lady's appearances at Pontevedra, Spain, on December 10, 1925, asking for the devotion of the Five First Saturdays and at Tuy, Spain, on June 12-13, 1929 to ask for the "collegial" consecration of Russia to the Immaculate Heart of Mary.

[11.] By 1982, when Pope John Paul II went to Fatima, had the conditions for the consecration of Russia (and consequently for its conversion) been complied with? Lucia did not seem to think so. Therefore, we continued to suffer from the evils of atheistic communism, a scourge used by God to punish the world for its sins. On March 25, 1984, in Saint Peter's Square in Rome, Pope John Paul II again renewed the Acts of Consecration made by Pope Pius XII in 1942 and in 1952, this time with all the bishops of the world joining with him in making the consecrations. However, Russia was not explicitly mentioned.

[12.] This is an unconditional promise, one which will certainly be fulfilled. However, we do not know when it will come true.

[13.] It is true that Jacinta, on account of her age, did not realize what is meant by this sin. However, this does not mean that, with her great intuition, she did not understand the seriousness of this sin.

[14.] Jacinta's love for the Immaculate Heart of Mary was like an "infused gift," as Lucia tells us, which can only be explained as a great mystic grace bestowed on her.

15. This "vision" of Jacinta about the Holy Father bears great resemblance to the renewal of the consecration of the world to the Immaculate Heart of Mary made by Pius XII in Saint Peter's Basilica on December 8, 1942, while "outside," that is, in various parts of Europe, he was furiously persecuted. It could also refer to conditions in Rome when Pope John Paul II renewed the Consecration in St. Peter's Square in 1984, while thousands of Communists marched in protest.

16. This could be a vision of the past as well as of the future. It is to be noted that the year 1917 fell during the pontificate of Pope Benedict XV. We think, however, that the vision in question points to the future and might happen to all the Popes especially from Pius XII to John Paul II.

17. There is every reason to assume that this refers to Pope Pius XII, the great Pope of the Immaculate Heart of Mary. However, *Jacinta's vision could be taken as applying to all the Popes since Fatima.*

18. This is the Second World War. Jacinta experienced this part of the secret mystically.

19. Jacinta is undoubtedly giving personal reaction to the terror which such visions inspired in her.

20. Although at times in danger, Portugal was actually spared throughout the entire Second World War.

21. These words might refer to the political and religious events in Portugal, 1975-1976, and continuing unrest after the loss of the territories in Africa.

22. It could not be said that Lucia's "prophecies" were "post eventum" simply because her superiors released her manuscripts for publication only after the events which had been announced in them. These manuscripts were, in fact, *already written prior to the events taking place.*

23. As regards the publication of the documents on Fatima, there was a wonderful "economia silentii," i.e., a special concern which can only be explained by an admirable Divine Providence governing everything that happened.

24. Jacinta's recommendation to promote the devotion to the Immaculate Heart of Mary throughout the world is truly remark-

able. For Lucia herself, this was to be a great stimulus in the years to come.

Lucia greets Pope Paul VI at Fatima, May 13, 1967

The International Pilgrim Virgin, which was brought to the U.S.
in 1947, was seen to shed tears more than 30 times.
On October 13, 1992, the statue was invited to Moscow,
thus coming to the climax of a forty-five year journey
across the world "to Russia." See Haffert's book:
Finally Russia!, 101 Foundation, 1993.

Chapter XV.

Comments On

LUCIA HERSELF

On October 7, 1941, Canon Galamba and the Bishop of Leiria went to see Lucia. They brought with them the Third Memoir which you have just read. The Bishop explained that Canon Galamba now desired to place further questions; His Excellency desired that Lucia should reply as she saw fit.

Actually Canon Galamba wanted the Bishop to command Lucia to write "*absolutely everything,*" and without delay. As we can see from the previous Memoirs, Lucia suffered greatly at the thought of revealing certain matters.

Bishop da Silva (whom I had the privilege of meeting many times and whom I came to appreciate and to love as a truly holy man) replied to Canon Galamba that he would not ask her to write absolutely "everything." "No, I will not ask her to do that," the Bishop said. Instead he made seven specific requests:

1) Canon Galamba had many questions which, due to lack of time, he would like her to answer in writing;

2) She was to write down everything she could remember in connection with Francisco, just as she had already done with regards to Jacinta;

3) She should write further details of the apparitions of the Angel;

4) She was to write a new and complete account of the apparitions of Our Lady;

5)   She was to put into writing further recollections of Jacinta;

6)   Canon Galamba wanted her to write down popular songs as they were sung in her village at the time;

7)   She was to read the book written by Father Fonseca and to put down anything she considered inaccurate.

Lucia was deeply grateful to the Bishop for his gentleness and thoughtfulness in not asking her to write "everything" but only to reply to seven specific questions. Indeed, as we review the life of Bishop Dom Jose Correia da Silva he appears to be a providential person in the history of Fatima. A prominent Marian leader in the United States once remarked:

"People think of four persons in relation to Fatima: Our Lady and the three children. But there are five: Our Lady, the three children and the Bishop."

When Dom Jose died, he was buried on the epistle side of the sanctuary of the Basilica. His successor, Bishop John Venancio, had the following simple and apt inscription engraved on the tomb:

"Here lies the Bishop of Our Lady."

Lucia spared no effort in dealing with all the Bishop's questions. She answered them with wonderful clarity and in great detail. When she was finished, she assured the Bishop:

"I believe I have written everything Your Excellency has asked me to write just now." (She withheld the third part of the secret.)

I have often been asked my personal impressions of Lucia, and I think what she says of herself is exactly the impression she gives:

"I am nothing, no one of importance... by chance an instrument in God's hands."

But what an instrument! May she never read these lines and have her humility offended by them, but she also impressed me as being an almost perfect instrument in every way... like Teresa of Avila or Therese of Lisieux. Certainly, she did not look on her apparitions as *personal* favors, but rather a responsibility placed upon her as "no more than a poor miserable instrument." We have good reason to believe much more of her.

Bishop Venancio told me of an extraordinary event which occurred before he had become successor to the first Bishop of Fatima. One day he was visiting his sister, whose husband had been suffering for years from a most painful affliction, chronic sciatica. He was speaking about Lucia when the husband, crying out in the desperation of his pain, said something most unexpected and surprising:

"Oh! If she really saw the Blessed Virgin, she could cure me!"

At that moment the pain left him, and never returned.

It was of course years later (after he had become Bishop of Fatima and we were traveling somewhere together) that Bishop Venancio told me this. At once the thought crossed my mind that this wonder had been performed by God because as the Bishop of Fatima he would have so many decisions to make, and God wanted him to know beyond any doubt that Lucia was truly what Our Lady had indicated: *Her messenger remaining on earth until the fullness of the Fatima Message should be known.*

I thought of it often. Then one day when I was again alone with the Bishop I said to him:

"Your Excellency, you recall having told me of your brother-in-law's remarkable cure from sciatica as you were talking about Lucia, and he exclaimed that if she had truly seen the Blessed Virgin she could cure him?"

The Bishop nodded, and I dared to add:

"I have always felt that God permitted this because you were destined to become the second Bishop of

Fatima, and He wanted you to have the consolation of knowing beyond any doubt that Lucia is truly Our Lady's messenger."

I was not surprised at the little twinkle that came into the Bishop's eyes and the smile that lit up his face, revealing that he had often thought the same.

When Our Lady told Lucia that she was to remain on earth and to "learn to read and write," we must conclude that she was to continue to be the voice of Our Lady in the world. Lucia was so afflicted to think that she would have to remain in the world that Our Lady was moved to console her at once with the words:

"Do not be sad. My Immaculate Heart will be your consolation and the way that will lead you to God."

There is no need for us to consider how Lucia must have suffered during the years that followed when it seemed that "nothing was being done" to make known the Message of Fatima. How her heart must have been afflicted when the Infant Jesus appeared to her on February 15, 1926, at Pontevedra, and asked:

"What is being done to establish in the world devotion to the Immaculate Heart of My Mother?"

When I saw her in July 1946, the "March of Pledges" (later the "Blue Army") had not yet begun. When I saw her again in The Carmel of Coimbra in 1952, the March of Pledges had become the Blue Army with over a million members.

In 1946 she seemed so serious... I might even say "weighed down" as though by some burden. Now, five years later, I could not help saying:

"Sister, I hope you don't mind my saying it, but you seem so much happier and even so much younger than when I saw you last!"

Her reply was one of gentle laughter. She spoke much about the importance of the family, of family Rosary and of the integrity of the family. I was with her for about an hour on this occasion. It was an unexpected visit and I had no important questions to

183.

ask, so I did what I had failed to do several years before: I rejoiced in looking into the eyes that had gazed into the eyes of Our Lady. I enjoyed listening to the voice that had responded to the voice of the Queen of the World.

Was Lucia so much happier now because something positive was being done to promote Our Lady's message on a worldwide scale? Was she happier because Our Lady Herself, as the Pope had put it, "had gone forth as though to claim Her dominion, and the favors She performs along the way are such that We can hardly believe what We are seeing with Our eyes?" Was she happier because the Blue Army was growing and already millions had signed the pledge, and now there were little cells developing in imitation of herself and Francisco and Jacinta, living the message in greater depth, so that fewer souls would be lost?

Her Life in Carmel

There is nothing in the memoirs about Lucia's life in Carmel because they were written before she entered, but we find a great deal of insight in her letters as well as from personal interviews. In a letter to a confessor of November 9, 1954, she wrote:

"When I had the good fortune of entering the Carmelite Order I was led to the cell, the best ornament of which is a single large wooden Cross. The Prioress asked me:

"'Do you know why the Cross has no statue?'

"Without giving me time to answer, she added:

"'It is so that you may crucify yourself on it.'"

"What a beautiful idea to be crucified with Christ! May He inebriate me with the folly of the Cross! Here lies the secret of my happiness... not to want or wish for more than to love and suffer for love..." She was impressed by the miseries of the world. In a letter of December 29, 1955, she wrote:

"Difficulties grow everywhere... The multitude of letters arriving here from all over the world bears witness to this. They do nothing but complain about the miseries that flood mankind. I become convinced that only those who like myself have the good fortune to be consecrated to Our Lord are the only happy people on earth." She added that the crosses of each day are a "part of being the chosen people" and "carried with love become a treasure of inestimable value."

When Our Lady had said that Lucia was to remain on earth "because God wishes to establish in the world devotion to My Immaculate Heart," could she have dreamed that her exile would be so long? Even though she speaks of the joy of loving God with all her heart, we can be sure that the sacrifices made each day were quite real. One of her sufferings was to know of all the suffering in the world and the delay of the collegial consecration. Her very love caused her to desire to alleviate every misery for which she was asked to pray.

Her exile in the world was to continue. Even though three times she would return to Fatima (at the command of Popes when the Pontiffs themselves would be in Fatima) the indifference of much of the world to Our Lady's message of warning even after the changes in Russia must have still weighed heavily on her heart.

†††

Chapter XVI.

In the Fourth Memoir —
Lucia Remembers

FRANCISCO

The Fourth Memoir begins with a short prologue and then continues with Lucia's remembrances of Francisco... throwing new light on the intimacy and importance of the visitations from Heaven.

†††

Confidence and Abandonment

Your Excellency,

After a humble prayer at the feet of Our Lord in the tabernacle and before the Immaculate Heart of Mary, our loving Heavenly Mother, asking the grace not to be permitted to write one word or even a single letter that is not for Their glory, I come now to begin this work happy and at peace as are those whose conscience assures them that they are doing in all things the will of God.

Abandoning myself completely into the arms of our heavenly Father and to the protection of the Immaculate Heart of Mary, I therefore once again place in Your Excellency's hands the fruits of my one tree... the tree of obedience.

Before making a start I thought of opening the New Testament, the only book I desire to have here in front of me in this remote corner of the attic lit by a single skylight, to which I withdraw whenever I can in order to escape as far as possible from all human eyes. My lap serves as a table and an old trunk as a chair.

But, someone will say, why don't you write in your cell? Our dear Lord has seen fit to deprive me even of a cell, although there are quite a few empty ones in the house.[1] As a matter of fact, the community room that we use for work and recreation would seem more suitable for the fulfillment of His designs. But, just as it is inconvenient for writing during the day, so is it all too conducive to drowsiness at night time.

But I am glad and I thank God for the grace of having been born poor, and for living more poorly still for love of Him. Dear Lord! That was not at all what I intended to say.

It Is God Who Works In You

I must return to what God presented to me when I opened the New Testament. In St. Paul's Letter to the Philippians 2:5-8, I read as follows:

"Let this mind be in you, which was also in Christ Jesus, who, being in the form of God, emptied Himself taking the form of a servant. He humbled Himself becoming obedient unto death." After reflecting awhile, I read also verses 12 and 13 of the same chapter:

"With trembling work out your salvation. It is God who works in you, both to will and to accomplish, according to His good will." Very well then, I need no more than this: obedience and abandonment to God who works within me.

I am truly no more than a poor and miserable instrument which He desires to use. In a little while, like a painter who casts his now useless brush into the fire so that it may be reduced to ashes, the Divine Artist will Himself reduce His now useless instrument to the ashes of the tomb until the great day of the eternal Alleluias. And I ardently desire that day, for the tomb does not annihilate everything, and the happiness of eternal and infinite love begins... now![2]

Unction of the Spirit

Your Excellency,

In Valenca on October 7, 1941, I was asked the following question by Rev. Dr. Galamba:

"Sister, when you said that penance had been done only in part, did you say this of yourself or was it revealed to you?"

I think, Your Excellency, that in such cases I never speak or write anything at all that comes from myself alone. I have to thank God for the assistance of the Divine Holy Spirit, whom I feel suggesting within me what I am to write or to say.

If at times my own imagination or understanding suggests something to me, I at once feel the lack of the divine unction and stop until I know in my inmost heart what it is that God wants me to say instead.[3] But why do I tell you all this? I do not know, The reason is known by God, who has inspired Your Excellency to command me to tell everything and not deliberately conceal anything.

Francisco's Character: His Spirituality

Therefore I am going to begin by writing what God wills to bring to my mind about Francisco. I hope that Our Lord will make him know in Heaven what I am writing about him on earth so that he may intercede for me with Jesus and Mary, especially during these coming days. The affection which bound me to Francisco was one of kinship,[4] and one which had its origin in the graces which Heaven deigned to grant us.

Apart from his features and his practice of virtue, Francisco did not seem at all to be Jacinta's brother.

Unlike her, he was neither capricious nor vivacious. On the contrary, he was quiet and submissive by nature. When we were at play and he won the game, if anyone made a point of denying him his rights as winner, he yielded without protest and merely said:

"You think you won? That's all right! I don't mind!"

He showed no love for dancing, as Jacinta did; he much preferred playing the flute while the others danced. In our games he was quite lively, but few of us liked to play with him as he nearly always lost.

I must confess that I myself did not always feel too kindly disposed towards him as his naturally calm temperament exasperated my own excessive vitality. Sometimes I caught him by the arm, made him sit down on the ground or on a stone, and told him to keep still.

He obeyed me as if I had real authority over him. Afterwards I felt sorry and went and took him by the hand and he would come along with me as good-humoredly as though nothing had happened. If one of the other children insisted on taking away something belonging to him, he said:

"Let them have it! What do I care?"

I recall how one day he arrived at my house holding a handkerchief with a picture of Our Lady of Nazare which someone had brought to him from the seaside. He showed it with great joy and all the children gathered round him to admire it.

The handkerchief, passed from hand to hand, in a few minutes disappeared. We looked for it but it was nowhere to be found.

I found it myself in another small boy's pocket and I wanted to take it away from him, but he insisted it was his own that someone had brought from the seaside for him. To end the quarrel, Francisco went up to him and said:

"Let him have it! What does a handkerchief matter to me?"

My own opinion is that, if he had lived to manhood, his greatest defect would have been his attitude of "never mind!"

When I was seven and began to take our sheep out to pasture he seemed quite indifferent. In the evenings he waited for me in my parents' yard with his little sister. But this was not out of affection for me but rather to please her. As soon as Jacinta heard the tinkling of the sheep bells she ran out to meet me, whereas Francisco waited for me on the stone steps leading at our front door.

Afterwards he came with us to play on the old threshing floor while we watched for Our Lady and the Angels to light their lamps. He eagerly counted the stars with us, but nothing enchanted him as much as the beauty of sunrise or sunset. As long as he could still glimpse one last ray of the setting sun, he made no attempt to watch for the first lamp to be lit in the sky.

"No lamp is as beautiful as Our Lord's," he used to remark to Jacinta, who much preferred Our Lady's lamp because, as she explained, "it doesn't hurt our eyes." Enraptured, he watched the sun's rays glistening on the window panes of the homes in the neighboring village, or glistening in the drops of water which spangled the trees and furze bushes of the serra, making them shine like so many stars. In his eyes these were a thousand times more beautiful than the Angels' lamps.

When he persisted in pleading with his mother to let him take care of the flock and therefore come along with me, it was more to please Jacinta than anything else, for she much preferred Francisco's company to that of her brother John. One day his mother, already quite annoyed, refused this permission and he answered with his usual tranquillity:

"Mother, it doesn't matter to me. It's Jacinta who wants me to go."

He confirmed this on yet another occasion. One of my companions came to my house to invite me to go with her, as she had a particularly good pasturage in view for that day. As the sky was overcast, I went to my aunt's house to inquire who was going out that day, Francisco and Jacinta or their brother John. In case of the latter, I preferred the company of my former companion. My aunt had already decided that John should go because it looked like rain. Francisco went to his mother again and insisted on going himself. He received a curt and decided "No," whereupon he exclaimed:

"It's all the same with me. It's Jacinta who feels badly about it."

When we were out on the mountains together, what Francisco enjoyed most was to perch on the top of the highest rock and sing or play his flute. If his little sister came down to run races with me, he stayed up there entertaining himself with his music and song. The song he sang most often went like this:

Chorus

I love God in Heaven.
I love Him also on earth,
I love the flowers of the fields,
I love the sheep on the mountains.

I am a poor shepherd girl,
I always pray to Mary;
In the midst of my flock
I am like the sun at noon.

Together with my little lambs
I learn to skip and jump;
I am the joy of the serra
And the lily of the vale.

He always took part in our games when we invited him, but sometimes he had no enthusiasm and would say:

"I'll go, but I know I'll be the loser."

The games we knew and found most entertaining were: pebbles, forfeits, pass the ring, buttons, hit the mark, quoits... and card games such as the bisca game, turning up the kings, queens and jacks, and so on. We had two packs of cards. I had one and they had the other. Francisco liked best to play cards, and bisca was his favorite.

Francisco Sees the Angel

During the Apparition of the Angel, Francisco prostrated like his sister and myself. He was carried away by the same supernatural force that moved us to do so, but he learned the prayer by hearing us repeat it since he told us he heard nothing of what the Angel said.

Afterwards when we prostrated to say that prayer, he was the first to feel the strain of such a posture, but he remained kneeling or sitting... and still praying until we had finished. Later he said:

"I am not able to stay like that for a long time like you. My back aches so much that I can't do it."

At the second Apparition of the Angel down by the well, Francisco waited a few moments after it was over and then asked:

"You spoke to the Angel. What did he say to you?"

"Didn't you hear?"

"No. I could see that he was talking to you. I heard what you said to him but what he said to you... I don't know."

As the supernatural atmosphere in which the Angel left us had not yet entirely disappeared, I told him to ask Jacinta or myself the next day.

"Jacinta, you tell me what the Angel said."

"I'll tell you tomorrow. Today I can't talk about it."

Next day, as soon as he came up to me, he asked me:

"Did you sleep last night? I kept thinking about the Angel, and what he might have said."

I then told him all that the Angel had said at the first and second Apparitions. But it seemed that he had not received an understanding of all that the words meant. He asked:

"Who is the Most High? What is the meaning of 'The Hearts of Jesus and Mary are attentive to the voice of your supplications... ?'"

Having received an answer he remained deep in thought for a while and then broke in with another question. My mind was not yet free so I told him to wait until the next day, because at that moment I was unable to speak. He waited quite contentedly but he did not miss the next opportunity of asking more questions. This made Jacinta say to him:

"Look! We shouldn't talk too much about these things."

When we spoke about the Angel, I don't know exactly how to describe what we felt.

"I don't know how I feel," Jacinta said. "I can no longer talk, or sing, or play. I haven't enough strength for anything."

"Neither have I," replied Francisco, "but what of it? The Angel is more beautiful than all this. Let's think about him."

In the third Apparition, the presence of the supernatural made itself felt still more intensely. For several days even Francisco did not venture to speak. Finally he said:

"I love to see the Angel but what's worse, we can't do anything afterwards. I couldn't even walk. I don't know what was wrong with me."

In spite of that, after the third Apparition of the Angel it was he who noticed it was getting dark and who drew our attention to the fact and thought we should take our flocks home. Once the first few days were over and we had returned to normal, Francisco said:

"The Angel gave you Holy Communion, but what was it that he gave to Jacinta and me?"

"It was Holy Communion, too," replied Jacinta, with inexpressible joy. "Didn't you see that it was the Blood that fell from the Host?" Francisco replied:

"I felt that God was within me, but I didn't know how!" Then, prostrating on the ground, he and his sister remained for a long time, saying over and over again the prayer of the Angel:

"Most Holy Trinity..."

Little by little, the atmosphere of the supernatural faded away. By May 13 we were playing with almost as much enjoyment and freedom of spirit as we had done before.

Impressions of the First Apparition

The Apparition of Our Lady plunged us once more into the atmosphere of the supernatural, but this time more gently. Instead of annihilation in the Divine Presence, which exhausted us even physically, it left us filled with peace and expansive joy which did not prevent us from speaking afterwards of what had happened. However with regard to the light communicated to us when Our Lady opened her hands (and everything connected with this light) we experienced a kind of interior impulse that compelled us to keep silent.

Afterwards we told Francisco all that Our Lady had said. He was overjoyed and expressed the happiness he felt when he heard of the promise that he would go to Heaven. Crossing his hands on his breast he exclaimed, "Oh, my dear Our Lady! I'll say as many Rosaries as You want!" From then on he made a habit of moving away from us, as though going for a walk. When we called him and asked him what he was doing, he raised his hand and showed his Rosary. If we told him to come and play, and say the Rosary with us afterwards, he replied:

"I'll pray then as well. Don't you remember that Our Lady said I must pray many Rosaries?" He said to me on one occasion:

"I loved seeing the Angel, but I loved still more seeing Our Lady. What I loved most of all was to see Our Lord in that light from Our Lady which penetrated our hearts. I love God so much! But He is very sad because of so many sins! We must never commit any sins again."

I have already said, in the second account about Jacinta, how he was the one who gave me the news that she had broken our agreement not to say anything. As he shared my opinion that the matter should be kept secret he added sadly:

"As for me, when my mother asked me if it was true, I had to say that it was, so as not to tell a lie." From time to time, he said:

"Our Lady told us that we would have much to suffer, but I don't mind. I'll suffer all that She wishes! What I want is to go to Heaven!"

One day, when I showed how unhappy I was over the persecution now beginning in both my family and outside, Francisco tried to encourage me with these words:

"Never mind! Didn't Our Lady say that we would have much to suffer, to make reparation to Our Lord and to Her Own Immaculate Heart for all the sins by which They are offended? Jesus and Mary are so sad! If we can console Them with these sufferings, how happy we shall be!"

When we arrived at our pasturage a few days after Our Lady's first Apparition, he climbed up to the top of a steep rock and called out to us:

195.

"Don't come up here; let me stay here alone!"

"All right." And off I went, chasing butterflies with Jacinta. We no sooner caught them than we made the sacrifice of letting them fly away, and we never gave another thought to Francisco. When lunch time came, we missed him and went to call him:

"Francisco, don't you want to come for your lunch?"

"No, you eat."

"And to pray the Rosary?"

"That, yes... later on. Call me again." When I went to call him again, he said to me:

"You come up here and pray with me." We climbed up to the peak, where the three of us could scarcely find room to kneel down, I asked him:

"But what have you been doing all this time?"

"I am thinking about God, who is so sad because of so many sins! If I could only give Him joy!"[5] One day we began to sing in happy chorus about the joys of the serra:

Chorus:

The earth and sky resound in song
All vie with me as though a dream,
While watching sheep on hill and dale
Or washing clothes in bubbling stream.

The goldfinch sings to wake me up
When brilliant sun dispels the night
From out the brambles where he hides
His happy song brings me delight.

The owl cries out to frighten me
When dark of night makes all forlorn.
But night is soft with moonlight rays
As maidens sing while shucking corn.

The many birds fill all the vale
With joyous trills and day-long song,
The doves with coos heard in the dale
And wheels of carts which squeak along!

The serra more than dales and hills
Becomes a garden where we run
With dew as jewels outshining rills
In mountains lit by God's bright sun.

We sang it right through once, and were about to repeat it when Francisco interrupted us:

"Let's not sing any more. Since we saw the Angel and Our Lady, singing doesn't appeal to me any longer."

Impressions of the Second Apparition

At the second Apparition on June 13, 1917, Francisco was deeply impressed by the light which, as I related in the second account, Our Lady communicated to us at the moment when She said:

"My Immaculate Heart will be your refuge and the way which will lead you to God."

At that time he did not seem to grasp the meaning of what was happening, perhaps because it was not given to him to hear the accompanying words. For that reason, he asked later:

"Why did Our Lady have a Heart in Her hand, spreading that great light which is God out over the world? You were with Our Lady in the light which went down towards the earth, and Jacinta was with me in the light which rose towards Heaven."

"That is because you and Jacinta will soon go to Heaven," I replied, "while I, with the Immaculate Heart of Mary, will remain for some time longer on earth."

"How many years longer will you stay here?" he asked.

"I don't know. Quite a lot."

"Was it Our Lady who said so?"

"Yes, and I saw it in the light that shone from Her Heart."

Jacinta confirmed the very same thing, saying: "It is exactly like that! That's just how I saw it, too!"

He remarked sometimes: "These people are so happy just because you told them that Our Lady wants the Rosary said, and that you are going to learn to read! How would they feel if they only knew what She showed to us in God, in Her Immaculate Heart, in that light? But this is a secret; it must not be spoken about. It's better that no one should know it." After this Apparition, whenever they asked us if Our Lady had said anything else, we began to give this reply:

"Yes, She did, but it's a secret." If they asked us why it was a secret, we shrugged our shoulders, lowered our heads and kept silent. But after July 13, we then said:

"Our Lady told us we were not to tell it to anybody," thus referring to the secret imposed on us by Our Lady.

Francisco Strengthens Lucia's Courage

In the course of this month the influx of people increased considerably, and so did the constant questionings and contradictions. Francisco suffered quite a lot from all this and complained to his sister, saying:

"What a pity! If you'd only kept quiet, no one would know! If only it were not a lie, we could tell all the people that we saw nothing, and that would be the end of it. But this can't be done!" When he saw me perplexed and in doubt, he wept, and said:

"But how can you think it is the devil? Didn't you see Our Lady and God in that great light? How can we go there without you, when it is you who does the talking?" That night after supper he came back to my house, called me out to the old threshing floor, and said:

"Look! Aren't you going tomorrow?"

"No. I've already told you I'm not going back there any more."

"But what a shame! Why is it that you now think that way? Don't you see that it can't be the devil? God is already sad enough on account of so many sins, and now if you don't go, He'll be sadder still! Come on, say you'll go!"

Impressions of the Third Apparition

In the third Apparition, Francisco seemed to be the one on whom the vision of hell made the least impression, though it did indeed have quite a considerable effect on him.

What made the most powerful impression on him and totally absorbed him was God, the Most Holy Trinity, perceived in that light which penetrated our inmost souls. Afterwards, he said:

"We were on fire in that light which is God, and yet we were not burnt! What is God?... We could never put it into words. Yes, that is something indeed which we could never express! But what a pity it is that He is so sad! If only I could console Him!...

One day I was asked if Our Lady had told us to pray for sinners, and I said She had not. At the first opportunity, while the people were questioning Jacinta, he called me aside and said:

"You lied just now! How could you say that Our Lady didn't tell us to pray for sinners? Didn't She ask us to pray for sinners, then?"

"For sinners, no! She told us to pray for peace, for the war to end... but for sinners, She told us to make sacrifices."

"Ah, that's true! I was beginning to think you had lied."

Francisco in Prison

I have already described how Francisco spent the day praying and weeping. He was perhaps even more upset than I was when my father received an order to present me before the Administrator at Vila Nova de Ourem.[6] In prison he was quite courageous and tried to cheer up Jacinta when she felt most homesick.

While we were saying the Rosary in prison he noticed that one of the prisoners was on his knees with his cap still on his head. Francisco went up to him and said:

"If you wish to pray, you should take your cap off." Right away the poor man handed it to him. He went over and put it on the bench on top of his own. During Jacinta's questioning he confided to me with boundless joy and peace:

"If they kill us as they say, we'll soon be in Heaven! How wonderful! Nothing else matters!" Then after a moment's silence, he added:

"God grant that Jacinta won't be afraid. I'm going to say a Hail Mary for her!" He promptly removed his cap and prayed. The guard, hearing him praying, asked him:

"What are you saying?"

"I'm saying a Hail Mary so that Jacinta won't be afraid." The guard made a scornful gesture and let him go ahead.

After our return from Vila Nova de Ourem we began to be aware of the presence of the supernatural all around us. We began to feel that we were about to receive some supernatural communication.

Francisco at once showed his concern over Jacinta's absence. "What a pity it would be," he exclaimed, "If Jacinta did not get here in time!"

He begged his brother to go quickly and get her, adding:

"Tell her to come running." After his brother left us, Francisco said:

"Jacinta will be very sad if she doesn't come in time." After the Apparition, his sister wanted to stay there the whole afternoon, so he said:

"No! You must go home, because Mother didn't let you come out with the sheep." And to encourage her, he went back to the house with her.

In prison, when we noticed that it was already past midday and they would not let us go to the Cova, Francisco said:

"Perhaps Our Lady will come and appear to us here." Francisco could not hide his distress. Almost in tears, he said:

"Our Lady must have been very upset because we didn't go to the Cova da Iria. She won't appear to us again. I would so love to see Her!"

While in prison, Jacinta wept bitterly because she was so homesick for her mother and all the family. Francisco tried to cheer her, saying:

"Even if we never see our mother again, let's be patient! We can offer it for the conversion of sinners. The worst thing would be if Our Lady never came back again! That is what hurts me most. But I offer this as well for sinners."

Afterwards, he asked me:

"Tell me! Will Our Lady not come and appear to us any more?"

"I don't know. I think She will."

"I miss Her so much!"

The Apparition at Valinhos was, therefore, a double joy for him. He had been tormented by the fear that She would never return. He told me later:

"Most likely She didn't appear on the 13th so as to avoid going to the Administrator's house, maybe because he is such a bad man."

Impressions of the Last Apparitions

After September 13, when I told Francisco that in October Our Lord would come as well, he was overwhelmed with joy. He said:

"Oh, how good He is! I've seen Him only twice,[7] and I love Him so much!" From time to time, he asked:

"Are there many days left till the 13th? I'm longing for that day to come so that I can see Our Lord again." Then he thought for a moment, and added:

"But listen! Will He still be so sad? I am so sorry to see Him sad like that! I offer Him all the sacrifices I can think of. Sometimes I don't even run away from all those people just in order to make sacrifices!"

After October 13, he said to me:

"I loved seeing Our Lord, but I loved still more seeing Him in that light where we were with Him as well. It's not long now and Our Lord will take me up close to Him and then I can look at Him forever."

One day, I asked him:

"When you are questioned, why do you put your head down and not want to answer?"

"Because I want you to answer, and Jacinta too. I didn't hear anything. I can only say what I saw. Then, supposing I said something you don't want me to say!"

Every now and then he went off and left us without telling us. When we missed him we went in search of him calling out his name. He answered from behind a little well, or a shrub or a clump of brambles, and there he was on his knees, praying.

"Why didn't you tell us so that we could come and pray with you?"

"Because I prefer to pray alone."

In my notes on the book called *Jacinta,* I've already related what happened on a piece of land known as Varzea. I don't think I need to repeat it here. On our way to my home one day we had to pass by my

*"I love God so much! But He is so sad because
of so many sins." (Francisco)*

godmother's house. She had just been making honeywater and called us in to give us a glass. We went in and Francisco was the first to whom she offered a glass. He took it and without drinking passed it on to Jacinta so that she and I could have a drink first. Meanwhile he turned on his heel and disappeared.

"Where is Francisco?" my godmother asked.

"I don't know! He was here just now."

When he did not return Jacinta and I thanked my godmother for the drink and went in search of Francisco. We knew without doubt that he would be sitting on the edge of the well which I have mentioned so often.

"Francisco, you didn't drink your glass of honeywater! My godmother called you so many times and you didn't appear!"

"When I took the glass I suddenly remembered I could offer that sacrifice to console Our Lord, so while you two were taking a drink, I ran over here."

Anecdotes and Popular Songs

Between my house and Francisco's lived my godfather Anastacio, who was married to an older woman whom God had not blessed with children. They were quite rich farmers and didn't need to work. My father was overseer of their farm and had charge of the day laborers. In gratitude for this they showed a special liking for me, particularly the lady of the house whom I called my godmother Teresa. If I didn't call in during the day I had to sleep there at night, because she couldn't get along without her little "sweetmeat," as she called me.

On festive occasions she delighted in dressing me up with her gold necklace and large earrings which hung down below my shoulders, and a pretty little hat decorated with immense feathers of different colors and fastened with an array of gold beads. At the "festas" there was no one better turned out than I. How my sisters and my godmother gloried in the fact! The other children crowded about me to admire the brilliance of my finery.

To tell the truth I myself greatly enjoyed the "festa," and vanity was my worst adornment. Everybody showed liking and esteem for me except a poor orphan girl whom my godmother Teresa had taken into her home on the death of her own mother. She seemed to fear I would get part of the inheritance she was hoping for, and indeed she would not have been mistaken had not Our Lord destined for me a more precious inheritance.

As soon as the news of the Apparitions spread, my godfather showed unconcern and my godmother was completely opposed to it all. She made no secret of her disapproval of such "inventions," as she called them. Therefore I began to keep away from her house as much as I could.

My disappearance was soon followed by that of the groups of children who had so often gathered there and whom my godmother loved to watch singing and dancing. She treated them to dried figs, nuts, almonds, chestnuts, fruit, and so on.

One Sunday afternoon when I was passing near her house with Francisco and Jacinta she called out to us:

"Come in, my little swindlers, come! You've not been here for a long time!" Once inside she lavished her usual attention on us. The other children seemed to guess we were there and began to come along as well.

My kind godmother, happy at seeing us all gathered in her house once again after such a long space of time, heaped delicacies upon us and wanted to see us sing and dance.

"Come on," we said, "what will it be, this one, or that?" My godmother made the choice herself. It was

"Congratulations Without Illusions," a party song for boys and girls.

Francisco, the Little Moralist

The women of the neighborhood no sooner heard the lively singing than they came over to join us. At the end they asked us to sing it through again. Francisco, however, came up to me and said:

"Let's not sing that song any more. Our Lord certainly does not want us to sing songs like that now." We therefore slipped away among the other children and ran off to our favorite well.

Meanwhile it was getting near Carnival time in 1918. The boys and girls met once again that year to prepare the usual festive meals and fun of those days. Each one brought something from home... such as olive oil, flour, meat, and so on... to one of the houses and the girls then did the cooking for a sumptuous banquet.

All those three days, feasting and dancing went on well into the night, and above all on the last day of the Carnival. The children under fourteen had their own celebration in another house. Several of the girls came to ask me to help them organize our "festa."

At first I refused, but finally I gave in like a coward, especially after hearing the pleading of Joseph Carreira's sons and daughter, for it was he who had placed his home in Casa Velha at our disposal. He and his wife insistently asked me to go there. I yielded then and went with a crowd of youngsters to see the place. There was a fine large room, almost as big as a hall well suited for the amusements, and a spacious yard for the supper! Everything was arranged.

I came home, outwardly in the most festive mood. But inwardly my conscience protested loudly. As soon as I met Jacinta and Francisco I told them what had happened.

"Are you going back again to those parties and games?" Francisco asked me sternly. "Have you already forgotten that we promised never to do that any more?"

"I didn't know what to do!"

There was indeed no end to the entreaties, nor to the number of girls who came insisting that I play with them. Some even came from far distant villages. From Moita came Rosa, Ana Caetano and Ana Broqueira; from Fatima, the two daughters of Manuel Caracol; from Boleiros, the two daughters of Manuel da Ramira, and two of Joachim Chapeleta as well; from Amoreira, the two Silva girls; from Currais, Laura Gato, Josefa Valinho, besides some others whose names I do not remember. Others came from Boleiros and Lomba de Pederneira, and so on, quite apart from all those who came from Eira de Pedra, Casa Velha, and Aljustrel.

How could I suddenly let down all those girls who seemed not to know how to enjoy themselves without my company, and make them understand that I had to stop going to these gatherings once and for all?

God inspired Francisco with the answer:

"Do you know how you could do it? Everyone knows that Our Lady has appeared to you. Therefore you can say that you have promised Her not to dance any more and for this reason you are not going! Then on such days we can run away and hide in the cave on the Cabeco. Up there nobody will find us!"

I accepted his proposal. And once I had made my decision nobody else thought of organizing any such gathering. God's blessing was with us. Those friends of mine, who until then sought me out to have me join in their amusements, now followed my example and came to my home on Sunday afternoons to ask me to go with them to pray the Rosary in the Cova da Iria.

†††

207.

1. She slept in a dormitory with other novices and therefore is writing in the only secluded spot available: a corner in the attic of the Novitiate House in Tuy. She could do only a few pages in the times allotted for silence, yet always picked up where she left off writing without going back and making any corrections.

2. This prologue reveals Lucia's literary taste, education and remarkable memory.

3. Lucia does not mean to say that she felt "inspired" in the scriptural sense of the word.

4. He was Lucia's cousin on her father's side.

5. It may well be said that Francisco had the gift of highest contemplation.

6. On August 11, Lucia was taken by her father to appear before the Administrator. Ti Marto, however, refused to take his children (Francisco and Jacinta).

7. He refers to the Apparitions in June and July. They saw Our Lord in the mysterious light which Our Lady communicated to them.

Mr. & Mrs. Marto with John Haffert and
Fr. Oliveira in July 1946.

Chapter XVII.

In the Fourth Memoir —
Lucia Remembers

FRANCISCO'S HOLY DEATH

In this chapter Lucia continues the account of her cousin Francisco. She describes his growth in holiness following the apparitions and the illness leading to his eventual death as predicted by Our Lady.

†††

Francisco did not talk much and when he prayed or offered sacrifices, he liked to hide even from Jacinta and myself. Quite often we surprised him hidden behind a wall or a clump of blackberry bushes whither he had ingeniously slipped away to kneel and pray, or "think," as he said, "of Our Lord who is sad on account of so many sins." If I asked him:

"Francisco, why don't you tell me to pray with you, and Jacinta, too?"

"I prefer praying by myself," he answered, "so that I can think and console Our Lord who is so sad!" I asked him one day:

"Francisco, which do you like better — to console Our Lord or to convert sinners so that no more souls will go to hell?"

"I would rather console Our Lord. Didn't you notice how sad Our Lady was that last month when She said that people must not offend Our Lord any more, for He is already much offended? I would like to console Our Lord, and after that, convert sinners so that they won't offend Him any more."

209.

Sometimes on our way to school, as soon as we reached Fatima he would say to me:

"Listen! You go to school and I'll stay here in the church, close to the Hidden Jesus. It's not worth my while learning to read as I'll be going to Heaven very soon. On your way home, come and call me."

The Blessed Sacrament was kept at that time near the entrance of the church on the left side, as the church was undergoing repairs.[1] Francisco went over there, between the baptismal font and the altar, and that was where I found him on my return.

Later when he fell ill, he often told me when I called in to see him on my way to school:

"Look! Go to the church and give my love to the Hidden Jesus. What hurts me most is that I cannot go there myself and stay awhile with the Hidden Jesus."

When I arrived at his house one day, I said goodbye to a group of school children who had come with me and I went in to pay a visit to him and his sister. As he had heard all the noise he asked me:

"Did you come with all that crowd?"

"Yes, I did."

"Don't go with them because you might learn to commit sins. When you come out of school, go and stay for a little while near the Hidden Jesus, and afterwards come home by yourself."

On one occasion, I asked him:

"Francisco, do you feel very sick?"

"I do, but I'm suffering to console Our Lord."

When Jacinta and I went into his room one day, he said to us:

"Don't talk much today, as my head aches so badly."

"Don't forget to make the offering for sinners," Jacinta reminded him. "Yes, but first I make it to console Our Lord and Our Lady, and then, afterwards for sinners and for the Holy Father."

On another occasion I found him very happy when I arrived.

"Are you better?"

"No. I feel worse. It won't be long now till I go to Heaven. When I'm there, I'm going to console Our Lord and Our Lady very much. Jacinta is going to pray a lot for sinners, for the Holy Father and for you. You will stay here, because Our Lady wants it that way. Listen, you must do everything that She tells you."

While Jacinta seemed to be solely concerned with the one thought of converting sinners and saving souls from going to hell, Francisco appeared to think only of consoling Our Lord and Our Lady, who had seemed to him to be so sad.

Francisco Sees the Devil

How different is the incident that I now call to mind. One day we went into a place called Pedreira, and while the sheep were browsing we jumped from rock to rock making our voices echo down in the deep ravines. Francisco withdrew, as usual, to a hollow among the rocks.

A considerable time had elapsed when we heard him shouting and crying out to us and to Our Lady. Distressed lest something might have happened to him, we ran in search of him calling out his name.

"Where are you?"

"Here! Here!"

But it took us some time before we could locate him. At last we came upon him trembling with fright, still on his knees, and so upset that he was unable to rise to his feet.

"What's wrong? What happened to you?" In a voice half smothered with fright, he replied:

"It was one of those huge beasts that we saw in hell. He was right here breathing out flames!"

I saw nothing and neither did Jacinta, so I laughed and said to him:

"You never want to think about hell so as not to be afraid... and now you're the first one to be frightened!"

Indeed, whenever Jacinta appeared particularly moved by the remembrance of hell he used to say to her:

"Don't think so much about hell! Think about Our Lord and Our Lady instead. I don't think about hell so as not to be afraid."

He was anything but fearful. He'd go anywhere in the dark alone at night without the slightest hesitation. He played with lizards and when he came across any snakes, he got them to entwine themselves round a stick, and even poured sheep's milk into the holes in the rocks for them to drink. He went hunting for foxes' holes and rabbits' burrows, for genets, and other creatures of the wild.

Francisco and His Feathered Friends

Francisco was very fond of birds and he could not bear to see anyone robbing their nests. He always kept part of the bread he had for his lunch, breaking it into crumbs and spreading them out on top of the rocks so that the birds could eat them. Moving away a little he called them, as though he expected them to understand him.

He didn't want any one else to approach lest they be frightened. "Poor wee things! You are hungry," he said, as though conversing with them. "Come, come and eat!"

And they, keen-eyed as they are, did not wait for the invitation but came flocking around him. It was his delight to see them flying back to the tree tops with their little craws full, singing and chirping in a deafening chorus in which Francisco joined with rare skill.

One day we met a little boy carrying in his hand a small bird that he had caught. Full of compassion, Francisco promised him two coins if only he would let the bird fly away. The boy readily agreed, but first he wished to see the money in his hand. Francisco ran all the way home from the Carreira pond, which lies a little distance below the Cova da Iria, to fetch the coins and so let the little prisoner free. Then as he watched it fly away, he clapped his hands for joy and said:

"Be careful! Don't let yourself be caught again!"

An old woman called Ti Maria Carreira, whose sons sent her out sometimes to take care of their flock of goats and sheep, lived thereabouts. The animals were rather wild and often strayed away in different directions. Whenever we met Ti Maria in these difficulties, Francisco was the first to run to her aid.

He helped her to lead the flock to pasture, chased after the stray ones and gathered them all together again. The poor old woman overwhelmed Francisco with her thanks and called him her dear guardian angel. When we came across any sick people, he was filled with compassion and said:

"I can't bear to see them, as I feel so sorry for them! Tell them I'll pray for them."

One day they wanted to take us to Montelo to the home of a man called Joaquim Chapeleta. Francisco did not want to go. "I'm not going because I can't bear to see people who want to speak and cannot." (This man's mother was dumb.)

When Jacinta and I returned home at nightfall, I asked my aunt where Francisco was. "How do I know?" she replied. "I'm worn out looking for him all afternoon. Some ladies came and wanted to see you, but you two were not here. He vanished and never appeared again. Now you go and look for him!"

We sat down for a bit on a bench in the kitchen thinking that we would go later to the Loca do Cabeco, certain that we would find him there, but no sooner had my aunt left the house than his voice came from the attic through a little hole in the ceiling. He had climbed up there when he thought that people were coming. From this vantage point he had observed everything. He told us afterwards:

"There were so many people! Heaven help me if they had ever caught me by myself! What ever would I have said to them?"

(There was a trap-door in the kitchen, which was easily reached by placing a chair on a table, thus affording access to the attic.)

Francisco's Love and Zeal

As I have already said, my aunt sold her flock before my mother disposed of ours. From that time, before I went out in the morning I let Jacinta and Francisco know the place where I was going to pasture the sheep that day. As soon as they could get away, they came to join me. One day they were waiting for me when I arrived.

"Oh! How did you get here so early?"

"I came," answered Francisco, "because... I don't know why. Being with you didn't matter much to me before, and I just came because of Jacinta... but now I can't sleep in the morning as I'm so anxious to be with you."

Once the Apparitions on each 13th of the month were over, he said to us on the eve of every following 13th:

"Look! Early tomorrow morning, I'm making my escape out through the back garden to the cave on the Cabeco. As soon as you can, come and join me there."

Oh dear! Forgive the wandering! There I was, writing things about his being sick and near to death, and now I see that I have gone back to the happy times we had on the serra, with the birds chirping merrily all around us. In writing down what I can remember, I am like a crab that walks backwards and forwards without bothering about reaching the end of its journey. I leave my work to Dr. Galamba, in case he can make use of anything in it... though I suppose he will find little or nothing.

I return, therefore, to Francisco's illness. But first I will tell you something about his brief schooling.

He came out of the house one day and met me with my sister Teresa, who was already married and living in Lomba. Another woman from a nearby hamlet had asked her to come to me about her son who had been accused of some crime which I no longer remember. If he could not prove his innocence he was to be condemned.

Teresa asked me insistently, in the name of the poor woman for whom she wished to do such a favor, to plead for this grace with Our Lady. Having received the message, I set out for school and on the way I told my cousins all about it. When we reached Fatima Francisco said to me:

"Listen! While you go to school, I'll stay with the Hidden Jesus and I'll ask Him for that grace."

When I came out of school, I went to call him and asked:

"Did you pray to Our Lord to grant that grace?"

"Yes, I did. Tell your Teresa that he'll be home in a few days' time." And indeed, a few days later the poor boy returned home. On the 13th, he and his entire family came to thank Our Lady for the grace they had received.

On another occasion I noticed, as we left the house, that Francisco was walking very slowly.

"What's the matter?" I asked him. "You seem unable to walk!"

"I have such a bad headache and I feel as though I'm going to fall."

"Then don't come! Stay at home!"

"I don't want to. I'd rather stay in the church with the Hidden Jesus while you go to school."

Francisco was already sick but could still manage to walk a little, so one day I went with him to the cave on the Cabeco and to Valinhos. On our return home we found the house full of people.

A poor woman was standing near a table pretending to bless innumerable pious objects: Rosary beads, medals, crucifixes and so on. Jacinta and I were soon surrounded by a crowd of people who wanted to question us. Francisco was seized upon by the would-be "blesser," who invited him to help her.

"I could not give a blessing," he replied very seriously, "and neither should you! Only priests do that."

The little boy's words went through the crowd as though spoken by a loudspeaker, and the poor woman had to make a quick departure amid a hail of insults from the people, all demanding back the objects they had just handed over to her.

I already related in my account of Jacinta, how he managed to go one day to the Cova da Iria; how he wore the rope and then handed it back to me; how he was the first, on a day when the heat was suffocating, to offer the sacrifice of not taking a drink; and how he sometimes reminded his sister about suffering for sinners, and so on. I presume, therefore, that it is not necessary to repeat these things here.

One day I was by his bedside keeping him company. Jacinta was there too. Suddenly his sister Teresa came to warn us that a veritable multitude of people were coming down the road and were obviously looking for us. As soon as she had gone out, I said to Francisco:

"All right! You two wait for them here. I'm going to hide."

Jacinta managed to run out behind me, and we both succeeded in concealing ourselves inside a barrel which was overturned just outside the door leading to the back garden. It was not long before we heard the noise of people searching the house, going out through the garden and even standing right beside the barrel... but we were saved by the fact that its open end was turned in the opposite direction.

When we felt that they had all gone away we came out of our hiding place and went to rejoin Francisco, who told us all that had happened.

"There were so many people and they wanted me to tell them where you were, but I didn't know myself. They wished to see us and ask us lots of things. Besides that, there was a woman from Alqueidao, who wanted the cure of a sick person and the conversion of a sinner. I'll pray for that woman and you pray for the others. There's such a lot of them.

Shortly after Francisco's death, this woman came to see us and asked me to show her his grave. She wished to go there and thank him for the two graces for which she had asked him to pray.

One day we were just outside Aljustrel on our way to the Cova da Iria when a group of people came upon us by surprise around the bend in the road. In order to see and hear us better, they set Jacinta and myself on top of a wall. Francisco refused to let himself be put there as though he were afraid of falling. Then little by little he edged his way out and leaned against a dilapidated wall on the other side. A poor woman and her son, seeing that they could not manage to speak to us personally as they wished, went and knelt down in front of Francisco. They begged him to obtain from Our Lady the grace that the father of the family would be cured and that he would not have to go to the war.

Francisco knelt down also, took off his cap and asked if they would like to pray the Rosary with him. They said they would and began to pray. Very soon all those people stopped asking curious questions and also went down on their knees to pray. After that they went with us to the Cova da Iria reciting a Rosary along the way. Once there, we said another Rosary and then they went away quite happy.

The poor woman promised to come back and thank Our Lady for the graces she had requested if they were granted. She came back several times, accompanied not only by her son but also her husband, who had by now recovered. They came from the parish of S. Mamede and we called them the Casaleiros.

Francisco's Illness

While he was ill Francisco always appeared joyful and content. I asked him sometimes:

"Are you suffering a lot, Francisco?"

"Quite a lot, but never mind! I am suffering to console Our Lord... and afterwards within a short time I am going to Heaven!"

"Once you get there, don't forget to ask Our Lady to take me there soon as well."

"That I won't ask! You know very well that She doesn't want you there yet." The day before he died he said to me:

"Look! I'm very ill but it won't be long now before I go to Heaven."

"Then do this: when you're there, don't forget to pray a great deal for sinners, the Holy Father, for me and for Jacinta."

"Yes, I'll pray. But look, you'd better ask Jacinta to pray for these things instead, because I'm afraid I'll forget when I see Our Lord... and then, more than anything else, I want to console Him." One day early in the morning, his sister Teresa came looking for me.

"Come quickly to our house! Francisco is very bad and says he wants to tell you something."

I dressed as fast as I could and went over there. He asked his mother and brothers and sister to leave the room, saying that he wanted to ask me a secret. They went out and he said to me:

"I am going to confession so that I can receive Holy Communion and then die. I want you to tell me if you have seen me commit any sins, and then go and ask Jacinta if she has seen me commit any."

"You disobeyed your mother a few times," I answered, "when she told you to stay at home, and you ran off to be with me or go and hide."

"That's true, I remember that. Now go and ask Jacinta if she remembers anything else." I went, and Jacinta thought for awhile, then answered:

"Well, tell him that, before Our Lady appeared to us he stole a coin from our father to buy a music box from Jose Marto of Casa Velha; and when the boys from Aljustrel threw stones at those from Boleiros, he threw some too!" When I gave him this message from his sister, he answered:

"I've already confessed those but I'll do so again. Maybe it is because of these sins that I had committed that Our Lord is so sad! But even if I don't die, I'll never commit them again. I'm heartily sorry for them now." Joining his hands, he recited the prayer:

"O my Jesus, forgive us. Save us from the fires of hell. Lead all souls to Heaven, especially those who are most in need." Then he said:

"Now listen, you must also ask Our Lord to forgive me my sins."

"I'll ask that, don't worry. If Our Lord had not forgiven them already, Our Lady would not have told Jacinta the other day that She was coming soon to take you to Heaven. Now I'm going to Mass and there I'll pray to the Hidden Jesus for you."

"Then please ask Him to let the parish priest give me Holy Communion."

"I certainly will." When I returned from the church, Jacinta was already up and was sitting on his bed. As soon as Francisco saw me, he asked:

"Did you ask the Hidden Jesus that the parish priest would give me Holy Communion?"

"I did."

"Then in Heaven, I'll pray for you."

"You will? The other day, you said you wouldn't."

"That was about taking you there very soon. But if you want me to pray for that, I will, and then let Our Lady do as She wishes."

"Yes, do. You pray."

"All right. Don't worry. I'll pray." Then I left them and went off to my usual daily tasks of lessons and work. When I came home at night I found him radiant with joy. He had made his confession and the parish priest had promised to bring him Holy Communion the next day.

Francisco to Heaven

On the following day after receiving Holy Communion, he said to his sister:

"I am happier than you are because I have the Hidden Jesus within my heart. I'm going to Heaven but I'm going to pray very much to Our Lord and Our Lady for them to bring you both there soon." Jacinta and I spent almost the whole of that day at his bedside. As he was already unable to pray, he asked us to pray the Rosary for him. Then he said to me:

"I am sure I shall miss you terribly in Heaven! If only Our Lady would bring you there soon, also!"

"You won't miss me! Just imagine! And you right there with Our Lord and Our Lady! They are so good!"

"That's true! Perhaps I won't remember!" Then I added:

"Perhaps you'll forget! But never mind!" That night I said goodbye to him.

"Goodbye, Francisco! If you go to Heaven tonight, don't forget me when you get there, do you hear me?"

"No, I won't forget. Be sure of that."

Then seizing my right hand, he held it tightly for a long time looking at me with tears in his eyes.

"Do you want anything more?" I asked him with tears running down my cheeks, too.

"No!" he answered in a low voice, quite overcome. As the scene was becoming so moving, my aunt told me to leave the room.

"Goodbye then, Francisco! Till we meet in Heaven, goodbye!..."

Heaven was drawing near. He took his flight to Heaven the following day in the arms of his Heavenly Mother.[2] I could never describe how much I missed him. This grief was a thorn that pierced my heart for years to come. It is a memory of the past that echoes forever unto eternity.

'Twas night and peacefully I dream'd
That on this happy longed-for day
He joined the angel choirs above
Who vie with us in praising Him.

What golden crown beyond all thought
Of flowers garnered here below
A crown of glory and reward
With earthly longings now all still.

The joy and smile from Mother's lips
Are his in Heav'n, there with God,
Afire with love and lasting joy
His years on earth so quickly pass'd.

Farewell!

✝✝✝

[1] The observation was made by Lucia herself.

[2] The "following day" was April 4, 1919, at 10:00 a.m.

Above: Mr. and Mrs. Marto, at the funeral of Francisco,
stand in front of their five surviving children: (left to right)
Anthony, Manuel, Joseph, John, Jacinta (April 5, 1919).

Left: Hundreds of thousands of pilgrims fill the Cova on
May 13, 1991, to join Pope John Paul II on the tenth
anniversary of the attempt on his life. His Holiness said he
had come back to Fatima on this anniversary not only to
thank Our Lady again for his life but also for the changes
in Eastern Europe. He called Fatima "the Marian Capital
of the World."

Chapter XVIII.

Comments On

SECRETS IN THE MEMOIRS

It is remarkable that Lucia speaks of the little attic room in which she wrote the memoirs, mentioning that *she did not even have a cell* at that time but slept in a dormitory. It is remarkable because she speaks so little about herself. She does not even mention in her memoirs that *Our Lady appeared to her on June 16, 1921, the last time she visited the Cova,* to say "goodbye."

During the Apparitions in 1917 three years before, Our Lady had told her *"I will come back here a seventh time."* On June 16, 1921, as she was making the heroic sacrifice of leaving her family to become an "orphan" under an assumed name in a far-off school, Our Lady appeared again to her in that same spot where She had revealed to her a message for the whole world. This time it was for Lucia's own consolation. Our Lady was keeping Her promise made to Lucia three years before:

"Do not be sad. My Immaculate Heart will be your consolation and the way that will lead you to God."

I was with Fr. Alonso (official documentarian of Fatima) and the Bishop of Fatima (Dom John Venancio) in that attic in the Dorothean convent in Tuy when we were negotiating the acquisition of the convent of the apparitions in Pontevedra to be taken over and administered by the Apostolate of Fatima (The Blue Army). The three of us were crowded under the sloping roof in that tiny space illuminated only by a small skylight.

"To think," Father Alonso said, "it was here that she wrote the memoirs — *never changing or deleting a word* in order not to make the notebook untidy!"

In that tiny space where these memoirs were written I felt a special closeness with the two special apostles of Fatima, Dr. Alonso and the Bishop. Both of them are now dead. It was Fr. Alonso who asked me to do this book.

Our Lady's Bishop

Bishop Venancio died on August 2, 1985. His successor, the Most Rev. Cosme do Amaral, preached the funeral sermon in the Leiria Cathedral with the Cardinal Patriarch of Lisbon, several bishops, and over a hundred priests attending. He said of Bishop Venancio:

"His entire spiritual life was centered in the Cova da Iria (where Our Lady of Fatima appeared) hidden in the confessional, before the Blessed Sacrament of the Chapel of Perpetual Adoration, or kneeling in the Chapel of the Apparitions..."

I had come to know and love Bishop Venancio over a period of more than twenty years. My love for him grew deeper day by day, month by month, year by year.

I was privileged to travel with him several times with the Pilgrim Virgin around the world, and Africa and South America, and to Australia... tens of thousands of miles with that miraculous image of Our Lady of Fatima which Pope Pius XII called The Messenger of Her Royalty! He certainly had no doubt that Lucia was left on earth by Our Lady to be Her messenger... Her voice.

Five days before Bishop Venancio died, I was in Paris reviewing the final version of a major motion picture film sponsored by the World Apostolate of Fatima (The Blue Army). I received a telegram which said he was already dead. I walked for hours from church to church praying for him... especially in the Chapel of Our Lady at St. Sulpice where St. Grignion De Montfort said his first Mass and in the Chapel of the Apparitions of the Miraculous Medal (Rue du Bac).

Two days later I awoke in the night recalling the time that a Blue Army international meeting in Fatima had a very close vote concerning the name "Blue Army." It was finally decided to have an alternate name: *World Apostolate of Fatima.* But the international leaders decided that the original name of Blue Army would also be kept.

Now "Understood"

Bishop Venancio said after the vote:

"I am glad they did not eliminate the Blue Army name. If they had, I would have vetoed their decision."

I was always impressed by this *because it was completely contrary to Bishop Venancio's custom and manner to veto any decision of a committee.* As I wrote in my book *Dear Bishop!,* I was convinced from that time on that the Bishop had some kind of message either from Our Lady or from Lucia concerning the name of the Blue Army.

Suddenly, there in Paris, after I had spent many hours of the previous day going from church to church in prayer for him, I seemed to understand *why.* I suddenly felt "comfortable" with the thought that at the present time the Holy See wishes that this Apostolate be known as *the World Apostolate of Fatima.* But in years to come the title *"Blue Army"* would become universally acceptable because this apostolate would be promoting not only the message as given by Our Lady at Fatima, but also that same message expanded through similar apparitions like the ones in Akita, Venezuela, and various others, which have received or await approval by the Church.

Was it just my imagination, or had Bishop Venancio just communicated this to me?

Astonishing "Message"

Two days later I was on the plane to Fatima, hoping to attend his funeral. In my handbag under my seat on the plane I had a book by Fr. Roschini on the Blessed Virgin. And the thought came to me:

"There is a message in that book for you from Bishop Venancio."

It seemed more than a passing thought. It seemed like *a message from the Bishop,* who I thought to be already dead as the telegram had stated. I reached under the seat, opened the handbag and took out the book and opened it... not in the middle where one might ordinarily open a book at random, but just a few pages from the end. And there at the top of the page I read:

"One is never so active for one's brethren as when one is no longer among them, but when one is light which has rejoined the Divine Light" (La Vierge Marie dans L'oeuvre de Maria Valtorta, p. 352).[1]

I turned back to the previous page so I could better understand. I read that after the Ascension, Our Lady longed ever more and more to rejoin Her Divine Son because of the certitude that She could do more for the Church and for each of Her children when She would be in Heaven... praying and interceding for them at the Throne of God. It then said Maria Valtorta had received this message from Our Lady Herself.

I closed the book in astonishment. When I arrived in Portugal, I learned that the Bishop had not died until I had arrived.

Two days later, Msgr. Luciano Guerra, Rector of the Shrine of Fatima, came to the Blue Army House to take Bishop Luna, who succeeded Bishop Venancio as President of the World Apostolate of Fatima (The Blue Army) and myself to the Cathedral in Leiria for the funeral.

I was privileged to arrange the cloth over the body and to help close the coffin and carry it to the grave. There was no sorrow. I had not lost a friend. I, and all the Fatima apostles in the world, now possessed him more intimately than ever.

"One is never so active for one's brethren as when one is no longer among them, but when one is light which has rejoined the Divine Light."

Bishop Venancio's Message

"The great and important task of the Blue Army of Our Lady of Fatima," said Bishop Venancio, *"is the interior renovation of the Church, the victory over atheistic Communism, and securing for the world a true and lasting peace."*

The saintly bishop saw this Apostolate as *a special opportunity* for "the great number of children, old people, invalids, and millions of parents, even though absorbed from morning to night in household chores with the care of their children, work in fields or factory, and without either time or possibility for the intense *organized work* of the apostolate." The bishop continued:

"In spite of physical or psychological incapacity *they are fully capable of responding to the requests made by the Queen of the Rosary.* They can pray, they can sacrifice themselves, they can expiate, and they can live and work according to the desires of the Immaculate Heart of Mary, thus contributing to the fulfillment of the essential part of the spirit of the message... the great work to which we are called."

Bishop Venancio as the Bishop of Leiria-Fatima saw the Message of Fatima as a message for the entire world and he saw the Blue Army as a providential Apostolate to carry the Message of Fatima to all nations... to all people. *The above statements of the bishop concerning the world mission of the Blue Army were published in the official newspaper of the Sanctuary of Fatima (Voz da Fatima) in October 1964.*

Just three years after this, Pope Paul VI journeyed to Fatima and the Bishop accepted the position of International President of the Blue Army. Bishop Venancio said in the same important article:

"The task of The Blue Army of Our Lady of Fatima consists in making known the Message of Fatima *to the whole world* by all the means at its disposal, *so that men of all nations will realize it in their personal lives.*"

Most Impressive

I remarked above that I felt privileged to place a last kiss on his coffin as I helped carry it to the grave and then lowered it into the tomb... feeling that I was lowering a precious relic of a dear friend now at the throne of Heaven with Our Lady, whose Bishop he had been.

After the death of St. Therese there was a veritable shower of roses... a "shower of miracles." After the death of Bishop Venancio there seems to have begun a "shower of power" upon our Apostolate! The very day he was buried, that same afternoon, we were able to break ground for the new wing of the International Center in Fatima — the cornerstone for which had been laid in his presence by his predecessor. The same day a generous donor gave $200,000 for the piece of land behind the Blue Army House, so that it would have sufficient area for the expansion!

We are not alone. Many who labored for the triumph promised at Fatima continue their work from Heaven.

More About the Church

Getting back to that meeting in the attic at Tuy where the Memoirs were written, one cannot help but think that the only reason Lucia did not delete that note about the attic is that she did not want to spoil the notebook.

As we were crowded in that tiny space there was obvious awe in the demeanor and voice of Father Alonso... a great intellectual, master of many languages, author of many books, and editor of the internationally prestigious periodical *Ephemerides Mariologicae.* He was himself a meticulous master of language who could speak fluently and without hesitation, even on complex matters, and he knew it was usual for writers to rethink a phrase, improve a sentence or substitute a better word.

He marveled that Lucia wrote in those difficult circumstances *without altering a word.* She did it as an act of obedience (and a very distasteful one at that). She must often have felt like deleting or changing something she had written!

Yet *in between all her other duties,* promptly interrupting even a word at the sound of a bell, sitting on an old trunk in that attic with her lap as her "desk," she wrote word after word, memoir after memoir, without a single change... and without ever repeating herself.

Aid of Holy Spirit

In this last memoir we find a personal revelation of great importance. *If she had the slightest doubt about what she was about to write* (at least about the appearance of Our Lady and Her message) she waited and prayed until she was *certain* in her heart *that the Holy Spirit was with her, assuring her of the exact truth.*

Is she saying that her memoirs are an "inspired" work? Of course not... at least not in the sense of the Scriptures being "inspired." She is merely telling the events and messages in their reality, but she is confident that the Holy Spirit is there to prevent her from error.

Father Alonso was always ready to point out that Lucia seemed to have almost total recall. Once when Francisco challenged her for telling a questioner that Our Lady had not asked her to pray for sinners, she reminded Francisco (somewhat to his amazement) that in referring to sinners Our Lady had asked only for sacrifices. This shows not only Lucia's almost *total* recall of every word Our Lady or the angel said, but also her scrupulosity in answering every question *exactly.*

Of course she knew, as Francisco did, that Our Lady *wanted* them to pray for sinners, especially the Rosary with the prayer:

"O my Jesus, save us from hell, *lead all souls to Heaven,* especially those most in need of Your Mercy," but since Our Lady had not said explicitly "pray for sinners," Lucia would not quote differently.

Lucia's Impression on Pope John Paul I

Pope John Paul I, just some months before he became Pope, had a meeting with Lucia in the Carmel at Coimbra. He wrote:

"She carries her years well as she herself assured me with a smile. But she did not add like Pius IX: 'I carry them so well that not one of them falls down on top of me.' *Her joviality, her ready speech, her intense interest for everything connected with the Church of today and its serious problems revealed her spiritual youthfulness."*

The Holy Father went on to say that he understood Portuguese because he had spent some time in Brazil.

He added that she spoke to him with "great energy and conviction" about the need for priests, religious, and all Christians to be as radical as the saints:

"It must be all or nothing if they want to belong seriously to God."

The three children of Fatima, instructed and formed by Our Lady Herself, exemplify this as we find some of the instances revealed to us in these memoirs. Our Lady inspired the children to holiness... even to heroism. We do not have to read between the lines of the memoirs to understand this. It seems proclaimed as with the sound of blaring trumpets in almost every line.

Also, there are secrets in these memoirs, all of which Lucia would dearly have kept, which little by little reveal themselves to the careful reader. Among them are secrets of Our Lord, of the Eucharist, and of the Holy Trinity.

The Appearances of Our Lord

The first "miracle" of Our Lady of Fatima was the light that shone from Her Heart upon the children after they had agreed to accept whatever sacrifices God would send them. The importance of this miracle of light from the Immaculate Heart of Mary is especially revealed in this past chapter of the fourth memoir in which Francisco says repeatedly that *this light impressed him more than all other events of Fatima.* His greatest joy was to recall what he experienced and *saw* in that light which shone from Our Lady's Heart: Jesus!

This miracle from the Heart of Mary happened twice, and *twice in that light the children saw Our Lord.* Lucia says merely that in that light they felt "lost in God" and were inspired to pray:

"O Most Holy Trinity, I adore Thee! My God! My God! I love Thee in the Most Blessed Sacrament!"

When Lucia told Francisco in September that Our Lord would come on October 13, Francisco was filled with joy because he had seen *Our Lord twice before* and now rejoiced that he would see Him again. Twice he mentioned that they *saw God* in that light from Mary's Heart, that "Jesus was sad," and that it was Francisco's greatest desire to console "the Hidden Jesus" (Our Lord in the Blessed Sacrament).

My own book, *The World's Greatest Secret,* emphasizes that the Message of Fatima is above all Eucharistic. How touched we must be as we read of the love of little Francis for the "Hidden Jesus"! Who of us can read of the heroism of the three children of Fatima without being deeply moved?

And how much more there is for us to learn! When Our Lady promises "the triumph of Her Immaculate Heart," does this mean that the light from Her Heart will shine upon us *all,* causing us *all* to feel "lost in God" and *to be suddenly aware of the TRUE PRESENCE of Jesus, One with the Father and the Holy Spirit, in the tabernacles of our nearby Chapels and Churches?*

As was said in the beginning, many books have been written on Fatima. Perhaps the most important are those which explain *the message.*

This has been my own preoccupation ever since I met with Sister Lucia about a half a century ago. I feel no shame in saying I would like to see everyone read my own books on the Eucharist (which is the center of the message) and on the Scapular and the Rosary (the two special devotions of Fatima).[2] All three books were a gift to the Apostolate of Fatima, so there is nothing self-serving in this recommendation.

The messenger is Lucia. She was left in the world specifically to be Our Lady's messenger. This was confirmed in a most dramatic and extraordinary way at Fatima on October 13, 1967, when Pope Paul VI went to Fatima and had Lucia beside him on the platform in front of the Fatima Basilica overlooking a crowd of hundreds upon hundreds of thousands.

"Presented" by the Pope

Suddenly the Pope stood back leaving Lucia before the vast crowd. Then the Pope spread his arms in a gesture of presenting her to the world (TV coverage was worldwide... see page i). This was not only an affirmation by the Pontiff of his own belief in Fatima, but also of his belief in *Lucia* as Our Lady's messenger.

Being shown in public was painful for Lucia... like the writing of her memoirs. It was made bearable as an act of obedience like so many sacrifices in her life.

In 1982 when Pope John Paul II came to Fatima he, too, had Lucia come. Bishop Venancio was with Lucia most of that day and he offered to have her visit the Chapel of the Apparitions and even her home. Lucia answered that she would do whatever she was told, but the bishop could see the pain in her face as he made the offer. She was hoping he would not ask her to show herself in public. Respecting her desire for self-effacement, he remained *alone* with her until the time for her return to the cloister.[3]

Those, like myself, who have met Lucia, describe her in very similar terms: natural, frank, completely unpretentious, apprehensive of being considered in any way "special." This writer's favorite picture of her is the one with Pope John Paul II, her hand clasped in the hand of the Pope and both of them praying together (see page viii).

Were they praying for peace? For the speedy triumph of the Immaculate Heart of Mary? For the Church?

Certainly all three... because to pray for one is to pray for all! The expressions on their faces seem to say that they *know* that "in the end" the Immaculate Heart of Mary will triumph. Even though Lucia did not get to Rome to see the Holy Father as she longed to do as a child, it was as though her little friends Francisco and Jacinta had arranged for Rome to come to her.

†††

1. *La Vierge Marie dans L'Oeuvre de Maria Valtorta,* edited by Pisani in 1983, is the French edition of Dr. Roschini's book on Mary as found in the works of Maria Valtorta. She wrote *The Poem of the Man-God,* revelations regarding the life of Christ. The text comprised 10 volumes in Italian, but was translated into 5 volumes in English. Latter available from the 101 Foundation.

2. 1) The book on the Eucharist is *The World's Greatest Secret.* It sold over 50,000 copies and has also been published in French.

   2) The book on the Scapular is *Sign of Her Heart.* It sold over 100,000 copies. The Portuguese edition was published by Lucia's own Carmelite community with a preface by the Archbishop of Coimbra.

   3) The book on the Rosary is *Sex and the Mysteries.*

3. Bishop Venancio himself related this to me.

*Below: St. Lucia with parents of
Francisco and Jacinta in 1946.*

Chapter XIX.

Comments On

THESE MEMOIRS IN THE LIGHT OF HISTORY

Let us remember that in 1917 Portugal was fighting at the side of England and France in the first world war, *until then the bloodiest war in history.* The year of the apparitions was the most desperate year of that war for Portugal and her allies. *Precisely on October 13, 1917,* the day of the great miracle of Fatima, *the first American troops landed in France* to fight what U.S. President Wilson called: *"A war to end all wars."*

On that day Our Lady prophesied what to many seemed impossible: *"The war will soon end."* As Our Lady had foretold a month before, St. Joseph appeared at Her side during the miracle "to bless the world and bring it peace."

The horror of this bloody war was felt even in the remote mountain parish of Fatima. As we read earlier in the Memoirs, Manuel, a brother of Francisco and Jacinta (see picture on page 222) had been reported killed in action and many who came to Fatima asked for the prayers of the three children for sons and brothers at the front. There is also the incident in Lucia's memoirs recalling that they were asked to pray for a young man who, for the sake of his family, wanted to be spared conscription. The favor was granted, as was a similar favor for Lucia's only brother.

In addition to the war, the atheist rule of Portugal at the time of the apparitions was of very great relevance to the Fatima events.

Lenin's grand plan went far beyond an atheist revolution only in Russia. He had planned a *world* revolution which called for an overthrow of governments simultaneously in Russia in the East, and Portugal in the West (or wherever the conditions were most favorable)... to be followed by a pincers movement across Europe.

In 1910, the first blood of Lenin's Marxist revolution was shed in Odessa where the uprising was quelled for the time by the Czarist forces. *In that same year* (1910) the *revolution in Portugal was successful.* The monarchy was overthrown. *Lisbon was proclaimed the "atheist capitol of the world."* The symbol of the revolutionaries was the red star.

Seven years later, *just before Lenin's final success in Russia* (with an attack on the Winter Palace in Petrograd, November 1917) Our Lady performed Her great miracle over the mountain of Fatima "so that all may believe" and foretold:

1) *Error will spread from an atheist Russia throughout the entire world;*

2) *The good* (honest persons who respect human rights and honor God) *will be persecuted;*

3) *The Pope will have much to suffer* (referring perhaps to *all* Popes since 1917, especially beginning with Pius XII);

4) *"Error from an atheist Russia"* spreading throughout the world will *"foment further wars";*

5) *"Several entire nations will be annihilated."*

From the dozens of books which have been written (and continue to be written) about Fatima, we learn not only many new details about the three children and about the relevance of this great supernatural event to Portugal and to the world, but we soon become acutely aware of a *most important relevance to the Church.*

This is the first time in history that God has permitted a *miracle* at a *predicted time and place* "so that all my believe." The only similar event in history (excluding miracles of Our Lord) is the fire called down from Heaven by Elias "so that all may know that God is God" (Kings III, 18).

Some may say that the greatest importance of Fatima is that the prayers of millions for world peace had been heard by Heaven with the end of the first world war. Others will say that the greatest importance of Fatima is the prediction of the worldwide Marxist revolution and a promise to turn it back through the conversion of Russia (explicitly promised by Our Lady of Fatima) and "an era of peace for mankind."

Still others may see the "nuclear connection" as the most important. The "great sign" predicted by Our Lady and seen by millions on January 24, 1938, was *identical to the false aurora created by a nuclear explosion,* a fact not discovered until 1985! Our Lady had foretold that the ultimate evil resulting from the worldwide revolution spreading from "an atheist Russia" will be "*the annihilation of several entire nations.*"

If the some one hundred thousand persons who saw the miracle of Fatima in 1917 had known about the atomic bomb (not discovered until more than a quarter of a century later), might they not have called it a "nuclear" miracle? When U.S. President Truman announced the "annihilation" of a Japanese city by the first atomic bomb he told the world:

"We have harnessed the power of the sun."

But ultimately when all is said and done, perhaps the greatest relevance of Fatima is to the Church.

Each and every Pope since 1917 has made one common and emphatically repeated statement about Fatima:

"It is a repetition of the Gospel."

Fatima is like a new Sinai... this time a reaffirmation not only of the Ten Commandments but *of all the essential doctrines of the Catholic Church.* Bishop John Venancio, the second Bishop of Fatima, published an abbreviation of the memoirs of Lucia and at the end enumerated the truths of the Faith reaffirmed at Fatima.

In addition to a reaffirmation of the truths of the Church, the message of Fatima concerned the crisis in the Church which became painfully evident to millions of faithful at the time of the second Vatican Council. Dr. Joachim Alonso, whom we have described before as the greatest authority on Fatima, published a little book concluding that *the third secret of Fatima concerned this crisis.*

As we have mentioned before, Pope John XXIII opened the secret in 1960 and soon after announced the Council. After promulgating the most important document of the Council four years later, his successor Paul VI (who had also read the secret) *mentioned Fatima in the Council* as he proclaimed Mary *"Mother of the Church."*

Now Collegiality

Consider the mystery of "collegiality." *We had heard little of "collegiality" before Vatican II,* but Our Lady of Fatima requested that *all the Bishops of the world join with the Pope* in an act of the consecration of Russia to the Immaculate Heart promising that when this collegial act was accomplished "Russia will be converted."

Pope Pius XII consecrated the world to the Immaculate Heart of Mary in 1942, the 25th anniversary of the apparitions. Ten years later he made a specific act of the consecration of Russia to the Immaculate Heart.

Twelve years later, in the presence of all the Bishops of the world, on November 21, 1964, Pope Paul VI renewed both of these consecrations. But it remained for Pope John Paul II to write to all the Bishops of the world to ask them to join with him in renewing these acts of consecration. His Holiness accomplished this at Fatima in 1982 and again (after another communication to the Bishops of the world) in 1984.[1]

Fatima Continues to Unfold

Fatima is *on-going*. For that reason, periodicals of the Fatima Apostolate have a special importance. For example, the interview with Lucia by Pope John Paul I was published in the Blue Army's Italian magazine *Il Cuore Della Madre.*

Much of the on-going news, including recent apparitions of Our Lady of Fatima (such as Akita) are found in these publications... the best known of which is *SOUL* magazine, published by the World Apostolate of Fatima (The Blue Army, USA).

Lucia's first comments on the collegial consecration of May 13, 1982, appeared in *SOUL.* She said the consecration would have its effect, but "the Blue Army will have much to do."

Our Lady of Fatima has continued to inform Lucia (still living in 1992) and *has been appearing in many parts of the world since 1917.* In the subsequent apparitions in which She appeared *specifically as Our Lady of Fatima, She has emphasized the importance of catechism* (at the same time repeatedly asking for devout recitation of the Rosary, as She did in 1917).

In Japan in 1973 She manifested Herself through a wooden statue in a convent of catechists in a suburb of Akita. The Bishop, who approved the event as supernatural (after two ecclesiastical commissions and eight years of study), when asked how he would summarize the message of Akita replied:

"It is the message of Our Lady of Fatima."

At Akita the *warning* of Our Lady was stressed. In an apparition of Our Lady of Fatima in Columbia, it was *the Rosary and catechism.*[2] In Nicaragua it was catechism and *the need for penance.*[3]

In addition to these apparitions approved by ecclesiastical authority, there are many, many more still under investigation which have nevertheless an important impact on the world. And all confirm what must be obvious: Our Lady did not return to Heaven after the miracle of 1917 and say:

"Well, now I have given the message to the world and proved it by a miracle, and if the world does not listen it is just too bad." As Bishop Constantino Luna, International President of the World Apostolate of Fatima (The Blue Army) never tires of saying:

"Our Lady of Fatima is an anxious Mother... continually working to save Her children from destruction." Fatima is an *on-going* event which will not end until "an era of peace will be granted to mankind." And even then (or perhaps *only* then) the message contained in the memoirs of Lucia may begin to be fully understood and appreciated.

The present writer first went to Fatima in 1946 with the idea of writing *the* book, but with each passing year it seemed more and more *impossible to contain all that needed to be said within two covers.* When all is said and done, *the* book on Fatima was written by Lucia herself.

Let us continue now with the most important part of her memoirs, to be followed by more recent personal interviews.

†††

241.

1. There has been much discussion as to whether or not these two consecrations by John Paul II satisfied the request of Our Lord for the Collegial Consecration of Russia to the Immaculate Heart of Mary (by the Holy Father and all the Bishops of the world).

An interview with Lucia (which took place within 24 hours after the 1982 consecration) was published in the SOUL Magazine, July-August 1982, pp. 6 & 7.

It is noteworthy that Lucia did not say that the consecration of 1982 was "complete." She merely said that the consecration would "have its effect." She said specifically that the World Apostolate of Fatima (The Blue Army) would still have much to do.

Some called this interview into doubt. Part of the confusion may have arisen from the fact that the person who interviewed Lucia was received as a member of her family rather than as an "interviewer." After carefully checking every word, he verified that Lucia's words were *exactly as was published in SOUL Magazine.*

2. In 1949, in Pasto, near Bogota, Columbia, Our Lady appeared to Brother John Aranguren, S.J. and told him: "Continue to teach the children Catechism, but also teach them how to pray the Rosary."

3. Our Lady appeared to the catechist, Bernardo Martinez in Cuapa, Nicaragua in 1981 and said that the Rosary must be prayed and especially in families. If not, the coming of the Third World War would be hastened.

Below: Bishop Jose Correia da Silva and Ti Marto (father of Francisco and Jacinta)

Chapter XX.

In the Fourth Memoir —
Lucia Remembers

THE APPARITIONS

We now come to the most important part of Lucia's memoirs. She had been requested by Bishop da Silva to write whatever else she remembered about the apparitions of the Angel and a new account of the apparitions of Our Lady. Lucia obeyed her Bishop's instructions, as seen from the following:

†††

Prologue

Now, Your Excellency, this is the most difficult part of all that you have asked me to write.

First of all, Your Excellency expressly asked me to write about the Apparitions of the Angel with every circumstance and detail, even (as far as possible) their intimate effects upon us. Then, along comes Dr. Galamba to ask you to command me also to write about the Apparitions of Our Lady.

"Command her, Your Excellency," he said a little while ago in Valenca. "Yes, Your Excellency, command her to write *everything*, absolutely *everything*. She'll have to do the rounds of purgatory many a time for having kept silent about so many things!"

As for purgatory, I have no fear of it from this point of view. I have always obeyed, and obedience deserves neither penalty nor punishment.

Firstly, I obeyed the interior inspirations of the Holy Spirit, and secondly, I obeyed the commands of those who spoke to me in His name. This was the first order and counsel which God deigned to give me through Your Excellency. Happy and content, I recalled the words I had heard long ago from the lips of the venerable Vicar of Torres Novas:

"The secret of the King's Daughter should remain within." Then, beginning to penetrate their meaning, I said:

"My secret is for myself." But now I can no longer say so. Immolated on the altar of obedience, I say rather:

"My secret belongs to God. I have placed it in His hands: may He do with it as best pleases Him." Dr. Galamba said then:

"Your Excellency, command her to say *everything, everything,* and to hide *nothing.*" And Your Excellency, assisted most certainly by the Holy Spirit, pronounced this judgment:

"No, I will not command that! I will have nothing to do with matters of secrets."[1] Thanks be to God! Any other order would have been for me a source of endless perplexities and scruples. Had I received a contrary command, I would have asked myself, times without number:

"Whom should I obey, God or His representative?" And perhaps, being unable to come to a decision, I would have been left in a state of real inner torment! Then Your Excellency continued speaking in God's name:

"Sister, write down the Apparition of the Angel and of Our Lady, because, my dear Sister, this is for the glory of God and of Our Lady." How good God is! He is the God of peace, and it is along paths of peace that He leads those who trust in Him.

I shall then begin my task, and thus fulfill the commands received from Your Excellency as well as the decrees of Rev. Dr. Galamba. With the exception of that part of the Secret which I am not permitted to reveal at present, I shall say everything. I shall not knowingly omit anything, although I suppose I may forget just a few small details of minor importance.

Apparitions of the Angel

Although I cannot give the exact date, it seems to me that it was in 1915 that the first Apparition took place. As far as I can judge, it was the Angel, although at that time he did not venture to make himself fully known. From what I can recall of the weather, I think that this must have happened between the months of April and October in the year 1915.

Three companions from Casa Velha (by name Teresa Matias, her sister Maria Rosa, and Maria Justino) were with me on the southern slope of the Cabeco. We were just about to start praying the Rosary when I saw, in the air above the trees that stretched down to the valley which lay at our feet, what appeared to be a cloud in human form, whiter than snow and almost transparent.

My companions asked me what it was. I replied that I did not know. This happened on two further occasions, but on different days. This Apparition made a certain impression upon me which I do not know how to explain. Little by little this impression faded away and were it not for the events that followed, I think I would have forgotten it completely.

I think that it must have been in the spring of 1916 that the Angel appeared to Francisco, Jacinta and me for the first time in our Loca do Cabeco. The dates I cannot set down with certainty because, at that time, I did not know how to reckon the years, the months, or even the days of the week.

As I have already written in my account of Jacinta, we had climbed the hillside in search of shelter. After having taken our lunch and said our prayers, we began to see, some distance off above the trees that stretched away towards the east, a light whiter than snow in the form of a young man. He was transparent, brighter than crystal pierced by the rays of the sun. As he drew nearer we could distinguish his features more and more clearly. We were surprised, absorbed, and struck dumb with amazement.

On reaching us, he said:

"Do not be afraid. I am the Angel of Peace. Pray with me."

Kneeling on the ground, he bowed down until his forehead touched the earth. Led by a supernatural impulse, we did the same and repeated the words which we heard him say:

"My God, I believe, I adore, I trust and I love You! I ask pardon of You for those who do not believe, do not adore, do not trust and do not love You!"[2]

Having repeated these words three times, he rose and said:

"Pray like that. The Hearts of Jesus and Mary are attentive to the voice of your supplications." Then he disappeared. The supernatural atmosphere which enveloped us was so intense for a long time that we were scarcely aware of our own existence, remaining in the same position in which he left us, continually repeating the same prayer.

The presence of God made itself felt so intimately and intensely that we did not even dare to speak to one another. The next day we were still immersed in this spiritual atmosphere, which only gradually began to disappear. It did not occur to us to speak about this Apparition, nor did we think of recommending that it be kept secret. The very Apparition itself imposed secrecy. It was so intimate that it was not easy to speak of it at all. The impression it made upon us was perhaps all the greater in that it was the first such manifestation we had experienced.

The second Apparition must have been in mid summer because the heat of the day was so intense that we had to take the sheep home before noon and only let them out again in the early evening. We went to spend the siesta hours in the shade of the trees which surrounded the well I have already mentioned several times. Suddenly, we saw the same Angel right beside us.

"What are you doing?" he asked. *"Pray! Pray much! The Hearts of Jesus and Mary have merciful designs upon you. Offer prayers and sacrifices constantly to the Most High."*

"How are we to make sacrifices?" I asked.

"Make of everything you can a sacrifice, and offer it to God as an act of reparation for the sins by which He is offended, and in supplication for the conversion of sinners. You will thus draw down peace upon your country. I am its Angel Guardian, the Angel of Portugal. Above all, accept and bear with submission the suffering which the Lord will send you."

These words were indelibly impressed upon our minds. They were like a light which made us understand Who God is, how He loves us and how much He desires to be loved, the value of sacrifice, how pleasing it is to Him and how, on account of it, He grants the grace of conversion of sinners.

It was for this reason that from then on we began to offer to the Lord all that mortified us, without, however, seeking out other forms of mortification and penance... except that we remained for hours on end with our foreheads touching the ground repeating the prayer the Angel had taught us. It seems to me that the third Apparition must have been in October or towards the end of September, as we were no longer returning home for siesta.

As I have already written in my account of Jacinta, we went one day from Pregueira (a small olive grove belonging to my parents) to the Lapa, making our way along the slope of the hill on the side facing Aljustrel and Casa Velha. There we said our Rosary and the prayer the Angel had taught us in his first Apparition.

While we were there the Angel appeared to us for the third time. He held a chalice in his hands with a Host above it. Some drops of blood were falling from the Host into the sacred vessel. Leaving the chalice and the host suspended in the air, the Angel prostrated himself on the ground and repeated this prayer three times:

"Most Holy Trinity, Father, Son and Holy Spirit, I adore you profoundly, and I offer You the most precious Body, Blood, Soul and Divinity of Jesus Christ, present in all the tabernacles of the world, in reparation for the outrages, sacrileges, and indifference with which He Himself is offended. By the infinite merits of His most Sacred Heart and the Immaculate Heart of Mary, I beg of You the conversion of poor sinners."[3]

Then, rising, he once more took the Chalice and the Host in his hands. He gave the Host to me, and to Jacinta and Francisco he gave the contents of the Chalice to drink, saying as he did so:

"Take and drink the Body and Blood of Jesus Christ, horribly outraged by the sins of ungrateful men. Repair their crimes and console your God."

Once again, he prostrated on the ground and repeated the same prayer with us three more times:

"Most Holy Trinity, etc...," and disappeared.

Impelled by the power of the supernatural that enveloped us we imitated all the Angel had done, prostrating ourselves on the ground as he did and repeating the prayers that he said. The force of the presence of God was so intense that it absorbed us and almost completely annihilated us.

It seemed to deprive us even of the use of our bodily senses for a considerable length of time. During those days, we performed all our exterior actions as though guided by that same supernatural being who was impelling us thereto. The peace and happiness which we felt were great but wholly interior. Our souls were completely immersed in God. A great physical exhaustion prostrated us.

Lucia's Silence

I do not know why, but the Apparitions of Our Lady produced in us very different effects. We felt the same intimate joy, the same peace and happiness... but instead of physical prostration, an expansive ease of movement; instead of this annihilation in the Divine Presence, a certain expansive liveliness; instead of the difficulty in speaking, we felt a certain communicative enthusiasm. Despite these feelings, however, we felt inspired to be silent, especially concerning certain things.

Whenever I was interrogated I experienced an interior inspiration which directed me how to answer, without either failing in truth or revealing what should remain hidden for the time being. In this respect, I still have just this one doubt:

"Should I not have said everything in the canonical enquiry?" But I have no scruples about having kept silence, because at that time I had as yet no realization of the importance of this particular interrogation. I regarded it, at the time, as being just like the many other interrogations to which I was accustomed.

The only thing I thought strange was the order to take the oath. But as it was my confessor who told me to do so, and as I was swearing to the truth, I took the oath without any difficulty. Little did I suspect, at that moment, that the devil would make the most of this in order to torment me with endless scruples later on. But, thank God, all that is over now.

There was yet another reason which confirmed me in my conviction that I did well to remain silent. In the course of the canonical enquiry, one of the interrogators, Rev. Dr. Marques dos Santos, thought he could extend his questionnaire and began to ask more searching questions. Before answering I looked enquiringly at my confessor. His Reverence saved me from my predicament and answered on my behalf. He reminded the interrogator that he was exceeding his rights in this matter.

Almost the same thing happened when I was questioned by Rev. Dr. Fisher. He had the authorization of Your Excellency and of Rev. Mother Provincial and seemed to have the right to question me on everything. But thank God he came accompanied by my confessor. At a given moment, he put to me a carefully studied question about the Secret. I felt perplexed and did not know how to answer.

I glanced towards my confessor; he understood and answered for me. The interrogator understood also and confined himself to picking up some magazines lying nearby and holding them in front of my face. In this way, God was showing me that the moment appointed by Him had not yet arrived.

I shall now go on to write about the Apparitions of Our Lady. I shall not delay over the circumstances that preceded or followed them, since Rev. Dr. Galamba has kindly dispensed me from doing so.

The 13th of May, 1917

High up on the slope in the Cova da Iria, I was playing with Jacinta and Francisco at building a little stone wall around a clump of furze. Suddenly we saw what seemed to be a flash of lightning.

"We'd better go home," I said to my cousins. "That's lightning; we may have a thunderstorm."

"Yes, indeed!" they answered.

We began to go down the slope, herding the sheep along towards the road. We were more or less half-way down the slope, almost level with a large holm oak that stood there, when we saw another flash of lightning. We had only gone a few steps further when, there before us on a small holm oak, we beheld a Lady dressed all in white.

She was more brilliant than the sun and radiated a light more clear and intense than a crystal glass filled with sparkling water when the rays of the burning sun shine through it.

We stopped, astounded, before the Apparition. We were so close, just a few feet from Her, that we were bathed in the light which surrounded Her, or rather, which radiated from Her. Then Our Lady spoke to us:

"Do not be afraid. I will do you no harm."

"Where are you from?"

"I am from Heaven."

"What do you want of me?"

"I have come to ask you to come here for six months in succession on the 13th day at this same hour. Later on, I will tell you who I am and what I want. Afterwards, I will return here yet a seventh time."[4]

"Shall I go to Heaven, too?"

"Yes, you will."

"And Jacinta?"

"She will go also."

"And Francisco?"

"He will go there too, but he must say many Rosaries." Then I remembered to ask about two girls who had died recently. They were friends of mine and used to come to my home to learn weaving with my eldest sister.

"Is Maria da Neves in Heaven?"

"Yes, she is." (I think she was about 16 years old.)

"And Amelia?"

"She will be in purgatory until the end of the world."[5] (It seems to me that she was between 18 and 20 years of age.)

"Are you willing to offer yourselves up to God and bear all the sufferings He wills to send you, as an act

of reparation for the sins by which He is offended, and for the conversion of sinners?"

"Yes, we are willing."

"Then you will have much to suffer, but the grace of God will be your comfort."

As She pronounced these last words *"the grace of God will be your comfort,"* Our Lady opened Her hands for the first time, communicating to us a light so intense that, as it streamed from Her hands, its rays penetrated our hearts and the innermost depths of our souls, *making us see ourselves in God, who was the light, more clearly than we see ourselves in the best of mirrors.* Then, moved by an interior impulse that was also communicated to us, we fell on our knees, repeating in our hearts:

"O most Holy Trinity, I adore You! My God, my God, I love You in the most Blessed Sacrament!"

After a few moments, Our Lady spoke again:

"Pray the Rosary every day in order to obtain peace for the world and the end of the war."

Then She began to rise serenely towards the east until She disappeared in the immensity of space. The light that surrounded Her seemed to open up a path before Her in the firmament. For this reason we sometimes said that we saw Heaven opening.

I think I have already explained in my account of Jacinta, or else in a letter, that the fear which we felt was not really fear of Our Lady, but rather fear of the thunderstorm which we thought was coming. It was from this that we sought to escape.

The Apparitions of Our Lady inspired neither fear nor fright, but rather surprise. When I was asked if I had experienced fear, and I said that we had, I was referring to the fear we felt when we saw the flashes of lightning and thought that a thunderstorm was at hand. It was from this that we wished to escape, as we were used to seeing lightning only when it thundered. Besides, the flashes of lightning were not really lightning, but the reflected rays of a light which was approaching. It was because we saw the light that we sometimes said we saw Our Lady coming... but, properly speaking, we only perceived Our Lady in that light when She was already on the holm oak tree. The fact that we did not know how to explain this and that we wished to avoid questions, caused us to say sometimes that we saw Her coming and other times that we did not. When we said we saw Her coming, we were referring to the approach of the light, which after all was Herself. When we said we did not see Her coming, we were referring to the fact that we really saw Our Lady only when She was on the holm oak.

The 13th of June, 1917

On June 13, as soon as Jacinta, Francisco and I had finished praying the Rosary with a number of other people who were present, we once more saw the flash reflecting the light which was approaching (which we called lightning). The next moment, Our Lady was there on the holm oak, exactly the same as in May.

"What do you want of me?" I asked.

"I wish you to come here on the 13th of next month, to pray the Rosary every day, and to learn to read. Later, I will tell you what I want."

I asked for the cure of a sick person.

"If he is converted, he will be cured within the year."

"I would like to ask you to take us to Heaven."

"Yes. I will take Jacinta and Francisco soon. But you are to stay here some time longer. Jesus wishes to make use of you to make me known and loved. He wants to establish in the world devotion to my Immaculate Heart"[6] (see important note #6).

"Am I to stay here alone?" I asked, sadly.

"No, my daughter. Do you suffer much? Do not be discouraged. I will never forsake you. My Immaculate

Heart will be your refuge and the way that will lead you to God."

As Our Lady spoke these last words She opened Her hands, and for the second time She communicated to us the rays of that same immense light. We saw ourselves in this light as though immersed in God. Jacinta and Francisco seemed to be in that part of the light which rose towards Heaven, and I in that part of the light poured out on the earth.

In front of the palm of Our Lady's right hand was a heart encircled by thorns which pierced it. We understood that this was the Immaculate Heart of Mary, outraged by the sins of humanity, seeking reparation.

You know now, Your Excellency, what we referred to when we said that Our Lady had revealed a secret to us in June. At the time, Our Lady did not tell us to keep it secret, but we felt moved to do so by God.

The 13th of July, 1917

By July 13, a few moments after arriving at the Cova da Iria near the holm oak (where a large number of people were praying the Rosary) we saw the flash of light once more. A moment later Our Lady appeared on the Holm oak.

"What do you want of me?" I asked.

"I want you to come here on the 13th of next month, to continue to pray the Rosary every day in honor of Our Lady of the Rosary in order to obtain peace for the world and the end of the war because only she can help you."

"I would like to ask you to tell us who you are, and to work a miracle so that everybody will believe that you are appearing to us."

"Continue to come here every month. In October, I will tell you who I am, and what I want, and I will perform a miracle for all to see and to believe."

I then made some requests, but I cannot recall now just what they were. What I do remember is that Our Lady said it was necessary for such people to pray the Rosary in order to obtain these graces during the year. She continued:

"Sacrifice yourselves for sinners. Say many times, especially whenever you make some sacrifice:

"'O Jesus, it is for love of You, for the conversion of sinners, and in reparation for the sins committed against the Immaculate Heart of Mary.'"

Vision of Hell

As Our Lady spoke these last words, She opened Her hands once more as She had done during the two previous months. The rays of light seemed to penetrate the earth, and we saw as it were a sea of fire.

Plunged in this fire were demons and souls in human form, like transparent burning embers, all blackened or burnished bronze, floating about in the conflagration, now raised into the air by the flames that issued from within themselves together with great clouds of smoke, now falling back on every side like sparks in huge fires, without weight or equilibrium, amid shrieks and groans of pain and despair, which horrified us and made us tremble with fear. (It must have been this sight which caused me to cry out, as people say they heard me.)

The demons could be distinguished by their terrifying and repellent likeness to frightful and unknown animals, black and transparent like burning coals. Terrified and as if to plead for help, we looked up at Our Lady, Who said to us, so kindly and so sadly:

"You have seen hell where the souls of poor sinners go. To save them, God wishes to establish in the world devotion to my Immaculate Heart. If what I say to you is done, many souls will be saved and there will be peace. The war is going to end. But if people do not

255.

cease offending God, a worse one will break out during the reign of Pius XI.

"When you see a night illumined by an unknown light,[7] know that this is the great sign given you by God that He is about to punish the world for its crimes, by means of war, famine, and persecutions of the Church and of the Holy Father.

"To prevent this, I shall come to ask for the consecration of Russia to my Immaculate Heart, and the Communion of Reparation on the First Saturdays. If my requests are heeded, Russia will be converted and there will be peace. If not, she will spread her errors throughout the world, causing wars and persecutions of the Church; the good will be martyred; the Holy Father will have much to suffer; various nations will be annihilated.

"Finally, my Immaculate Heart will triumph. The Holy Father will consecrate Russia to me, and she will be converted, and a era of peace will be granted to the world. In Portugal, the dogma of the Faith will always be preserved; etc... Do not tell this to anybody.

"Francisco, yes, you may tell him.

"When you pray the Rosary, say after each mystery: O my Jesus, forgive us our sins, save us from the fires of hell. Lead all souls to heaven, especially those most in need"[8] (see important note #8).

After this, there was a moment of silence, and then I asked:

"Is there anything more that You want of me?"

"No I do not want anything more of you today."

Then, as before, Our Lady began to ascend towards the east until finally She disappeared in the immense distance of the firmament.

The 13th of August, 1917

I have already said what happened on August 13[9] so I will not delay over it here but pass on to the

Apparition which, in my opinion, took place on the 15th in the afternoon.[10] As at that time I did not yet know how to reckon the days of the month, it could be that I am mistaken... but I still have an idea that it took place on the very day that we arrived back from Vila Nova de Ourem.

I was accompanied by Francisco and his brother John. We were with the sheep in a place called Valinhos when we felt something supernatural approaching and enveloping us. Suspecting that Our Lady was about to appear and feeling sorry that Jacinta might miss seeing Her, we asked her brother to go and call her. He was unwilling so I offered him two small coins and off he ran. Meanwhile, Francisco and I saw the flash of light which we called lightning. Jacinta arrived and a moment later we saw Our Lady on a holm oak tree.

"What do you want of me?"

"I want you to continue going to the Cova da Iria on the 13th, and to continue praying the Rosary every day. In the last month, I will perform a miracle so that all may believe."

"What do you want done with the money that the people leave in the Cova da Iria?"

"Have two litters made. One is to be carried by you and Jacinta and two other girls dressed in white; the other one is to be carried by Francisco and three other boys. The money from the litters is for the Feast of Our Lady of the Rosary, and what is left over will help towards the construction of a chapel which is to be built."

"I would like to ask You to cure some sick persons."

"Yes, I will cure some of them during the year."

Then, looking very sad, Our Lady said:

"Pray, pray very much, and make sacrifices for sinners; so many souls go to hell because there is no one to pray and to make sacrifices for them."[11]

She began to ascend as usual towards the east.

The 13th of September, 1917

By September 13, as the hour approached I set out with Jacinta and Francisco. Because of the crowds around us we could advance only with difficulty. The roads were packed with people. Everyone wanted to see us and speak to us. There was no human respect whatsoever. Simple folk, even ladies and gentlemen, struggled to break through the crowd pressing around us. No sooner had they reached us than they threw themselves on their knees before us, begging us to place their petitions before Our Lady. Others who could not get close to us shouted from a distance:

"For the love of God, ask Our Lady to cure my son who is a cripple!" Yet another cried out: "And to cure mine who is blind!... To cure mine who is deaf!... To bring back my husband, my son, who has gone to the war!... To give me back my health as I have tuberculosis!" and so on.

All the afflictions of poor humanity were assembled there. Some climbed up to the tops of trees and walls to see us go by and shouted down to us. Saying yes to some, giving a hand to others and helping them up from the dusty ground, we managed to move forward, thanks to some gentlemen who went ahead and opened a passage for us through the multitude.

Now, when I read in the New Testament about those enchanting scenes of Our Lord's passing through Palestine, I think of those which Our Lord allowed me to witness, while yet a child, on the poor roads and lanes from Aljustrel to Fatima and on to the Cova da Iria! I give thanks to God, offering Him the faith of our good Portuguese people, and I think:

"If these people so humbled themselves before three poor children just because they were mercifully granted the grace to speak to the Mother of God, what would they not do if they saw Our Lord Himself in person before them?"

Well, none of this was called for here! It was a distraction of my pen leading me away where I did not mean to go. But, never mind! It's just another useless digression. I am not tearing it out, so as not to spoil the notebook.

At last we arrived at the Cova da Iria, and on reaching the holm oak we began to pray the Rosary with the people. Shortly afterwards, we saw the flash of light and then Our Lady appeared on the holm oak.

"Continue to pray the Rosary in order to obtain the end of the war. In October Our Lord will come, as well as Our Lady of Sorrows and Our Lady of Carmel. Saint Joseph will appear with the Child Jesus to bless the world. God is pleased with your sacrifices. He does not want you to sleep with the rope on, but only to wear it during the daytime."

"I was told to ask You many things, the cure of some sick people, of a deaf-mute..."

"Yes, I will cure some, but not others. In October I will perform a miracle so that all may believe."

Then Our Lady began to rise as usual and disappeared.

The 13th of October, 1917

On the 13th of October we left home quite early expecting that we would be delayed along the way. Masses of people thronged the roads. The rain fell in torrents. My mother, her heart torn with uncertainty as to what was going to happen and fearing it would be the last day of my life, wanted to go with me.

On the way, the scenes of the previous month, still more numerous and moving, were repeated. Not even the pelting rain and muddy roads could prevent these people from kneeling in the most humble and suppliant of attitudes. We reached the holm oak in the

Cova da Iria. Once there, moved by an interior impulse, I asked the people to shut their umbrellas and pray the Rosary. A little later we saw the flash of light and Our Lady appeared on the holm oak.

"What do You want of me?"

"*I want to tell you that a chapel is to be built here in my honor. I am the Lady of the Rosary. Continue to pray the Rosary every day. The war is going to end and the soldiers will soon return to their homes.*"

"I have many things to ask You: the cure of some sick persons, the conversion of sinners, and other things..."

"*Some yes, but others, no. They must amend their lives and ask forgiveness for their sins.*" Looking very sad. Our Lady said:

"*Do not offend the Lord our God any more, because He is already much offended.*" Then opening Her hands, She made them reflect on the sun. As She ascended, the reflection of Her own light continued to be projected on the sun itself.

This will explain, Your Excellency, why I cried out to look at the sun. My purpose was not to draw the attention of the crowd, of which I was not even aware. I did it because I was impelled by an interior force.

After Our Lady had disappeared into the immense distance of the firmament, we beheld St. Joseph with the Child Jesus and Our Lady robed in white with a blue mantle, beside the sun. St. Joseph and the Child Jesus appeared to bless the world, for they traced the Sign of the Cross with their hands.

When a little later this apparition disappeared, I saw Our Lord and Our Lady... it seemed to me that it was Our Lady of Sorrows. Our Lord appeared to bless the world in the same manner as St. Joseph had done. When this apparition vanished I saw Our Lady once more, this time apparently as Our Lady of Carmel.[12]

Here, then, Your Excellency, you have the story of the Apparitions of Our Lady in the Cova da Iria in

Above: Picture of Our Lady of Mt. Carmel in the parish church at Fatima. Jacinta remarked that in the very last vision on October, 13, 1917, Our Lady (holding a Scapular) looked "like the picture in the parish church."

Above: Detail of the crowd at Fatima, October 13, 1917

1917. Whenever and for whatever motive I had to speak of them, I sought to do so in as few words as possible, with the desire of keeping to myself alone those more intimate aspects which were so difficult for me to reveal. But as they belong to God and not to me, here they are.

I return what does not belong to me. To the best of my knowledge I keep nothing back. I think I have only omitted some minor details referring to the petitions which I made.

As these were merely material things, I did not attach such great importance to them, and it is perhaps because of this that they did not make such a vivid impression on my mind... and then there were so many of them, so very many! It was possibly because I was so anxious to remember the innumerable graces that I had to ask of Our Lady, that I was mistaken when I understood that the war would end on that very 13th.[13]

✝✝✝

[1] This is the reason why Lucia does not write down the third part of the secret in this portion of her Fourth Memoir.

[2] The word "trust" could be translated more literally by the word "hope." After much deliberation it was decided that because of the diverse meanings of "hope" in English, the angel's prayer would be translated more accurately by the verb to "trust." This translation was approved by the Bishop of Fatima, Dom Jose Correia da Silva, to whom these memoirs are addressed. In order to avoid future differences in translation, the Bishop published the angel's prayer using the word "trust" in the English edition of Voz da Fatima.

[3] In the First Memoir she was writing primarily about Jacinta, because this is what Bishop da Silva had asked her to do. However, in the Fourth Memoir she was told to recall all that is important.

Therefore, we find one word inserted in this Prayer of the Angel which does not appear in the prayer of the Angel in Lucia's Second Memoir. It is the word "profoundly." The Angel had prostrated himself before the Blessed Sacrament suspended in the air and gave the children such an overwhelming impulse to bow down profoundly in adoration with him at this point, that Lucia felt it was an important element to the prayer itself. Therefore, in this more careful version (since the Bishop had commanded her to recall with exactitude everything of importance concerning the Apparitions) this thought is inserted.

Lucia has explained that each word spoken by the Angel was indelibly impressed upon the minds of each of the children. But apparently the word "profoundly" was rather an impression or idea conveyed by the attitude of the Angel than a specific word. She therefore omitted it altogether in the Second Memoir, but feels constrained to add it to this version. And when first released by the Bishop, the translation of this word was phrased "I bow down before you, I adore You." But this has been summarized to "I adore You profoundly" (now the version most widely used).

It is also to be kept in mind that Lucia has been having a series of visions ever since 1917, and wherever she had the slightest doubt, especially when she was told to write something under obedience, she would ask Our Lord or Our Lady for clarification. Thus many more details have come to light even since Lucia first wrote her Memoirs, especially as concerns the relative roles of the Scapular and the Rosary which Our Lady held in Her hands in the series of final visions during the miracle of the sun on October 13, 1917, and about the collegial consecration of Russia to the Immaculate Heart of Mary.

4. This "seventh time" probably refers to June 16, 1921, on the eve of Lucia's departure to Vilar do Oporto. When Lucia went to the Cova to say "goodbye" at the place of the Apparitions, Our Lady appeared to her again. The Apparition in question had *a personal message* for Lucia which she did not consider necessary to relate here.

5. Everyone thought Amelia had led a holy life and few prayers had been said for her. Immediately after this, many prayed for her and thus the revelation of Our Lady was a great act of mercy and reminds us all not to presume that all who seem to have led good lives will have a brief purgatory. The words of Scripture remain: "It is a holy and wholesome thought to pray for the dead" (2 Mac. 12:45).

6. Because she was in a hurry, Lucia omitted the end of the paragraph which, in other documents, reads as follows:

"I promise salvation to those who embrace it, and those souls will be loved by God like flowers placed by me to adorn His throne."

7. This was what the press called an aurora borealis on the night of January 25-26, 1938, which was unusual, and always regarded by Lucia as the God-given sign which had been promised.

8. Often the words "of Thy Mercy" are added because this is understood to be Our Lady's meaning. However it might also be understood to mean "in need of *this prayer*."

9. This is the day the children were kidnapped by the administrator of Ourem and imprisoned.

10. It had been earlier thought by many writers that the apparition of Our Lady to the three children at Valinhos took place not on August 15, but on the following Sunday, August 19.

Lucia shows great delicacy as she insists that she is quite sure it was August 15. Before his death, Msgr. Canon Galamba established that the apparition at Valinhos actually occurred on August 15, as Lucia has stated (see Chapter 5).

11. Lucia could not refer to the previous Memoirs written long before. It is noteworthy that her quotations of what Our Lady said are repeated exactly from her memory.

12. Often called "Our Lady of the (Brown) Scapular."

13. Lucia did not really mean to say that the war would be over on the same day; the mistake was due to the many pressing questions she was asked.

Valinhos

Chapter XXI.

Comments On

THE WORDLESS VISIONS DURING THE MIRACLE OF THE SUN AND ST. JOSEPH

Without comment Lucia describes *three final visions* while the sun whirled and people within 32 miles thought the world was ending.

First there appeared St. Joseph with the Holy Child blessing the world. Our Lady stood beside Her holy spouse clothed in white tunic and blue mantle.

Next Our Lord appeared in His glorified manhood. He blessed the world "as St. Joseph had done." Beside Him was His Co-Redemptrix, Our Lady of Sorrows, to whom He had "entrusted the peace of the world" (Jacinta).

Finally Our Lady came under Her ancient title of "Mount Carmel... *where Elias had performed a miracle "to show that God is God,"* even as She had just done on this mountain of Fatima. She held the Child Jesus in Her arms while holding the Scapular down to the world (see picture on page 259).

Would Fill Entire Books!

As I write this in my 77th year, having read hundreds of books and having prayerfully thought of these events for so long a time, I feel that if I were to live another lifetime of prayer and study I would never be able to put into words all that these wordless, final visions of Fatima have to say. Their meaning may be expected to unfold in the time of the triumph of Love... the triumph of the Immaculate.

The Appearance of St. Joseph

A tiny example of some of the riches in these last "visions without words" is an interesting story about the way St. Joseph actually appeared. There seemed to be "contradictions" when Dr. Formigao interrogated the children just after the October 13 visions concerning St. Joseph. At one point it was said that the Holy Child was standing beside the Saint, and at another that St. Joseph held Him in his arms.

I had the impression, before I went to speak to Lucia 29 years later, that St. Joseph stood on one side, Our Lady on the other, and that the Holy Child was between them. I had a drawing made to show to Sr. Lucia for her comment. When she saw the picture she sat straight up, her face became animated. She exclaimed: "It was not like that! The Child Jesus was *standing elevated with the arm of St. Joseph around Him* while He and St. Joseph gave the blessing." Therefore, both "contradictory" statements of the children made just after the event were correct!

As we shall see, similarly the Holy Child later appeared with Our Lady at Pontevedra: elevated, so that His Face was beside Hers even though He was so much smaller. In the appearance during the miracle of the sun with His father, His face was beside St. Joseph's.

The Special Statue

The fiftieth anniversary of the apparitions of Fatima was a great occasion. The Pope (Paul VI) came to Fatima despite great opposition (outcries that Portugal was a colonial power, etc.). This was a time when Popes rarely left Rome. His predecessor, John XXIII, *was the first Pope to leave Rome in a hundred years,* and that was just to go across Italy to Loreto to pray in the Holy House for the success of the Council.

On this important golden jubilee of Fatima it was suggested to the Bishop that St. Joseph had never been sufficiently honored. Indeed it seemed no one had ever thought to have a statue made of him as he had appeared: with the Child embraced by the Saint's left arm, while father and Child blessed the world "to bring it peace."

The Bishop had already agreed to lead a peace flight around the world with the Pilgrim Virgin immediately after the jubilee ceremonies of October 13 (the Pope had been there in May)... and would it not be fitting for St. Joseph to go along? A special statue was made exactly according to Lucia's description. It was the first.

In the presence of hundreds upon hundreds of thousands, as an official part of the jubilee ceremonies, the Bishop solemnly blessed the statue recalling that fifty years before over this holy place the saintly Patriarch had appeared with the Holy Child to bless the world. The Bishop announced that as the pilgrim Virgin had gone forth from Fatima to proclaim Her message of Peace, so this statue of Her holy spouse would now go forth with Her on a jubilee peace flight around the world. This was done. The statue is now in a replica of the Holy House of Nazareth at the Blue Army national center in Washington, N.J. (USA)

St. Joseph at Pontevedra

We may expect to hear a great deal about St. Joseph in the coming times so it seems fitting to speak of how this great saint has shown himself a most powerful patron of Our Lady's Fatima Apostolate. It is as though all *those who respond* to the appeal of Her Immaculate Heart *can obtain almost anything they ask of St. Joseph.*

The Pontevedra convent (where the Child Jesus appealed for reparation for the offenses against the

Immaculate Heart of Mary and where Our Lady made the promise of the five First Saturdays) was abandoned by the Dorothean Sisters because of termites. On the very day we signed the contract to purchase the convent (with the intention of preserving the place of the apparitions), before entering the abandoned building Bishop Venancio and I acquired a statue of St. Joseph.

We prayerfully installed it in the termite ridden convent, entrusting it to St. Joseph. The result cannot be considered less than miraculous. *When workers came to restore the convent, despite the fact that there had been no exterminating treatment the termites had left.*

The entire story of the Pontevedra Convent, in which are now commemorated the "final visions" of Fatima (of the first Saturdays and of the request for the Collegial Consecration), is extraordinary. The small room in which Lucia had the apparition of the First Saturdays is now the sanctuary of a small chapel of the apparition; and the main convent chapel contains all the original furnishings of the chapel of Tuy.

Lucia had shown a special predilection for the Pontevedra convent as though she foresaw that it would one day be an international center commemorating these important, climactic visions and messages from Heaven. She wrote to her confessor on May 18, 1936:

"Here we are waiting for the day when they will close this house... the thought of returning to Portugal mitigates the sacrifice." It was indeed a great sacrifice for her to leave the house where she had been so lovingly visited by Our Lady and the Divine Infant.

When the Pontevedra convent was reopened, the great apostle of St. Joseph, Rev. Christopher Rengers, OFM Cap, decided "on an inspiration" that the original wooden model of the Medal of St. Joseph (now widely known) should be installed there.

Above: Main Chapel in Pontevedra. Altar and aches from convent of Tuy figured in the "last vision of Fatima" there. Below: Chapel of the "five Saturdays vision," also in the convent in Pontevedra.

Pontevedra

Father Rengers came personally to the opening ceremony to present this precious gift. Later when the Archbishop of Santiago came to bless the two chapels of the convent (which commemorate the apparitions both of Pontevedra and Tuy), the large original carving of the St. Joseph medal was carried in procession and remains to this day as a perpetual sign of the "special presence" of Our Lady's spouse in that sacred place where the Child Jesus appealed to the world for devotion to Her Immaculate Heart.

Thus the hearts of all those who honor St. Joseph through the medal must have a special place in the Hearts of Jesus and Mary revealed at Fatima and in Pontevedra in the flames of Their Love.

St. Joseph at Fatima

In 1951 no funds whatever were available for building the international center of the apostolate at Fatima. Msgr. Colgan and I, who had begun to promote the apostolate on a large scale only a year before, put a plaster statue of St. Joseph in a field which had been discovered for us by Lucia's sister and on which we had put a down payment. It was just behind the Basilica of Fatima.

In the words of Blessed Andre of Montreal we asked St. Joseph: "Please build a roof over your head for Our Lady" (for Her World Apostolate of Fatima).

The very first funds were used to order a marble statue of St. Joseph which we intended to place in front of the building when it would be finished. A larger statue of the "Blue Army Madonna" (Our Lady crowned as Queen, showing Her Immaculate Heart and holding forth the Scapular and the Rosary) was to be placed on top.

In less time than I would ever have dreamed possible, without having to borrow even a single dollar the building was completed. When it was indeed finished and about to be dedicated by a Legate of Pope Pius XII, it was found that the statue of Our Lady was too heavy so St. Joseph went on top... and there he stands overlooking the Basilica and the Cova every bit like his appearance in the sky during the great Fatima miracle, blessing the world together with the Holy Child. It would seem that Our Lady outdid our efforts to honor St. Joseph, and at the same time to honor our Apostolate. The Blue Army international center has the glory of being the only place in all Fatima where the appearance of St. Joseph during the miracle of the sun is so commemorated.

St. Joseph in Washington, NJ

Sister Mary Miranda, OSF, a Felician sister who played a key role in the planning and building of the Shrine and convent at the Blue Army national center in Washington, NJ, was one of St. Joseph's angels. No matter how small or large the project, it was entrusted to the Carpenter Saint of Nazareth.

Up went the convent and up went the Shrine, and as each bill came in so did the money. We will carry to the secrecy of the grave our *awe and wonder* because of the "impossibilities" which we saw blown away again and again like dust in the wind by the breath of St. Joseph.

There is an entire chapter in the book *Sign of Her Heart* about the Scapular and St. Joseph. Examples and quotations of great authorities and saints are used to show that the Scapular is a special sign of St. Joseph for all who wear it. Since by the Scapular Our Lady has "adopted" me as Her "special child" (as the Church sings in the special Preface of the Mass of Our Lady of Mount Carmel), it makes me also a special child of St. Joseph.

Our Lady's Rosary, especially in the first chaplet, teaches me to follow in the footsteps of St. Joseph.

Consider his devotion and respect for Mary even when he had not yet been told that Her conception was a miracle. What an example he gives to all husbands to trust their wives and to be ready to forgive even when they feel wronged! And the same of course is true for wives towards husbands.

Consider his anguish at not being able to provide proper shelter for Mary and Jesus in Bethlehem and his humble acceptance of God's Will. He was at Her side when Simeon said a sword would pierce her Heart "so that out of many hearts thoughts would be revealed." He was there with Our Lady in the agonizing search when Jesus separated Himself for three days.

Then Jesus went down to Nazareth *"and was subject to them."* God willingly subjected Himself to a man like you and me... setting *an example for families* and an example for all souls who may not yet see this great light rising over the world from Fatima... a light inviting us to union, like St. Joseph, in the Sacred Heart of Jesus through the Immaculate Heart of Mary.

An Important Reason

We have inserted these remarks about St. Joseph because they are the kind of details which seem to flow in the spirit of Lucia's memoirs and because it is so important to realize that far more was "said" in those final and wordless visions than words can tell. But there is a "bottom line." There is a door to all these mysteries. There is a door to the triumph of the Immaculate Heart of Mary. There is a door to the "era of peace for mankind." And Lucia's primary mission was to point to that door.

As Cardinal Ottaviani said in his press conference on the Secret of Fatima (in Rome, February 11, 1962): What is most important in the message of Fatima is what Lucia has revealed about it. She has told us in basic, simple terms how we can open the door. We are given an inkling of what is behind the door.

†††

Statue of St. Joseph atop the World Center of the Blue Army at Fatima, with Byzantine dome in background.

Chapter XXII.

Comments On

THE TWO HEARTS

From Fatima a new light has begun to shine into the world. It is the great Love of the Eucharistic Heart of Jesus reflected from the Immaculate Heart of Mary. Obviously it is not a new devotion but rather a light shining with new brilliance, illuminating devotion to the Hearts of Jesus and Mary with an invitation for all hearts to be become afire in Their Love.

The light began to shine even before the apparitions of Our Lord to St. Margaret Mary Alacoque. It shone brighter as St. John Eudes succeeded in establishing the liturgical Feasts of the Hearts of Jesus and Mary. It became ever brighter at the Rue du Bac and in the writings of saints like Francis de Sales, Grignion de Montfort, Alphonsus Ligouri, Maximilian Kolbe, and others.

But at Fatima the light begins to shine like a sun to dazzle the whole world. One of Jacinta's last exhortations to Lucia was to proclaim to the world:

"The Heart of Jesus wants the Immaculate Heart of His Mother to be venerated at His Side."

The Light From Her Heart

The first "miracle" of Fatima was a light from the Immaculate Heart of Mary in which the children saw the Eucharistic Jesus saddened by unrequited love. Little Francisco said that nothing in all the events of Fatima impressed him more than the experience of that light from Mary's Heart in which he saw the sadness of the "Hidden Jesus." Bathed in that light the children felt "lost in God" and were inspired to cry out:

"O Most Holy Trinity, I adore Thee! My God, my God, I love Thee in the Most Blessed Sacrament!"

Difficulty of Words

The problem about a light is finding words to describe it. It is something to be experienced rather than read about, but many words have been written about it. St. John Eudes heard Jesus say:

"I have given you this admirable Heart of My dearest Mother *which is but one with Mine, to be truly your heart also* so that the children may have but one Heart with their Mother... *that so you may adore, serve and love God with a Heart worthy of His infinite Greatness.*"[1]

The children of Fatima experienced this in the light from the Immaculate Heart of Mary. We know why and how they obtained the favor of this experience, but before we speak of that, more about the brilliance of this light rising over the world.

God Wills It

Our Lady said at Fatima: *"God wishes to establish in the world devotion to My Immaculate Heart."*

One of the conditions for the conversion of Russia was that all the Bishops of the world should unite with the Pope in the act of Consecrating that nation to Our Lady's Immaculate Heart. And when Lucia asked Our Lord why He insisted on this collegial consecration (which took over fifty years to be realized!) He answered:

"Because I want My entire Church to know that it is through the Immaculate Heart of My Mother that this favor is obtained (i.e. the conversion of Russia)... *so that devotion to Her Immaculate Heart may be placed alongside devotion to My Own Sacred Heart."*

The consecration took place on March 25, 1984, and gradually the new light begins to shine over the world as mankind enters the 21st century and a new era: the era of the triumph of that Immaculate Heart through which came the Heart of God Incarnate.

Is It Miraculous?

We know what that triumph will be. The children of Fatima experienced a foretaste of it in the light from Mary's Heart: An awareness of *God with us* (the Eucharist)... *an awareness of a Great Love which transforms the lives of those who experience it.* It is to be a triumph of love... more difficult to describe even than the light from Our Lady's Heart. Much of mankind is to experience this *great love of God* which at once conveys a horror of sin and transforming love for Him and neighbor. We are talking about a *miracle of grace* as transforming as the light which caused St. Paul on the road to Damascus to fall blinded from his horse and to hear the words of Jesus:

"Why do you persecute Me?" And still blind from the light, he rose from the ground... the great persecutor became the great Saint.

Why and How

Why did the children of Fatima experience this? First, they earned it by a simple "Yes" to the most fundamental question in anyone's relationship to God: *"Will you be willing?"* That was Our Lady's first question to them: *"to accept whatever God wills to send you and to offer it up...?"*

Second, they were chosen... as children... to show that this light from Mary's Heart is ready to shine on everyone who says, "Yes." The first and simplest way to do this is to make the Morning Offering and mean it. To be really transformed in that light we need but renew the Offering when daily duty, God's Commandments, require our saying "no" to sin and "yes" to the loving Hearts of Jesus and Mary.

Made Easy

Our Lady of Fatima makes this easy for us with two devotions: One a sign of Her constant protection and presence; the other a twenty minute devotion leading us into the mysteries of our salvation.

The "tool" of the first devotion is the Scapular of Mt. Carmel which She held out of the sky at the climax of Her Fatima appearances and which Lucia said is "The sign of consecration to Her Immaculate Heart." The second "tool" is the Rosary which She asks us to say with attention to the mysteries.

"Keep me company," Our Lady adds, "on the First Saturday of the month" by: a) Saying the Rosary; b) spending 15 minutes thinking about the mysteries; c) going to confession; d) receiving Holy Communion; e) offering these four acts "in reparation for the offenses committed against My Immaculate Heart."

Greatest and most common of those offenses are perhaps careless Communions and sins against purity.

The very thought of the "Immaculate" Heart tends to make us detest impure thoughts and actions and if we use Our Lady's devotions (Scapular, Rosary, First Saturdays) with good will *the light from Her Immaculate Heart* will drive back the darkness of evil and fill us with the joy of the triumph She has promised for us and for the world.

Is it difficult to think of "my" heart as "one" with the Hearts of Jesus AND Mary... or even that it COULD be ONE with Theirs?

279.

A Model

Jesus is God even though also Man and Mary was conceived Immaculate. Sin never touched Her, but sin has certainly touched me. I live in a world which seems even to have lost its sense of sin. But whom do I see in the sky of Fatima as the great miracle of the sun begins? *It is St. Joseph,* with one arm around the Child Jesus and the other arm raised in blessing. And Our Lady, in white tunic and blue mantle, smiles at their side as we remember Her words:

"In October I will perform a great miracle so that all may believe... I will bring St. Joseph and the Child Jesus to bless the world and bring it peace."

St. Joseph is not God-Man, nor was he immaculate. He was born in original sin like each of us. *But his heart became one with the Immaculate Heart of Mary and the Sacred Heart of Jesus.* He is the first example of the message which St. John Eudes heard from the Eucharistic Jesus:

"I have given you this admirable Heart of My Mother, which is but One with Mine, to be truly YOUR heart also... so that you may adore, serve and love God with a heart worthy of His infinite Greatness." How perfectly this was fulfilled in St. Joseph, my model of union with the Sacred Hearts of Jesus and Mary!

Rosary and Scapular

We find St. Joseph at Mary's side in all the joyful mysteries of the Rosary, a living and real example to lead us into the depths of these mysteries: God with us, through Mary.

As the Scapular obtains for us the effect of Mary's presence in our lives, it does this also with St. Joseph. "If Joseph is the father of those of whom Mary is the Mother," said the Rev. Joseph Andres, SJ, "he is necessarily *the special father of those who wear the*

Scapular."[2] The devout Gerson (quoted by St. Alphonsus Ligouri) exclaimed:

"O beautiful, amiable and adorable Trinity: Jesus, Mary and Joseph. United by such bonds of love and charity, you are truly worthy of the love and adoration of the children of God." [3]

St. Joseph is more than just a model. He is *truly* my loving spiritual *father. Like Our Lady he wants me to be plunged into the Love of Jesus. He stands ready at every moment to bless me... and to bring me the peace of which the angels sang over Bethlehem.*

Greatness of St. Joseph

As we said in Chapter XXI, one reason we have dwelt in some detail on the meaning of the vision of St. Joseph during the miracle of the Sun is to show the value and need for prayerful study of the "wordless visions" of Fatima... almost too important for words. The angelic doctor, St. Thomas Aquinas wrote:

"There are three things God cannot make greater than He has made them: The Humanity of Our Lord, the glory of the elect, and the incomparable Mother of God, of whom it is said that God can make no mother greater than the Mother of God. You may add a fourth in honor of St. Joseph. God cannot make a greater father than the father of God."[4]

Father Huguet, in his wonderful book *The Power of St. Joseph* (16th med.) wrote: "Happy is the soul who can say like St. Joseph that Mary lives in her and that she lives in Mary!... and so becomes more and more like her divine model, more and more united to God!"

Special Aids

In summary... Our Lady not only invites us into union though Her Heart to the Heart of Jesus as God invited St. Joseph, but She gives us four special aids:

281.

1) The Morning Offering;

2) The Scapular, sign of Her constant nearness and intercession as I strive to follow Her path of light;

3) The Rosary, revealing to me the mysteries of God's Love and inspiring me along that path of light;

4) The First Saturday devotion for monthly renewal of my purpose... and by the First Friday-First Saturday devotions (especially vigils) to hasten me to the end of that path of light into the Great Love waiting to fill me and the world with joy and peace.

✝✝✝

[1.] Sign Of Her Heart, by John Haffert, p. 16.

[2.] Ibidem, p. 159

[3.] Ibidem, p. 153

[4.] Ibidem, p. 159

Below: Rare photo of the three children.

Chapter XXIII.

In the Fourth Memoir —
Lucia Remembers

REFLECTION OF OUR LADY IN
FRANCISCO AND JACINTA

Lucia says that she sought to fulfill the Bishop's wishes "in as few words as possible." She also repeatedly reveals her desire "of keeping to myself alone those more intimate aspects which were so difficult for me to reveal."

When this book seemed to be getting rather long there was thought of eliminating details which might be considered "unimportant." But in all her words Lucia is giving us a lucid, beautiful view of Our Lady and Her message... seen in the mirror of the three children who saw Her and responded to Her words.

After describing (indeed in very few words!) the apparitions of Our Lady, Lucia completes her memoirs with a final look into the mirror.

†††

Not a few people have expressed considerable surprise at the memory God has deigned to give me. Through His infinite goodness I have indeed been favored.

Where supernatural things are concerned this is not to be wondered at, for these are imprinted on the mind in such a way that it is almost impossible to forget them. At least the meaning of what is made known is never forgotten, unless it be that God also wills that this, too, be forgotten.

Furthermore, Rev. Dr. Galamba has asked me to write down any other favor that may have been obtained through Jacinta. I have thought about it and can recall only two instances.

At Least One Hail Mary!

The first time Senhora Emilia (of whom I spoke in the second account of Jacinta) came to take me to the priest's house in Olival, Jacinta went there with me. It was already night when we reached the village where the good widow lived.

The news of our arrival quickly spread and Senhora Emilia's house was soon surrounded by a crowd of people. They all wanted to see us, question us, ask for graces, and so on.

It happened that a certain devout woman from a little village nearby was accustomed to recite the Rosary in her own home, in company with any of the neighbors who wished to join her. She invited us to go and pray the Rosary in her house.

We excused ourselves, explaining that we were going to pray it with Senhora Emilia, but she spoke so insistently that there was nothing to do but yield to her request. When the news got around that we were going there, crowds of people hurried to the good woman's house in the hope of securing a good place. This was all the better for us, since we found the road comparatively free.

On our way to the house a girl about twenty years old came out to meet us. Weeping, she knelt down and begged us to enter her house and say at least one Hail Mary for the recovery of her father who for three years had been unable to take any rest on account of continual hiccups.

In such circumstances it was impossible to refuse. I helped the poor girl to her feet. It was already late into the night and we were finding our way along by the light of lanterns. I told Jacinta to remain there and I would go on ahead to pray the Rosary with the people (at the widow's house) and would call for her on my return. She agreed.

Grace Received

When I came back and went into the house I found Jacinta sitting on a chair facing a man also seated. He was not so very old but he looked emaciated. He was weeping with emotion, Some persons were gathered around him... members of his family, I should think. On seeing me Jacinta got up, said goodbye and promised that she would not forget him in her prayers. Then we returned to Senhora Emilia's house.

Early the next morning we set out for Olival and only came back three days later. When we returned to Senhora Emilia's house we found the happy girl accompanied by her father.

He now looked much better and had lost all trace of the nervous strain and extreme weakness. They came to thank us for the grace they had received. They said he was no longer troubled by the annoying hiccups.

The Prodigal Son

The other favor was received by an aunt of mine called Vitoria, married and living in Fatima. She had a son who was a real prodigal. I do not know the reason, but he left his father's house and no one knew what had become of him.

In her distress, my aunt came to Aljustrel one day to ask me to pray to Our Lady for this son of hers. Not finding me, she asked Jacinta instead, who promised to pray for him. A few days later he suddenly returned home, asked his parents' forgiveness, and then went to Aljustrel to relate his sorry story.

He told us that, after having spent all that he had stolen from his parents, he wandered about for quite a while like a tramp until, for some reason I have now forgotten, he was put in jail in Torres Novas. After he had been there for some time, he succeeded in escaping one night and fled to the remote hills and unfamiliar pine groves.

Realizing he had completely lost his way, and torn between the fear of being captured and the darkness of a stormy night, he began to pray. He said that only some minutes had passed when Jacinta appeared to him, took him by the hand and led him to the main road which runs from Alqueidao to Requengo, making a sign for him to continue in that direction.

When morning dawned he found himself on the road to Boleiros. Recognizing where he was, he was overcome with emotion and headed straight home to his parents.

He declared that Jacinta had appeared to him, and that he had recognized her perfectly. I asked Jacinta if it was true that she had gone there to guide him. She answered that she had not... that she had no idea at all of the location of the pine woods and hills where he had been lost.

"I only prayed and pleaded very much with Our Lady for him, because I felt so sorry for Aunt Vitoria." That was how she answered me. How, then, did it happen? I don't know. Only God knows.[1]

There remains one more question of Dr. Galamba's which I have yet to answer:

"How did people feel when they were in Jacinta's presence?" It is not easy to reply, for ordinarily I do not know what goes on within other people and therefore I do not know how they feel. This means that I can

only say what I felt myself and can describe only
exterior manifestations of other people's feelings.

Jacinta, Reflection of God

What I myself usually felt was much the same as
anyone feels in the presence of a holy person who
seems to be in continual communication with God.
Jacinta's demeanor was always serious and reserved,
but always friendly. All her actions seemed to reflect
the presence of God in the way proper to people of
mature age and great virtue. I never noticed in her
that frivolity or childish enthusiasm for games and
ornaments so typical of small children.

This of course, was after the Apparitions; before
them, she was the personification of enthusiasm and
caprice! I cannot say that the other children gathered
around her as they did around me. This was probably
due to the fact that she did not know as many songs
or stories with which to teach and amuse them, or
perhaps that there was in her a seriousness far
beyond her years. If in her presence a child, or even
a grown-up, were to say or do anything unseemly, she
would reprimand them, saying:

"Don't do that, for you are offending the Lord our
God, and He is already so much offended!"

If, as sometimes happened, the child or adult
answered back and called her a "pious Mary" or a
plaster saint, or some other such thing, she would
look at them very seriously and walk away without a
single word. Perhaps this was one of the reasons why
she did not enjoy more popularity.

If I was with her, dozens of children would gather
around us in no time. But if I went away, she would
soon find herself alone. Yet when I was with her they
seemed to delight in her company. They would hug
and kiss her in the affectionate way of innocent
children. They loved to sing and play with her.

Sometimes they begged me to go and look for her when she had not come out to play. If she told them that she did not want to come because they were naughty, they promised to be good if only she would come out:

"Go and get her, and tell her that we promise to be good if she'll come."

Jacinta, Model of Virtue

When I went to visit her during her illness, I often found a large group waiting at the door hoping to be able to come in with me to see her. They seemed to be held back by a certain sense of respect. Sometimes before I left, I asked her:

"Jacinta, do you want me to tell some of them to stay here with you and keep you company?"

"Oh, yes! But just the ones who are smaller than myself!" Then they all vied with each other, saying:

"I'll stay! I'll stay!" After that she entertained them by teaching them the Our Father, the Hail Mary, how to bless themselves, and to sing. Sitting on her bed or, if she was up, on the floor of the living room, they played "pebbles" using crab apples, chestnuts, sweet acorns, dried figs and so on... all of which my aunt was only too happy to supply so that her little girl might enjoy the children's company.

She prayed the Rosary with them, and counseled them not to commit sin and so avoid offending the Lord our God and going to hell. Some of them spent whole mornings and afternoons with her and seemed very happy in her company... but once they had left her presence, they did not dare to go back in the trusting way so natural to children.

Sometimes they came in search of me begging me to go in with them, or they waited for me outside the house, or else they waited at the door until my aunt or Jacinta herself invited them in to see her. They seemed to like her and to enjoy her company, but they felt themselves held back by a certain shyness or respect that kept them somewhat at a distance.

Grown-ups also went to see her. They showed clearly how much they admired her demeanor, which was always the same, always patient without being in the least demanding or complaining.

Whatever the position in which she was lying when her mother left her, this was how she remained. If they asked her whether she felt better, she answered:

"I'm much the same," or "I think I'm worse, thank you very much." There was an air of sadness about her as she lay silent in the presence of visitors.

People stayed sitting by her bedside for long periods at a time and looked as though they felt happy to be there. It was there also that Jacinta had to undergo detailed and exhausting interrogations. She never showed the slightest impatience or repugnance, but merely told me later:

"My head aches so much after listening to all those people! Now that I cannot run away and hide, I offer more of these sacrifices to Our Lord." The neighbors sometime brought along clothes they were making, so that they could sit and sew by her bedside.

"I'll work a little beside Jacinta," they would say; "I don't know what it is about her, but it is good to be with her."

They brought their little ones along too. The children amused themselves by playing with Jacinta and their mothers were thus left free to do their sewing. When people asked her questions, she answered in a friendly manner, but briefly. If they said anything which she thought improper, she promptly replied:

"Don't say that; it offends the Lord our God." If they related something unbecoming about their families, she answered:

"Don't let your children commit sin, or they could go to hell." If there were grown-ups involved, she said:

"Tell them not to do that, for it is a sin. They offend the Lord our God, and later they could be damned." People who came to visit us from a distance, either out of curiosity or from devotion, seemed to sense something supernatural about Jacinta. At times when they came to my house to speak to me, they remarked:

"We've just been talking to Jacinta and Francisco... when with them we feel that there is something supernatural about them." Sometimes, they went so far as to want me to explain why they felt like that. As I did not know, I simply shrugged my shoulders and said nothing. I have often heard people commenting on this.

One day two priests and a gentleman came to my home. While my mother was opening the door and inviting them to come in and sit down, I climbed into the attic to hide. My mother, after showing them in, left them alone while she went out into the yard to call me, for she had left me there but a moment before. While my mother was outside searching for me the good gentlemen were discussing the matter:

"We'll see what this one will tell us."

"What impressed me," remarked the gentleman, "was the innocence and sincerity of Jacinta and her brother. If this one does not contradict herself, I'll believe. I don't know what it is I felt in the presence of those two children!"

"It's as though one feels something supernatural in their presence," added one of the priests.

"It did my soul good to talk to them."

My mother did not find me and the good gentlemen had to resign themselves to taking their departure without having been able to speak to me.

"Sometimes," my mother told them, "she goes off to play with other children and nobody can find her."

"We're very sorry! We greatly enjoyed talking to the two little ones, and we wanted to talk to your little girl as well... but we shall come back another time."

One Sunday, my friends from Moita (Maria, Rosa and Ana Caetano, and Maria and Ana Broqueira) came after Mass to ask my mother to let me go and spend the day with them. Once I received permission, they asked me to bring Jacinta and Francisco along too. I asked my aunt and she agreed, and so all three of us went to Moita.

After the mid-day meal Jacinta was so sleepy that her little head began to nod. Mr. Jose Alves sent one of his nieces to go and put her to bed. In just a short while she fell fast asleep. The people of the little hamlet began to gather in order to spend the afternoon with us. They were so anxious to see Jacinta that they peeped in to see if she was awake.

They were filled with wonder when they saw that, although in a deep sleep, she had a smile on her lips... the look of an angel... and her little hands were joined and raised towards Heaven. The room was soon filled with curious people. Everyone wanted to see her, but those inside were in no hurry to come out and make room for the others. Mr. Jose Alves, his wife and nieces all said:

"This must be an angel." Overcome, as it were, with awe, they remained kneeling beside the bed until, about half past four, I went to call her so that we could go and pray the Rosary in the Cova da Iria and then return home. Mr. Jose Alves' nieces are the Caetano girls mentioned above.

Francisco Was Different

In contrast to Jacinta, Francisco was quite different. He had an easy manner and was always friendly and smiling, playing with all the children without distinction. He did not rebuke anyone. All he did was to go aside whenever he saw anything that was not as it should be. If he was asked why he went away, he answered:

"Because you're not good," or... "Because I don't want to play anymore."

During his illness the children ran in and out of his room with the greatest freedom, talked to him through the window and asked him if he was feeling better, and so forth. If he was asked whether he wanted some of the children to stay with him and keep him company, he used to say that he preferred not as he liked to be alone. He would say to me sometimes:

"I like just having you here, and Jacinta too."

When grown-ups came to see him he remained silent, only answering when directly questioned, and then in as few words as possible. People who came to visit him, whether they were neighbors or strangers, often spent long periods of time sitting by his bedside, remarking: "I don't know what it is about Francisco, but it feels so good to be here!"

Some women from the village commented on this one day to my aunt and my mother, after having spent quite a long time in Francisco's room:

"It's a mystery one cannot fathom! They are children just like any others, they don't say anything to us, and yet in their presence one feels something one can't explain and that makes them different from all the rest."

"It seems to me that when we go into Francisco's room, we feel just as we do when we go into a church," said one of my aunt's neighbors, a woman named Romana, who apparently did not believe in the Apparitions. There were three others in this group also: the wives of Manuel Faustino, Jose Marto and Jose Silva.

I am not surprised that people felt like this, being accustomed to find in most people only preoccupation with material things which goes with an empty, superficial life. Indeed, the very sight of these children was enough to lift their minds to Our Heavenly Mother, with whom the children were believed to be in communication; to eternity, for they saw how eager, joyful and happy they were at the thought of going there; to God, for they said that they loved Him more than their own parents; and even to think of hell, for the children warned them that people would go there if they continued to commit sin.

On the outside, so to speak, they were children like all others. But if these good people so accustomed to the material side of life had only known how to elevate their minds a little, they would have seen without difficulty that in these children there was something that marked them out as being different.

I have just remembered something else connected with Francisco, and I am going to relate it here. A woman called Mariana, from Casa Velha, came one day into Francisco's room. She was most upset because her husband had driven their son out of the house. She was asking for the grace that her son would be reconciled with his father. Francisco said to her in reply:

"Don't worry. I'm going to Heaven very soon, and when I get there I will ask Our Lady for that grace."

I do not recall just how many days remained before he took his flight to Heaven, but what I do remember is that on the very afternoon of Francisco's death the son went for the very last time to ask pardon of his father who had previously refused it because his son would not submit to the conditions imposed.

The boy accepted everything that the father demanded and peace reigned once again in that home. This boy's sister, Leocadia by name, later married a brother of Jacinta and Francisco and became the mother of their niece, whom Your Excellency met in the Cova da Iria when she was about to enter the Dorotheans.

Epilogue

I think, Your Excellency, I have written everything you have asked of me for now. Up to this time I did all I could to conceal the more intimate aspects of Our Lady's Apparitions in the Cova da Iria. Whenever I found myself obliged to speak about them, I was careful to touch on the subject very lightly in order to avoid revealing what I wanted so much to keep hidden. But now that obedience has required this of me, here it is!

I am left like a skeleton stripped of everything, even of life itself, placed in the National Museum to remind visitors of the misery and nothingness of all passing things. Thus despoiled, I shall remain in the museum of the world reminding all who pass, not of misery and nothingness, but of the greatness of the Divine Mercies.

May the Good God and the Immaculate Heart of Mary deign to accept the humble sacrifices which They have seen fit to ask of me, in order to revive in souls a spirit of Faith, Confidence and Love.

Tuy, 8th December, 1941.

✝✝✝

[1.] At this juncture of the memoirs Lucia gives a lengthy answer to Dr. Galamba's request that she make observations and, if necessary, any corrections to the book *Our Lady of Fatima* by the Rev. Luis Gonzaga Aires da Fonseca, S.J.

We have omitted this since it would be meaningful only to those who might compare her comments and corrections to the original.

She also speaks of her interrogation by a layman, Antero de Figueiredo, which she found extremely difficult because of his pointed questions. Figueiredo succeeded little in his effort to pry secrets but the subsequent book he wrote is considered one of the source books on Fatima.

Chapter XXIV.

Comments On

THE END OF THE MEMOIRS

Lucia completes the memoir with these two stories about Jacinta because she had been asked to write down any other favors (beyond those in the first memoir) she knew to have been obtained through Jacinta's prayers. When Jacinta was asked whether she had actually been "transported" to the young man lost in the woods she seemed to know nothing about it.

Elsewhere we told that while Bishop Venancio was speaking to his sister about Lucia, his brother-in-law suffering from acute chronic pain cried out: "If she saw Our Lady, she could cure me." And at that moment he was instantly and permanently cured.

How does one explain these events? And why does it happen that Lucia seems inspired to end all four of her important memoirs with these unusual favors?

Could it be to remind us of the reality of the Mystical Body and the power of the Communion of Saints: *union and interaction* of all in the state of grace? Will this become characteristic of the coming time of the triumph of the Immaculate Heart? Will we be more aware of our spiritual interdependence and of *the power of shared faith and prayer?*

Once again we are surprised by "her own words"... and made to think.

They Were Normal Children

Finally Lucia speaks of Jacinta's virtues (truly extraordinary in a nine year old) and adds:

"This was of course after the apparitions. Before them she was the personification of enthusiasm and caprice!"

Does this mean that the three children lost their sense of humor and joy after the apparitions? Absolutely not. A very wrong impression is created by the famous photograph of the three children taken at the time of the apparitions. They seem to have a dour expression. (Unfortunately most representations of Jacinta and Francisco are taken from that photo.)

But the look is not one of severity. It is apprehension. They had never known of photographs and often the persons who wielded cameras in their faces frightened them.

I remember as late as 1946 when I was making a movie of their parents, the whirring of the camera seemed to frighten them. Their expression showed apprehension. After all, the lives of the children had been threatened more than once and the enemies of Fatima and of the apparitions were often frightening indeed!

Joyous

My impression of Lucia in 1946 (and she was certainly like Francisco and Jacinta) was of a person who did not take herself to be at all important. She appeared self-composed, balanced, well poised... and if she was serious I felt that it was only because my questions were serious. (I was striving to pin down the basic minimum Our Lady required to convert Russia and bring about the era of peace, asking many direct and important questions which had never been previously addressed.)

But as I have said previously, when I saw Lucia several years later in the Carmel of Coimbra *with no questions to ask*, my most vivid memory of that visit is of her pealing, pure laughter. The message of Our Lady is a joyous one.

Not only does it bear the promise of a TRIUMPH of love in the world, but the very basic condition of that triumph is joyous in itself and in its effect on those who live it. Can there be any greater joy than the sanctification of daily duty, as there is no greater misery than the slavery of sin?

More Than Just a Pledge

The wholehearted and therefore joyous response of the children of Fatima to Our Lady's requests shows far more than simple commitment. It shows a *daily, conscious effort* to unite one's heart to the Immaculate Heart of Mary by *purifying each action of the day*. This results in what Her thorn-encircled Heart has come to ask of us: Co-redemption.

Cause of Tears

While Our Lady gave us a great message at Fatima confirmed by a great miracle, *She gave us an equally great message in the example of these little children* and She left Lucia in the world to describe how they took it seriously.

At Akita Our Lady used miracles of tears to affirm that "Consecration to the Immaculate Heart of Mary is not taken seriously... You must attach great importance to the First Saturdays... Pray with fervor not only because of your own sins but *in reparation for the sins of all men.*" Many have not responded at all and very few have responded as generously as did the children who *saw hell* and understood what saving souls really means. And they saw the thorn-encircled

Heart of Mary pleading for prayers for sinners. In my book *The Meaning of Akita* I wrote:

"By a miracle of tears flowing from a wooden statue (at Akita) Our Lady plunges us into Her mystery as Co-redemptrix. She condenses the reason for Her sorrow in one phrase: "Because so many souls are lost!"[1]

In the Plan of Redemption

There is a paradox in the joy of drying Our Lady's tears. Reason fails us before the mystery of the joy in Heaven over one sinner doing penance and the anguish of Calvary. In a previous chapter we used many words to delve into a mystery for which Lucia used only a sentence: *St. Joseph appeared.* We could do far more with the sentence which followed: *Our Lady of Sorrows appeared.*

In the liturgy of September 15, Feast of Our Lady of Sorrows, we are plunged into the mystery of Fatima, the mystery of Co-redemption. Father A. M. Lepicier says:

"This liturgical emphasis on the Sorrows of Mary *following the Feast of the Exaltation of the Holy Cross* shows the primordial place given by the Church to Our Lady *in the plan of redemption* and what place She should have in the devotion of Christians redeemed by the Blood of Christ and *by the tears* of His dear Mother."[2]

What we read in almost all Lucia's words is that Our Lady called her and her cousins, and She calls us, to *share in this mystery.* And this will be the cause of our joy, and of the joy of the world.

†††

[1] *The Meaning of Akita*, Haffert, 101 Foundation, pp. 14-15.

[2] *Notre Dame des Sept Douleurs*, Lepicier, Published 1950, p. 10

Chapter XXV.

Comments On

CONVERSION OF RUSSIA AND THE FIRST SATURDAYS

In 1946, when I asked what was necessary for the conversion of Russia and world peace, Lucia promptly answered that the principal request of Our Lady was contained in Her very first request to the children:

"Will you be willing to accept whatever God will send you and to offer it up in reparation for sin and for the conversion of sinners?"

Lucia went on to explain that the Rosary was important because in meditating upon its mysteries and using the power of its prayer, we were able to strengthen ourselves to respond affirmatively to this all-important question. For the same reason it was important that we be consecrated to Our Lady and to wear the Scapular, which is the sign of that consecration.[1]

The First Saturdays are also important because in making the First Saturdays, examining our consciences, confessing, receiving Communion, and spending fifteen minutes meditating on the mysteries of the Rosary, we purify and strengthen ourselves to continue our response to Our Lady's primary request (sanctification of daily duty) for yet another month.

The interview led to a "pledge" to include the essential requests of Our Lady:

1)   To sanctify one's daily duty by making the Morning Offering and remembering it in moments of temptation;

2)   To wear the Scapular as a sign of consecration to Our Lady's Immaculate Heart, imitating the virtues it signifies;

3)   To say the Rosary daily (5 decades) with attention to the Mysteries;

4)   To renew our purpose monthly, by the devotion of the Five First Saturdays.[2]

The Appearance of Our Lady

In that interview of 1946, I asked Lucia about the appearance of Our Lady. I showed her various pictures, asking which most resembled the vision. She *rejected all* the pictures as inadequate.

Father Thomas McGlynn, O.P., an accomplished sculptor, was asked by Bishop da Silva to do the monumental marble statue now in the niche on the front of the Basilica at Fatima. To do this Father McGlynn was privileged to meet with Lucia day after day as he worked on a clay model.

Perhaps far more important than the great and beautiful statue which Father McGlynn sculpted is the book he wrote describing these meetings with Lucia. Try as he would to change the image to suit her desires, it was never enough. In the end, she squeezed the clay of Our Lady's face in absolute frustration as though wanting to reduce it to nothing. *It seemed impossible to reproduce in words or clay the actual beauty which Lucia and her cousins had seen.* That is why she spoke of it so little, or almost not at all.

One of the highlights of my own visit with her in 1946 occurred in the following manner.

Just before my meeting with her, Bishop da Silva had told me of two recent apparitions Lucia had. Since they were not contained in the Memoirs, I asked her about them. She seemed surprised by what the Bishop had told me and said she was not permitted to speak about anything except what had happened in 1917.

"Well, Sister," I said, "could you tell me whether I understood the Bishop correctly?" She hesitated a moment, and then said quietly, "yes."

"Sister," I then asked, "when Our Lady appears to you now, does She appear the same as She did in 1917?" At that moment (and it was the *only* such moment in four hours!) she seemed to forget my presence. With a wistful expression which would be difficult to describe she almost whispered:

"Yes, yes... always the same."

At that moment I had some slight understanding of the great loneliness she must have been almost continually feeling when not seeing Our Lady... *the loneliness that caused all three children to want to die so that they could "see Her always"*... and which caused Lucia to explain that when she learned she had to remain on earth to learn to read and write, it was *"like a sword piercing my heart."*

She was to remain, and on May 13, 1967, Pope Paul VI had her come from her Carmel in Coimbra and stand at his side before a crowd of a million people, thus publicly affirming his belief, and the belief of the Church in general, in all that Lucia was left on earth "to write" in order that the will of God might be fulfilled to *"establish devotion to the Immaculate Heart of Mary in the world."*

The 1929 Vision

As we have already said, again on May 13, 1982, she was at Fatima when Pope John Paul II came there to fulfill a request Our Lady had made to Lucia in the convent at Tuy on June 13, 1929. In a letter which she had written to the Holy Father (Pope Pius XII), Lucia describes that vision in the following words:

"Suddenly the whole chapel was illumined by a supernatural light, and a cross of light appeared above the altar, reaching to the ceiling.

"In a bright light at the upper part of the cross could be seen the face of a man and his body to the waist (*Father*), on his breast there was a dove also of light (*Holy Spirit*) and nailed to the cross was the body of another man (*Son*).

"Somewhat above the waist, I could see a Chalice and a large Host suspended in the air, onto which drops of blood were falling from the face of Jesus crucified and from the wound in His side. These drops ran down onto the Host and fell into the Chalice. Our Lady was beneath the right arm of the cross (it was Our Lady of Fatima with Her Immaculate Heart within a crown of thorns and flames). Under the left arm of the cross, large letters, as of crystal clear water which ran down over the altar, formed the words *Grace and Mercy.*

"I understood that it was the Mystery of the Most Holy Trinity which was shown to me, and I received lights about this Mystery which I am not permitted to reveal.

"Our Lady then said to me:

"*'The moment has come when God asks the Holy Father, in union with all the bishops of the world, to make the consecration of Russia to my Heart, promising to save it by this means.'*"

Why the Delay?

Eleven years later when the Collegial Consecration had not yet been made, writing to her confessor on July 15, 1940, Lucia expressed her concern and sorrow:

"*As for the consecration of Russia to the Immaculate Heart of Mary... it will be done, but not for the moment. God wants it this way for now to punish the world for*

Above: The words "Graces and Mercy" flowed like water.
Our Lady said that NOW was the time for the collegial
consecration of Russia to Her Immaculate Heart and for
the first Saturday Communions of reparation.

its crimes. We deserve it. Afterwards He will listen to our humble prayers. I am really sorry that it was not done. In the meantime so many souls are being lost!"

Lucia wrote again on August 18, 1940:

"The Holy Father will not do it yet. Our good Lord could through some prodigy show clearly that it is He who asks for it, but He takes this opportunity to punish the world with His Justice for so many crimes and to prepare it for a more complete turn towards Him."

Pope John Paul II Called for the Memoirs

On May 13, 1981, precisely at the time of the apparition of Our Lady of Fatima, an assassin's bullet tore into the body of Pope John Paul II as he was blessing a crowd in Saint Peter's Square. At that same moment the Pope felt a special protection of Our Lady.

In the weeks which followed, as he lingered between life and death in the Gemelli Hospital in Rome, *the Pope asked for Lucia's Memoirs.* It was Mother Mary Ludovica, National Secretary for the Blue Army in Italy, who took the manuscripts to the Holy Father in the hospital.[3] The following March (1982), a letter went from the Vatican to every bishop in the world, enclosing copies of the Acts of Consecration of the World *and of Russia* to Mary's Immaculate Heart and informing the bishops that *on the following May 13, 1982, His Holiness, in spiritual union with them, would renew these consecrations at Fatima.*[4]

That day Lucia met at length with the Holy Father. She explained to His Holiness that in order to completely fulfill the desires of Our Lord, the bishops of the world should *join* with the Pope in this Act of Consecration.

The following September, at a Synod of Bishops in Rome, the Pope renewed the Acts of Consecration and spoke to the bishops of his intention to renew this consecration again. And on December 8 of that year

Above:

Much of the world first learned of Fatima when, in October of 1942, 25th anniversary of the Miracle of Fatima, Pope Pius XII responded to the appeal from Lucia by consecrating the world, with an oblique mention of Russia, to the Immaculate Heart of Mary.

This solemn event, captured in the photo above, was broadcast on Vatican Radio (note microphones) in addition to being recorded in the Acts of the Holy See.

At the extreme left is Cardinal Montini, who succeeded Pius XII and who renewed the consecration in the presence of the entire Vatican Council in 1964.

In 1982 Pope John Paul II sent a copy of the consecration, plus a later specific consecration of Russia made by Pius XII in 1952, to all the Bishops of the world in preparation for the collegial act which was finally accomplished on March 25, 1984.

(1983), His Holiness again wrote to all the bishops of the world, this time *asking them to join with him* on the following March 24-25, 1984 in the renewal of the Acts of Consecration.

Was Lucia's mission finally complete?

In the apparition of July 13, 1917, Our Lady had said *She would come back* to ask for the consecration of Russia to Her Immaculate Heart. As we have said Our Lady came to ask for the consecration of Russia on June 13, 1929. During that vision Our Lady said:

"The moment has come in which God asks the Holy Father, in union with all the bishops of the world, to make the consecration of Russia to my Immaculate Heart, promising to save it by this means. There are so many souls whom the justice of God condemns for sins committed against me that I have come to ask reparation: sacrifice yourself for this intention and pray."

Collegial Consecration

It was in 1929 that Our Lord promised the conversion of Russia when there would be a collegial consecration of that nation to the Immaculate Heart of Mary. Over a period of more than half a century one Pope after the other (five times in all) made the act of consecration, but without first asking all the Bishops of the world to join with him. Only on March 25, 1984, was the consecration finally made in that way as Our Lord required.

We recall once again that, when asked why all the previous consecrations (made without participation of all the world's Bishops) had not sufficed, Lucia answered that Our Lord insisted on the collegial act of consecration (i.e., consecration of Russia by the Holy Father together with ALL the Bishops of the world) because:

"I want My entire church to know that this favor (the conversion of Russia) was obtained through

the Immaculate Heart of My Mother so that it may extend this devotion *later on* and put the devotion to this Immaculate Heart beside the devotion to My Sacred Heart" (Letter of Lucia, May 18, 1936... emphasis added).[5]

In July 1981, Pope John Paul II *did personally experience a prodigy* when he was on the brink of death following the attempt on his life on May 13, 1981. His Holiness then made the Collegial Act of Consecration on May 13, 1982, at Fatima, and again on March 25, 1984, in Rome. *His Holiness urged renewal of this consecration in all dioceses and parishes of the world.*

Pleasing To The Two Hearts

Concerning the importance of diocesan and parish consecration, in a letter of December 1, 1940, Lucia had written to a religious superior:

"I was so pleased at the inspiration you had for the renewal of the consecration of all dioceses and parishes to the Immaculate Heart of Mary. This very much pleases Our Lord and the Heart of our heavenly Mother." Lucia added:

"They (Our Lord and Our Lady) frequently complain about the sinful life of the majority of people, even of those who call themselves practical Catholics. Above all, They complain very much about the lukewarm, indifferent and extremely comfortable life of the majority of the priests and members of the religious congregations. The number of souls He meets through sacrifice and an intimate life of love is extremely small and limited."[6]

The acts of Collegial Consecration seem to give Our Lady special power to help souls... to crush Satan and to turn back the tidal wave of evil. For the last consecration made by the Holy Father after notification to all the bishops of the world on March 24 and 25, 1984, the Holy Father had the statue of Our Lady of Fatima flown from Fatima to Rome. This was the same statue which Pius XII had crowned on May 13, 1946, proclaiming Our Lady of Fatima "Queen of the World."

After he accompanied the statue in solemn procession across St. Peter's Square and finally to the "confessional" over Saint Peter's tomb, the Pope joined with all the bishops of the world in that solemn and Collegial Act of Consecration... a solemn affirmation of Our Lady's Queenship and of Her *rights* over the Church and over all redeemed by the Cross.

It Will Be Late

Lucia commented to Our Lord that the Holy Father would probably not believe her unless He Himself would move the Pope with a special inspiration. Our Lord answered:

"The Holy Father. Pray very much for the Holy Father. He will do it, but it will be late. However, the Immaculate Heart of Mary will save Russia. It has been entrusted to her."

Lucia subsequently explained that the consecration of 1984 was "too late" to have prevented the spread of error from an atheist Russia throughout the entire world. *But it was not "too late" for the conversion of Russia.* As Moses was able to turn back the destruction of the people of Israel by his prayer, now those who believe *can turn back the annihilation of nations* in union with Our Lady as She intercedes for us before the throne of God in this terrible hour.

Lucia made clear, over and over, that *it was because of the world's failure to respond to the Message of Fatima that the Holy Father was not moved to make the Collegial Consecration sooner.* Several years before, Lucia had written in a letter to her confessor:

"In an intimate communication, Our Lord complained to me, saying:

"'They did not wish to heed My request. Like the King of France, they will repent and do it, *but it will be late. Russia will have already spread her errors throughout the world, provoking wars, and persecutions of the Church; the Holy Father will have much to suffer.'*"

As we have already explained, in 1942 Pope Pius XII consecrated the world to the Immaculate Heart, and in 1952 he consecrated Russia. These acts were renewed by Pope Paul VI in the Vatican Council on November 21, 1964, but the bishops *were not asked* to join in these consecrations.

Therefore, when on May 13, 1982, Pope John Paul II first renewed the consecration at Fatima "in spiritual union with all the bishops of the world" *after having sent them copies of the complete Acts of Consecration of the World (1942) and of Russia (1952)*, Sister Lucia said that it would have its effect, but for the prevention of nuclear war, the effect would depend on the response of the world to this consecration.

The great fact and miracle of Fatima must awaken the world to a realization of Our Lady's very words:

"War is a punishment for sin... error will spread from an atheist Russia through the entire world... several entire nations will be annihilated..."

"Now is the time," said Our Lady as She appeared beneath the cross, while from the pierced hand of Her Son there flowed down "like water" the words:

"Grace and Mercy."

"Now is the time."

✝✝✝

---

1. *Dear Bishop!*, p. 6.

2. *Dear Bishop!*, Chapter 3

309.

3. Mother Mary Ludovica, foundress of the Sister Oblates of the Immaculate Heart of Mary, personally confirmed this fact to the author.

4. It is important to note that there were two separate documents from the Acts of the Holy See, each several pages long. *The second was specifically the consecration of Russia* (so named). All the Bishops of the world were again informed on Dec. 8, 1983, that the Pope asked them to join with him the following March 25, 1984, in a renewal of these consecrations. There is no doubt that the latter act was collegial and Russia was included. The Pope did not see a need to mention the name again. Indeed it seemed more appropriate to specify "those nations for whom this act is especially intended" (which all the Bishops of the world knew specifically included Russia) so that it included all those nations to which militant atheism had spread in the more than 50 years since this collegial consecration had been requested.

5. *Documentos*, p. 415.

6. *Documentos*, p. 439.

7. The Intelligence Officer was Vincent Allen. Retired in Melbourne, Florida, he reported this in *Florida Today*, Dec. 28, 1991, p. 11a.

House of Lucia's Parents

Father John De Marchi with Sister Lucia in 1946 in Fatima. Sister Lucia was than a Dorothean sister.

Chapter XXVI.

Comments On

RESPONSE TO THE FATIMA REQUEST

As was said before, when the "formula" (now known as the "Blue Army Pledge") was prepared under the direction of Lucia in July 1946, and the very next day presented to the Bishop of Leiria/Fatima for his approval, the Bishop responded in these solemn words:

"You may promulgate this as coming from me."

It was Lucia herself who, in the parlor of the Dorothean Convent on the outskirts of Porto in 1946, spelled out precisely *the fundamental requests* of Our Lady which must be fulfilled to bring about the triumph of Her Immaculate Heart.

The foundation on which the World Apostolate of Fatima is built is that simple pledge. This is what Catholics all over the world are asked to do. This is their essential commitment as members of "the Blue Army." More than twenty-five million around the world have made that commitment.

Example of the Children

The other requests of Our Lady are all tied to that basic pledge out of which develops, almost of necessity, the spiritual "cells" of holiness, the second — or next higher degree — of Blue Army membership. This spirituality of the Blue Army cells, as Father Joachim Alonso of Madrid has so beautifully expressed, is *"the spirituality of Fatima as evidenced in the lives of the children whom Our Lady Herself instructed."*

It might be said that the first Bishop of Leiria/ Fatima, the most Reverend Jose Correia da Silva, was the real founder of The Blue Army. It was he who had the inspiration and, above all, the courage to evaluate the pledge at a time when the essential conditions of Our Lady of Fatima had not yet been specified, and to say with all the authority of the Bishop of the place of the apparitions:

"You may promulgate this as coming from me."

Was there anyone more concerned in the development of the Blue Army than this venerable prelate? How could we forget that during the last months of his life, the very first question he asked his secretary each morning was:

"What new development is there today about the Blue Army?"

Indeed his interest in the apostolate was so great that I remember begging Our Lady that he would live to see the building of the Blue Army International Center in which he seemed even more interested than the completion of the buildings at the Shrine itself (although this could be a subjective exaggeration on my part).

Certainly one of the most memorable days in the history of the Blue Army was when the old Bishop in a wheelchair, pushed and guided by Bishop Venancio who was to be his successor, crossed the Cova behind the Basilica to bless the cornerstone of the Blue Army International Center and to preside at the corner-stone ceremony during which Monsignor Harold Colgan and Father John Loya (a Byzantine priest) sealed the stone. (I cannot refrain from recalling here with joy that I was privileged to add a bit of the mortar.)

Importance of the Scapular

Some people felt that the introduction of the Brown Scapular into the "formula" was unnecessary. The Blue Army in France wanted to substitute the Miraculous Medal, but the Bishop of Fatima replied that it was the Brown Scapular of Mount Carmel "and no other" which is the preferred sign of consecration to Mary's Immaculate Heart.

Doubt persisted. On August 15, 1950, the Very Reverend Father Howard Rafferty, O. Carm., Provincial of the Third Order of Carmelites in the United States, was delegated by the prior General of the Carmelite Order to interview Lucia on this point. During the interview he remarked that "some books on Fatima do not make a mention of the Scapular as part of the message." Lucia replied:

"Oh, but they are wrong!" Then Father Rafferty asked why Our Lady appeared as Our Lady of Mount Carmel. And Lucia answered:

"Our Lady wants everyone to wear it. As the Holy Father said, the Scapular is the sign of our consecration to the Immaculate Heart of Mary."[1]

Father Rafferty then inquired if the Scapular was necessary in order to fulfill the Message of Fatima. When Lucia said it was, he asked:

"Would you say that it is *as necessary* as the Rosary?" Lucia answered:

"The Rosary and the Scapular are inseparable."[2]

Perhaps the reluctance of many to accept the Scapular and the Rosary as important to the turning back of the tide of evil in the world is because they are such *simple* devotions. Even some prominent clergymen have expressed contrary views and called these devotions "irrelevant."

In the Memoirs themselves Lucia never mentioned the Scapular. Obviously this is one of the reasons she was to remain on earth — because the fullness of the

Message would only gradually be revealed. In traveling around the world several times with the second Bishop of Fatima, I was impressed that His Excellency found it difficult to speak on the Message in less than an hour because he did not want to leave out any one of these important parts of Our Lady's Message.

Invariably His Excellency would add that it was not so difficult to believe that Our Lady could convert Russia and bring peace to the world *as it was to believe that for such simple things She would obtain this triumph of Her Immaculate Heart!*

He gave the example of the Syrian general who had leprosy and went to a prophet in Israel to be cured. When the great man was told simply "to bathe in the river" he became indignant and was going to return home. His servants insisted that since he had come so far should he not do the simple thing the prophet had asked? If the prophet had asked their master to do something *great and difficult,* would he not have done it? Finally persuaded, the Syrian general descended from his carriage and entered the River Jordan. Instantly he was miraculously healed so that his flesh "became like that of a baby."

Bishop Venancio pointed out that the Blue Army Pledge is literally little more than bathing in the River Jordan "*where we are.*" The Scapular and the Rosary are such simple sacramentals, *easily at hand.* Does it seem possible that two such simple devotions would obtain the spiritual strength to live up to the duties of our daily life and to enter into the full Sacramental life of Jesus?

We can certainly believe this as we witness the *wave of holiness* we have seen in the wake of this apostolate around the world. Who would have dreamed of a day when tens of thousands around the world would spend entire nights in prayer before the Blessed Sacrament? And yet that is what we are witnessing in the wake of this apostolate.

Abraham asked the Lord whether Sodom and Gomorrah would be spared if ten such persons were found in the city. God answered that He would spare the cities if just ten persons were found.

In the wake of the World Apostolate of Fatima (The Blue Army), a literal wave of holiness is sweeping across the world to counteract the tide of evil, and in city after city hundreds are now making All-Night Vigils especially on the first Friday-Saturday.

Avoiding the Chastisement

When Our Lady spoke of "several entire nations" *not* being annihilated if her requests were heard, can we not hope that instead of a nuclear winter we shall indeed have a nuclear peace? We cannot "take back" the atom bomb. We cannot restore into oblivion our knowledge of the power of the atom, or the technique of harnessing it into a force sufficiently destructive to wipe out all life on earth.

Everything is possible with God. The miracle of Fatima, so much like a nuclear explosion (which caused all who saw it to think that it was the *end of the world)* ended in a triumph of faith and joy. At almost the last moment, when the crowd at the Cova da Iria at Fatima on that October 13, 1917, thought they were about to be destroyed, the great ball of fire *gathered back into itself* and rose into the sky.

Suddenly the sun was shining clearly. The surrounding earth and even the garments of the people were instantly dried. And to think that this great miracle was performed in our own century: "so that *everyone may believe!*"

As we pointed out before, Lucia does not describe the miracle in the Memoirs because during the twelve minutes that this incredible event was taking place she was seeing a series of visions: the Holy Family, Our Lady of Sorrows, and Our Lady of Mount Carmel.

Science and the Church intervened to confirm what happened.

Thirteen years later, when the investigations were complete, on October 13, 1930, the Bishop of Leiria/Fatima declared that the miracle and the visions of the children at Fatima were "worthy of belief." Literally thousands of pages of testimony had been taken. But the Bishop chose quite simply to state that the miracle had occurred "as described in the secular press." His Excellency declared:

This phenomenon, which no astronomical observatory registered and which therefore was not natural, was witnessed by persons of all categories and of all social classes, believers and unbelievers, journalists of the principal Portuguese newspapers, and even by persons some miles away — facts which annul any explanation of collective illusion.[3]

Miracle Without Precedent

Also as we have said before, perhaps if those people on the mountain at Fatima in 1917 had known what an atomic explosion was, they might not have called the miracle "a miracle of the sun" but rather an "atomic miracle!" A ball of fire was so hot and so bright that they thought it was the sun. Yet it could not have been the sun.

It was no more than two miles above the earth, seen up to a distance of only 32 miles. A few who saw it were so filled with faith that they were not afraid even though they thought it was the end of the world. But most were terrified. Some fainted. *All* the dozens upon dozens of witnesses whom I interrogated when I wrote a book about this phenomenon said that *they thought it was the end of the world.*

Every "hypothesis" offered by scientists makes natural explanation impossible. There is nothing gentle about this miracle! It was of terrifying awe-

317.

someness. If we put ourselves in the place of the witnesses we might ask:

"How would I feel if I were convinced, *at this moment the world was about to end?*"

People wept, knelt in the mud, cried their sins aloud, pleaded for mercy. Yes, this happened! This writer looked into the eyes and listened to the voices of dozens upon dozens of witnesses — and has seen and heard the fear in their eyes and in their voices.

But perhaps what a frightened atomic age should note particularly about this miracle, this very special sign from God to this age, is that just as the crowd expected to be destroyed, *it was suddenly spared.* Even the discomfort experienced for hours in a cold, pelting rain was suddenly lifted. Their anguish and fear was instantly transformed into a great joy of the "supernatural."

If the Message of Fatima is "terrible," it is also filled *with the greatest hope* that the atomic age could also have. If this Message... which Lucia was left on earth to give to the world... is fulfilled, there will be "an era of peace." After Pope John Paul II went to Fatima on May 13 to make the collegial consecration, we wondered whether that would now mean that Russia was about to be converted and an era of triumph about to begin.

As was explained in the last chapter, Lucia said "the consecration will have its effect, but it is too late..." *There has been a tidal wave of evil and a proliferation of nuclear weapons. If we are now to avoid nuclear war, "The Blue Army will have much to do."*

†††

318.

1. The importance of the scapular as a sign of consecration to the Immaculate Heart was also revealed at Pellevoisin in 1876. In these apparitions, which were finally approved by the Church in 1983, Our Lady spoke of the Scapular as "My livery and that of My Son." Kissing the small Scapular that Our Lady wore in the apparitions (upon which the living Heart of Jesus appeared) the visionary experienced an ineffable sensation of union with the Heart of Jesus through and with the Immaculate Heart of His Mother. See Haffert's: *Her Glorious Title.*

2. This statement by Fr. Rafferty was verified by him shortly before his death in 1990. When this statement (after many years) was called into question, the celebrated Carmelite exclaimed:
"But I am absolutely sure of each word. I wrote it down at once," and he referred to a tape recording made at the time. Furthermore these words to Fr. Rafferty were published in *Sign of Her Heart*, a book *translated into Portuguese in Lucia's own Carmel.* Indeed the book was actually published in Portugal at the request of the Coimbra Carmel.

3. *Meet the Witnesses*, AMI Press, 1961

Extreme left: Canon Galamba and John Haffert with group at Lucia's house visiting her sister (extreme right), Maria dos Anjos.

Chapter XXVII.

Comments On

WHAT IS BEING DONE

On December 10, 1925, Our Lady appeared with the Child Jesus in Lucia's tiny room in the Dorothean convent in Pontevedra in fulfillment of the promise she made in 1917 to "come back" and ask for the devotion of the Five First Saturdays. Lucia speaks of herself in the third person as she describes the apparition:

"On December 10, 1925, the most holy Virgin appeared to her. By her side, elevated on a luminous cloud was a Child. The most holy Virgin rested Her hand on her shoulder. As She did so, She showed her a Heart encircled by thorns which She was holding in Her other hand. At the same time, the Child said:

"'Have compassion on the Heart of your most holy Mother, covered with thorns, with which ungrateful men pierce it at every moment, and there is no one to make an act of reparation to remove them.'

"Then the most holy Virgin said:

"'Look, my daughter, at my Heart, surrounded with thorns with which ungrateful men pierce it at every moment by their blasphemies and ingratitude. You at least try to console me and say that I promise to assist[1] at the hour of death, with the graces necessary for salvation, all those who, on the first Saturday of five consecutive months, shall confess, receive Holy Communion, recite five decades of the Rosary, and keep me

company for fifteen minutes while meditating on the mysteries of the Rosary, with the intention of making reparation to me.'"

Before we go further, I should like to remark on the great intimacy of Our Lady and Our Lord in this First Saturday apparition which took place in a tiny room almost filled by a bed leaving an open space only three feet wide.

In that close area the Holy Child was elevated next to His Mother so that His Eyes were level with Hers. It was thus comfortable for Lucia to gaze at both Mother and Child.

As Jesus appealed for reparation to the thorn-pierced Heart of Mary, *Our Lady reached out and put Her hand lovingly on Lucia's shoulder.*

Perhaps we may say: "Oh, she was a saintly nun. She deserved such a sign of Our Lady's affection." But does not this gesture speak to each of us of Our Lady's loving nearness, Her Motherly caresses every time we may kiss Her Scapular or say Her Rosary? Jesus said to Lucia:

"Have compassion on the Heart of your most holy Mother!"

This is our loving, intimate Mother given to us by Jesus from the Cross, offering us Her Heart.[2]

Is it not touching that Jesus, standing so close to His Mother and pleading that the thorns be removed from Her pierced Heart, should urge compassion on "*your* most holy Mother?"

How intimately we are bound with Him in "our" Mother's Immaculate Heart! Not content with giving Himself in the Eucharist He also gives us His Mother as truly our Mother also.

This apparition of the Five First Saturdays is the most intimate of any apparitions of this importance. And this special message for all the world was linked with the prevention of a chastisement (announced ten years before it happened).

321.

In most apparitions there is a distance between the Queen of Heaven and those seeing Her, as in the earlier apparitions of Fatima and those of La Salette, Lourdes, Pontmain, Pellevoisin, Beauraing, Banneux, Akita, and others. An exception would be that of St. Catherine Laboure who approached Our lady as She was seated in a chair and then knelt and rested her hands in Our Lady's lap.

This apparition at Pontevedra seems to convey that Our Lady is indeed my real, loving Mother. As St. Therese said, seeing in the strings of the Scapular Her embracing, protecting arms: "More a Mother than a Queen." She has stooped from Heaven again and again, always an anxious and loving Mother. But now as She places Her arm around Lucia, Her Divine Son, who has entrusted to Her the peace of the world, presents Her to us with a most plaintive appeal:

"Have COMPASSION on the Heart of your most holy Mother, covered with thorns by ungrateful men."

Our Mother suffers because every person is Her child. Billions of them are in danger of the destruction man has prepared for himself before She can muster enough of Her devoted and believing children to help Her bring a wave of Merciful Divine Grace to drive back the tide of evil.

Jesus does not ask us to have compassion on ourselves and on our children as, foreseeing the destruction of Jerusalem, He did on the way to Calvary. He asks us to have compassion on the thorn-pierced Heart of our loving, anxious Mother in whose Heart *are reflected the needs of each and every one on earth,* including most especially those who do not know Jesus and those in danger of being lost.

When St. Catherine Laboure looked up into Our Lady's eyes in the chapel of the Rue du Bac she was amazed to see tears forming there while Our Lady spoke of the Divine chastisement made necessary by the sins of men. Then Our Lady was transformed and appeared on a golden globe crushing the serpent. In Her hands She held a smaller globe. She said it represented "each person in particular." She held the globe over Her Heart.

Each one of us in particular is in the loving Hands and Heart of our Heavenly Mother. She came at Fatima *carrying the golden globe around Her neck as She revealed Her Immaculate Heart* and said:

"I will come back to ask for the consecration of Russia to My Immaculate Heart and for the Communion of Reparation on the First Saturdays."

Now, ten years later at Pontevedra, She is keeping that promise.

She comes to tell us exactly what reparation will suffice to mitigate the merited chastisement. She explains the four practices to be performed on five consecutive First Saturdays.

Apparition Room Spared

It was remarked earlier that the convent of the apparitions in Pontevedra had been abandoned because termite destruction was apparent everywhere, especially throughout the wooden floors, door jambs, window sills.

Not having had experience with termite damage, when I became the person responsible for the building I thought it would be just a matter of replacing some beams and putting in new floors. It was a sad shock when the Dean (who represented the Archbishop of Santiago) informed us that no patchwork was possible. He had had to renovate other buildings in the same area and the only solution was to remove the roof, gut the entire stone structure and completely rebuild the interior.

That meant the complete destruction of the little room of this important, intimate apparition of the Immaculate Heart of Mary with Her Divine Child. I could not bring myself to this. I decided that whoever succeeded me would have to do it, sad that so holy a place should be falling into ever greater ruin.

Not long afterwards a doctor's wife in Chicago had a dream of a convent in Spain falling into ruins and that she should contact me. When I received her call I thought she wanted to contribute to the purchase of the convent and told her no further contribution for that was needed. "But," she said, "I understand that I am to send money for its repair." The amount she offered was far too small for the work but it gave me an idea: to ask permission of the Dean of Pontevedra for permission to make temporary repairs so the convent could be used at least for a few years until the major repairs might be undertaken.

The permission was granted. And, having myself seen other termite damage in old buildings of Pontevedra and convinced that rebuilding would ultimately be necessary, I tremble today to think with what almost careless abandon I ordered one wall of the apparition room torn down, opening it into a larger room. (That is now a chapel and the actual room of the apparition is the sanctuary.)

Although nothing had been done to exterminate the termites in the years since the convent was abandoned, the termites had left. And when the workmen began the "temporary" repairs they found that all structural beams of the building were not only intact but showed no sign of termites. To our further astonishment, exactly the amount of money given by the woman who had the dream covered the entire rehabilitation of the convent.

In the years which followed, the building was improved with accommodations for pilgrims. The furnishings of the chapel of Tuy [3], place of the vision in which Our Lady asked for the collegial consecration of Russia to Her Immaculate Heart, were brought to Pontevedra and placed in the main chapel.

Now both of these important apparitions are commemorated at Pontevedra. They are the two visions in which Our Lady fulfilled Her promise after foretelling the chastisements which would befall the world: "To prevent this I shall come to ask for the consecration of Russia to My Immaculate Heart and the Communion of reparation on the First Saturdays.[4]

When the repairs at Pontevedra were finished the Dean, who had personally overseen the work with utter amazement, literally jumped up and down on the upper floor and said: "This building is now forever!"

We used so much space to tell about this not only to give personal witness but most of all because it gives us the impression that God wanted us to have this lasting memorial of a vision so personal and meaningful to each and every one of us.

The urgency and plaintiveness of this apparition became even more apparent two months after the vision in the little room. It was February 26, 1926.

The convent cesspool had no connection with the sewer in the street outside the garden gate. Lucia had been told to empty it.

She was carrying the filthy, smelly waste by bucket. So little is said of herself in the memoirs that we would certainly not have known that she was given this kind of work were it not for the apparition which took place. One is reminded of the life of Bernadette of Lourdes in the convent of Nevers.

Lucia had to go back and forth between the cesspool and the trap in the street. A little boy came along and paused at the gate. He was silent and sad, watching Lucia.

"Don't you have anyone to play with?" she finally asked.

The little fellow seemed to reply only by his sadness.

"Do you know the Hail Mary?"

Still there was the same air of sadness that tugged at her heart. But she had her duties to fulfill. What could she do to console him?

"Why don't you go around the corner," she suggested, "to the Church of St. Mary Major and ask Our Lady to give you the Child Jesus to keep you company?"

At that the little boy was transformed. She suddenly saw Him as He had appeared up in her little room two months before when He appeared with His Mother and said: "Have compassion on the Heart of your Mother" and then stood at His Mother's side as She appealed for Communions of reparation on the First Saturdays.

It was Jesus. And although transformed, He was still sad as He asked:

"What is being done to promote the devotion to the Immaculate Heart of My Mother in the world?"

Pausing in astonishment from her lowly work, struck by the same sadness, Lucia answered:

"I told the Mother Superioress and she said there was nothing she could do." The Holy Child replied:

"Of herself, no. But with My Grace she can do it all."

May those words of the Child Jesus at Pontevedra echo in our hearts as we come to the end of these pages. "What is being done?"

We have read of the extraordinary sacrifices of the little children of Fatima. What is asked of us is so simple and so little by comparison!

The response necessary to bring the world into the era of peace without the need for a "Divine Correction" or chastisement remains always the same: Repentance, reparation. But the wonder of Fatima is something new: We are given specific means of repentance and reparation.

The repentance is the sanctification of daily actions. And many will succeed in making it if they wear the Scapular and say the Rosary.

The reparation is the First Friday-First Saturday devotion to the Hearts of Jesus and Mary. This cries out for more attention. After the privilege of reading the original words of Lucia and of Our Lord and Our Lady, how will we respond?

We began to reply with a few chapters but realized that this is far too important to be dismissed by a simple statement or even a chapter or two. Therefore this book has a sequel titled *To Prevent This*. The title is taken from Our Lady's own words when She told of the terrible afflictions which were about to befall mankind and said: "To prevent this, I shall come to ask..."

So far only one of the afflictions She came to prevent has not yet befallen the world: "Several entire nations will be annihilated." And we may presume that this last is the most important of all since none of the others were prevented.

Personal opinions are of little importance, but after my interview with Lucia in 1946 I was convinced that this last prophecy is the one most to be prevented. When I asked what she thought would happen next (and I had in mind a nuclear war) she said she thought the next thing that would happen would be the collegial consecration and the "conversion" of Russia. (This statement will be found in my book *Russia Will Be Converted* written in 1948.) And that left the threat of nuclear war AFTER the changes in Russia. I do not say this is what Lucia meant. It was my impression.

In the sequel we look more closely at what we now feel reasonably sure is what Our Lady meant by the term "conversion" of Russia and why we can believe that the "annihilation of several entire nations" may be a part of the 1960 secret of Fatima and is still to happen if Our Lady's requests are not heard.

The critical time following dissolution of the Soviet Union is the urgent time for the First Saturday Communions of reparation.

327.

May Her Own Words, in themselves and as reflected in the lives of the innocent children to whom She appeared, persuade us without delay to respond to Our Lady's merciful desire to save the world from a chastisement by fire which would be "worse than the deluge."

God's Merciful Love has sent Her to prevent this.

How will each of us answer the plaintive question of Jesus:

"What is being done?"

The Third Secret

Only if there is an adequate world response now to the First Saturdays can the world avoid what may be in the 1960 secret but which is clearly revealed by Our Lady at Akita: Chastisement. There are some who feel that the world has some kind of right to know the contents of the last secret of Fatima.

But for the average person it is enough that four successive Popes have agreed one after another not to make it known. And the secret still serves a special purpose. It still attracts attention. It still says: "There remains more to the message of Fatima than you know." And apparently the Popes decided that if Our Lady wants the secret to be known She will make it known, *as may be the case in the tears and message of Akita.*

The Secret Remains

Seven years passed after Pope John XXIII opened the secret and decided not to make it public. Meanwhile the Church had been preoccupied with the second Vatican Council and many began to think that perhaps there had been no secret.

Everything about Fatima seemed in question. Recognizing the adverse effects of the long silence (since the world had been expecting the secret to be revealed in 1960). Pope Paul VI instructed the Cardinal Prefect of the Holy Office to call a press conference in Rome on February 11, 1972, to give an explanation.

What Is Important?

The Cardinal explained that the secret had indeed been opened by the Pope in 1960 but that after consultation with others (himself included) it was decided that the message was not to be made known to the general public.

"What is important," the Cardinal said, "is the part of the Fatima message already made public." To emphasize this, Pope Paul VI personally went to Fatima three months later under unusual circumstances. His Holiness had Lucia come from her Carmelite cloister and stand at his side as he reaffirmed before the world the importance of the Fatima events and message.

Question Remains

But the World continued to be haunted by the question of the secret. Did the Pope decide not to reveal it because it spoke of some terrible catastrophe? But what could be more terrible than the prophecies of Fatima already revealed: the second world war, further wars fomented by the spread of Communism through the world, persecutions and finally that "several entire nations will be annihilated?"

Father Alonso, greatest of the Fatima experts, deduces that the secret concerns a crisis in the Church. Others claim it refers to a cleansing of the world by chastisement if enough persons fail to cleanse it by reparation (and Father Alonso does not rule this out).

The answer, as we just said, may be found in the message of Our Lady at Akita, given on the anniversary of the miracle of Fatima (October 13) in 1973. The message speaks both of a crisis in the Church and of a chastisement "worse than the deluge."

It states that so far Our Lady has been able to hold back the chastisement (because of the response of a few generous souls and by offering the Passion of Her Son to the Father)... but that greater response is urgently needed.

†††

[1.] In Portuguese the word for assist as used here has the connotation of present aid, i.e., of presence.

[2.] We recall that when Catherine Laboure was taken to the chapel on the Rue du Bac in Paris by her guardian angel and saw Our Lady in the retreat master's chair, she instinctively ran up and knelt to rest her hands in Our Lady's lap. (In these Paris apparitions, too, Our Lady revealed Her Immaculate Heart next to the Sacred Heart of Jesus.)

[3.] Even the floor-to-ceiling arches which separated the main chapel from the sanctuary were transported to Pontevedra. Perhaps most important is the main altar over which the vision took place while the words "Grace and Mercy" flowed from the Hand of the Crucified Jesus "down over the altar." A part of the altar was also brought to the U.S. and is the main altar of the convent at the national center of the Blue Army in Washington, N.J.

[4.] The World Apostolate of Fatima (Blue Army) acquired this entire convent to make it a center of devotion to the Immaculate Heart of Mary. The room of the apparition has been converted into a chapel. The street has been renamed in honor of Lucia.

Oddly enough one will encounter critics (who seem to seek anything in the apparitions of Fatima with which to find fault) who say that the apparitions of Tuy and Pontevedra were never approved by the Church because they are in the Archdiocese of Santiago outside the jurisdiction of Fatima. But the Archbishop of Santiago personally blessed the two chapels in Pontevedra and approved the cult there. One is the chapel of the First Saturday apparitions and the other of the so called "final vision" which took place in nearby Tuy.

Above: In tears in Akita on October 13, 1973, (anniversary of the Fatima miracle) Our Lady foretold a chastisement of the world. When the Bishop of Akita (who approved the apparitions in 1984) was asked what message Our Lady was conveying to the world by Her miracles and messages, the Bishop said: "It is the message of Fatima."

Chapter XXVIII.

Comments On

THE UNANSWERED QUESTIONS

So many questions remain.

What else did the Cardinal Prefect of the Holy Office say in that press conference in Rome about the 1960 Fatima Secret? What happened to Arturo Santos, the unbeliever who jailed the three children of Fatima and threatened to kill them? What happened to the atheists who ruled Portugal at the time of the apparitions and who declared Lisbon to be the *Atheist capital of the world?*

The chilling answer to this last question is found in Costa Brochado's *Fatima in the Light of History.*[1] It should be especially meaningful to all practical atheists today, whether or not in Masonic lodges as those men were. Similar men have flocked into the spiritual vacuum of Eastern Europe.

Changes in Russia

What more do we know about the special love and concern of Our Lady for Russia?

Relative to this there is perhaps no more amazing story than that of the Icon of Kazan — an Icon so deeply involved in the entire history of Russia that it seems to represent the very *soul* of Russia. Recognizing this, Lenin's militant atheists destroyed the Basilica of Our Lady of Kazan on Red Square to prove once and for all to the Russian people that "there is no God."

How did the Icon of Kazan come to be enshrined in a Byzantine Chapel *at Fatima* in the International Center of the world Apostolate of Fatima (The Blue Army)? Part of the answer is in my own book, *Dear Bishop!.*

And why all these tantalizing questions?

Because there is much more to know than will be found in this book. Fatima is not something which "happened" in the past but which began in 1917 and continues now. In 1982, when Pope John Paul II called upon the Church to prepare for the year 2000 "with Mary" as an advent for the bimillennium of Christianity His Holiness said:

"Fatima is more urgent now than ever." On May 13, 1991, His Holiness added: "Fatima is the Marian Capital of the world."

The Pilgrim Virgin

One of the ongoing wonders of Fatima is the Pilgrim Virgin, in itself a major wonder of our time. Pope Pius XII said of the Pilgrim Virgin that it was "*as though Our Lady Herself went forth to claim Her Dominion* (as Queen of the World) and the favors She performs along the way are such that *we can hardly believe what we are seeing with our own eyes.*"

We get some idea of the scope of these favors when we learn that Canon Barthas (whose several books answer many interesting questions)[2] wrote an entire book on just one phenomenon of the statue of Our Lady as it traveled: *The Miracle of the Doves.* And after traveling the world for 45 years, in October of 1992 the Pilgrim Virgin was finally to arrive at Her destination: Russia!

What about the effect of the great Miracle of Fatima itself... the first miracle in history at a predicted time and place... upon Portugal as a nation? *Why have these events had so little press coverage outside Portu-*

gal? (These questions are addressed in the book *Meet the Witnesses.)*

We say all this because we hope that the reader will not finish reading *Her Own Words* and feel that that there is nothing more of importance to know about Fatima. Indeed, of so many more questions one of the most important must be: *What is being done, as Our Lord Himself asked Lucia* on February 15, 1921, *to make the Fatima message known throughout the world and to establish the devotion of the Five First Saturdays?* What chances are there that enough persons may respond in time to avoid the annihilation of nations?

Mohammedans

Archbishop Fulton Sheen raised another important question: Why did Our Lady choose the name *Fatima, the name of the daughter of Mohammed?* Is Bishop Sheen right when he says it was because Mohammedans are to be intimately involved in the "triumph" and in the "era of peace to mankind" promised at Fatima? Endeavoring to answer this I wrote the little book *Hand of Fatima.*

Is Our Lady of Fatima, as Paul VI seemed to say, the Woman of the Apocalypse? And what did Pius XII mean when he proclaimed Her Queen of the World in 1954 saying that *"in the doctrine and devotion of Mary's Queenship lies the world's greatest hope for peace?"* (The book exploring this question is *Who is the Woman of the Apocalypse?)*

Another important question concerns Our Lady of Mount Carmel. In the Memoirs we learn simply that Our Lady asked for consecration to Her Immaculate Heart and appeared at the climax of the October 13 Miracle as *Our Lady of Mount Carmel* holding the scapular out of the sky. From subsequent statements of Lucia we know that "Our Lady wants everyone to wear it" (the Scapular) and that "the Rosary and the Scapular are inseparable."

But why? From the Memoirs and interviews we know only the bare essentials.

To understand the importance of the Scapular of Our Lady of Mt. Carmel in the Message of Fatima it is necessary to read books like *Sign of Her Heart* and *Her Glorious Title.*

First Saturdays

And what about the First Saturdays? Suggested homilies are available from The Blue Army for priests to help the faithful with the necessary fifteen minutes of meditation. Many rosary aids are available, such as the book: *Sex and the Mysteries.*

For the First Friday-First Saturday vigils there is the book *Night of Love.* These all night vigils in honor of the Two Hearts could be the last weight in the balance of Justice and Mercy to enable to Sacred Hearts to prevent the great chastisement "now ready" (Our Lady's words at Akita) to fall upon the world.

Yet so few know that these vigils of reparation are taking place in churches often within traveling distance of their own homes. So few know what a beautiful and profound "experience" of the Hearts of Jesus and Mary such vigils prove to be. So few know...

Lucia, Our Lady's messenger, tells us what we must do. *It is up to us* to find out what is necessary in order *to do it* and to do it well. One book is not enough.

Devotion to the Pope

In *Her Own Words,* there are several references to the Pope: The Pope will have much to suffer... the Pope in union with all the Bishops of the world... the Pope is to place devotion to the Immaculate Heart of Mary alongside devotion to the Sacred Heart of Jesus.

Volumes could be written about the Popes and Fatima! There is an entire volume of 204 pages of what Pope John Paul II alone said during his visit to Portugal and Fatima in 1982. An entire book deals solely with the relationship of Pius XII to Fatima![3] Not only was this Pope consecrated a Bishop at the very time Our Lady first appeared at Fatima, but he accepted to be called "the Pope of Our Lady of Fatima."[4]

He saw a reenactment of the Miracle of the Sun[5] over the Vatican in the Holy Year of 1950. He decided to *close the Holy Year for all the world outside of Rome* in Fatima on the following October 13. In his address to Fatima on this occasion the Pope spoke of the almost incredible wonders of the Pilgrim Virgin.

Paul VI *mentioned Fatima in the Council* before *all the Bishops of the world* at perhaps the most solemn moment of the Council: Just after the proclamation of *Lumen Gentium.*[6] A year later this Pope went in person to Fatima at a time when it was extremely rare for the Pope to leave Rome.

John XXIII instituted the Feast of Our Lady of Fatima. Pope John Paul I, who reigned only a short time, answered to those who belittled Fatima as a "private revelation" saying:

"An article of faith contained in the Gospel is also the following: Signs will be associated with those who believe (Mark 16: 17)... I think I may lawfully be allowed to refer to the sign of October 13, 1917 to which even non-believers and anti-clericals bore witness."

As many pages as there are in this entire book could hardly contain all that Pope John Paul II said about Fatima. Many would say that he could be even more aptly called "the Pope of Fatima" than Pius XII.

Shelves are lined with books about Fatima in a variety of languages, and *each and every one* delves deeper into the dimensions of this divine intervention for the atomic age. Several of these books deal with the third secret showing that even *speculation about the secret* contributes to a deeper understanding of the importance of Fatima to the future of every man, woman and child on the face of the earth.

The "last word" was spoken back in 1967 by Cardinal Ottaviani in that press conference commanded by Pope Paul VI: "*What is important is the part of the Fatima Message already made public.* Nothing else is essential."

This book gives a summary of the *truths of Heaven* affirmed at Fatima for the atomic age... truths which can save us from nuclear destruction... truths which can lead us to "an era of peace for mankind." However, we cannot just close this book and feel that now we *know* all that is important! Consider just one single phrase of Jacinta concerning Our Lady and Her Immaculate Heart:

"*God has entrusted the peace of the world to Her.*"

What does that mean? Our Lady repeated almost the same words at Akita, in Japan, in 1973.[7] What is the significance of the almost shocking statement at Akita concerning a Divine chastisement: "*Only the Blessed Virgin can save you?*"

Fiery chastisement of "several entire nations" was emphasized by *miracles of blood and tears.* (See the authoritative book *Akita, The Tears and Message of Mary* by Fr. Teiji Yasuda, available from the 101 Foundation.)

Surely only God can perform miracles and only God can save. Why would God delegate such powers to Mary? And even if He has, why has He chosen to make this known to us now?

What is the official view of the Church... conveyed by the Popes especially in the Marian Years of 1954 and 1987-88? Does not just that *one* phrase cry out to each of us: *How little I know* of this great Message from Heaven in the atomic age, even though I may be an educated person! How ill-equipped I am to understand what God is saying to the world in *Her Own Words* and in the veritable wave of miracles which caused the Pope to exclaim: "*We can hardly believe what we are seeing with our eyes.*"

The Two Hearts

Then there are two other little phrases spoken by Our Lord when Lucia asked (under obedience) why He insisted on the collegial consecration of Russia to the Immaculate Heart of Mary to be followed by the conversion of Russia.

Our Lord answered first that it was because He wanted "*My entire Church to know* that this favor was obtained *through the Immaculate Heart of Mary*" (to whom He had entrusted the peace of the world!), and second: "*So that afterwards the Holy Father may place devotion to the Immaculate Heart of My Mother alongside devotion to My Own Sacred Heart.*"

In 1982 and again in 1984, Pope John Paul II made the collegial consecration. The following year His Holiness began to speak of the "Alliance of the Two Hearts" and became personally involved in a meeting of some of the top theologians of the Church which took place in Fatima in the Fall of 1986 and culminated in a week long seminar in Manila in 1987 at which Cardinal O'Connor of New York City was the Pope's legate.

The World Apostolate of Fatima (The Blue Army) was deeply involved in these events which opened a whole new dimension on the Alliance of the Hearts of Jesus and Mary and *how each of us* is called today to *enter into that Alliance.* Indeed, this is the deepest meaning of Fatima! It is the reason I wrote a sequel to this book (*To Prevent This!*).

††††

1. Costa Brochado was the secretary of the National Assembly of Portugal and his important book was published in Lisbon in 1948 by Portugalia Editora, titled *Fatima A Luz da Historia*. Unfortunately the English edition is out of print.

2. As we have mentioned before, Canon Barthas produced some of the very best books on Fatima. One of the most complete is *Fatima — 1917-1968*, published by Fatima Editions, Toulouse, France, 1969, 439 pages, including many historical pictures and 20 pages devoted to the history of the Pilgrim Virgin.

3. *Portugal, Message of Fatima*, St. Paul Editions, Daughters of St. Paul, Boston, MA 02130 (USA), c1983.

4. On June 4, 1951, Pius XII, speaking at the inauguration of a new church in Rome said: "This great date (May 13th) so important in our life, without our knowing it, was perhaps in the secret designs of providence to prepare us for an even more important date, that when the Lord wished to weigh upon our soldiers the care of the universal Church. At that very hour, on a mountain at Fatima, there occurred the first apparition of the White Queen of the Most Holy Rosary, as if the Mother of Mercy had wished to signify to us that these stormy times in which our Pontificate would unfold, in the midst of one of the greatest crises of world history, we would always have Her maternal and vigilant assistance as the great conqueror in all of God's battles to envelope us, protect us and guide us."

It was at the end of this sermon that someone present cried out spontaneously: "Long live the Pope of Fatima." And Pius XII, with a large smile answered to the entire throng: "That I am."

5. Pope Pius XII saw the sign of God: 30 and 31st of October, and 1st and 8th of November 1950 (see *L'Osservatore Romano* of October 13 and November 17, of 1951). For a time these miraculous occurrences were not made public, although the Pope shared them with some of the Cardinals. His Holiness decided to close the Holy Year of 1950 at Fatima for all the world outside of Rome. It was at the closing of this Holy Year on October 13, 1951, that Cardinal Tedeschini, the Pope's legate, made the prodigies public.

6. The importance of the action of Pope Paul VI is often overlooked. The Pope apparently had intended to convoke all of the Bishops in St. Mary Major the day after the Council closed, in order to renew the consecration of the world and of Russia to the

Immaculate Heart of Mary "in the presence of all the Bishops of the world." But many of the Bishops had already made their plans to return to their dioceses in different parts of the world and it was apparently for this reason that the Pope took this unprecedented action. But it must have been God's Will that this singular distinction (to have been mentioned in the Council itself) should have been given to the Fatima message, so important to the Church and to the world.

7. See the Pastoral Letter published by the Bishop of the Diocese of Niigata, Japan in SOUL Magazine, January-February 1987, p. 6. In his Pastoral Letter, declaring the events at Akita to be supernatural, the Bishop said he had made two trips to Rome to consult the Sacred Congregation of the Doctrine of the Faith and that were it not for the miraculous events surrounding Akita, it would be almost impossible for us to believe a message which conveyed such a serious warning to the world. Two ecclesiastical commissions of inquiry preceded the Bishop's Pastoral Letter of approval. When asked to summarize the message of Akita, the Bishop said simply: "It is the message of Fatima."

Below: Icon of Our Lady with Scapular and Rosary in Chapel at Blue Army International Center in Fatima.

Chapter XXIX.

Comments On

THE BATTLE CRY

Our Lady is the "Cause of our joy," and the final word is *hope.*

My most vivid final impression of Lucia was of a joyful person... a person really FULL of joy, even though the memoirs that we have just read tell of sacrifice and tears.

The voluntary sacrifices surprise us: little Jacinta, a gaping wound in her chest, dragging herself from bed to prostrate herself on the floor to repeat the Eucharistic prayer of the angel; cords worn tightly about the waist and piercing the skin so that Our Lady Herself had to tell them not to practice such a difficult penance without relief; days on end in the hottest time of the summer without a drop of water. Who could believe this of three little children... so anxious to prevent souls from falling into hell... so ready not only to offer their very lives, as they did in the prison of Ourem, but always seeking ways of pain and mortification because Our Lady said:

"So many souls are lost because there is NO ONE to pray and make sacrifice for them."

But all this was done in joy. Each of these sacrifices was an act of love. Each was to console "the Hidden Jesus" and to save souls. Perhaps even more difficult were the involuntary sacrifices.

When Lucia was publicly humiliated by the parish priest in front of everyone because she had not come when his sister had sent for her she accepted it all in silence, her heart torn by the threat that he would not give her Communion and that on a certain day... which was almost impossible for her... she was to come to him to confession. And she bore it all. Then, apparently inspired by Our Lady, a priest who witnessed this said that perhaps there was a reason she had not answered the priest's summons; perhaps she had an order from her mother. And only then was her humiliation mitigated... although the attitude of the priest remained unchanged.

Page After Heroic Page

She could have defended herself with a word. But she was silent. Imagine the effect on such a sensitive soul to be told by the priest that she was tricked by the devil and could go to hell! And the anguish of being commanded by her mother to admit she had lied and repeatedly beaten not just with the bottom of the broom but with the wooden handle! And this from a mother who had always been so tender and whom the little girl loved with all her heart.

Page after heroic page we read, in words so modest that they almost conceal the facts, of almost incredible sacrifice "in reparation for sin and in reparation for the offenses against the Immaculate Heart of Mary." What are those offenses? Jacinta herself said:

"Most souls go to hell because of sins of *impurity.*" Oh! What can save our world today in which so many souls are lost in the awful darkness of sins of impurity? And the darkness is so dense that these lost souls do not even recognize sin for sin.

Many even claim a RIGHT to sin: A right to abortion, a right to "birth control" by unnatural means, a right to do with their bodies as they please. Thus the sins of impurity become unforgivable sins against the Holy Spirit (see *The Meaning of Akita* by Haffert, 101 Foundation, p. 48).

Is there *anything*, any movement, any power which can dispel this darkness and save these millions of lost souls? Yes, there is one which according to Lucia bears the solemn promise of the triumph of the Immaculate Heart of Mary.

It was first called the "March of Pledges." The pledge in question contains the three essential conditions for the triumph of the Immaculate Heart of Mary in the world. No great sacrifice is entailed. Indeed it is so simple, so easy, that the Most Rev. John Venancio, successor to the first Bishop of Fatima, said that one of the greatest obstacles to the success of this apostolate is that it is difficult to believe that it *could* be so simple.

But we might add that this simple formula has an effect on many who make it... similar to the effect of the apparition of Our Lady on the children of Fatima. Many of them become heroic. It is a formula that works magic in souls away from the Sacraments.

For the Spiritually Crippled

It is a *formula* of conversion rather than catechism, of light for those in darkness rather than more light for those in light. It is for the spiritually crippled to whom Our Lady offers crutches of Scapular and Rosary and the solid ground of daily duty.

The World's Greatest Secret, a book on the reality and importance of the Eucharist, offers the metaphor of food on a table at the base of which starving people are too weak to reach up for the Saving Bread.

At Fatima Our Lady of the Eucharist holds down the chain of Her Rosary and the cords of Her Scapular to draw them up.

Catechism alone cannot do it. Preaching alone cannot do it. *Only Our Lady's simple devotions* are the magic formula. *The importance of these devotions was not only affirmed by Lucia,* Our Lady's messenger, *but more solemnly affirmed by the second Vatican Council: The two devotions to our Lady most to be fostered in the Church today are the Rosary and the Scapular of Mt. Carmel* (Pope Paul VI, speaking of Par. 67 of Lumen Gentium).

The magic formula is completed by the *primary purpose of these devotions: Sanctification of our daily duty.* Thus the starving people on the floor around the Eucharistic table receive not only chains and cords but nourishment.

Those in darkness receive not only light, but light to a specific path. The crippled are supplied not only with crutches but also solid ground beneath them. This formula of holiness is a masterpiece of Our Heavenly Mother which took almost 800 years to prepare. It was at the beginning of the 13th century that St. Dominic foresaw it and prophesied:

"One day, through the Rosary and the Scapular, Our Lady will save the world."[1]

Rallying Cry: Russia!

For fifty years the rallying cry of the apostolate of this formula of holiness had been "RUSSIA WILL BE CONVERTED." But now the Soviet Union is no more.

What will be the battle cry of Our Lady's apostles in the 21st century? How will they muster the spiritual forces needed before the danger of "annihilation of several entire nations" (predicted by Our Lady at Fatima) as tensions rise in the dissolving Soviet Empire and even small nations have or are acquiring nuclear bombs?

Perhaps Our Lady Herself gave us the ultimate battle cry with Her ultimate promise: "Finally Russia will be converted; My Immaculate Heart will triumph and *an era of peace will be granted to mankind."*

Many of the leaders of this apostolate, who began by making the simple pledge, now lead lives of great holiness. Thousands spend the night of first Friday-first Saturday in prayer before the Blessed Sacrament. Tens of thousands attend daily Mass for which they prepare by recitation of the Rosary. And will not their Victorious Queen inspire them, in rapidly succeeding events, with ever new battle cries?

Above all it is necessary to keep our eyes on the goal... and the specific means Our Lady has given to reach it. In very recent years some seemed to forget that the intention of Lucia and of those who first launched the original "March of Pledges" (which was later named the Blue Army and then "World Apostolate of Fatima") was to obtain commitment (from the greatest possible number) to fulfill the three basic conditions specified by Lucia for the triumph of Her Immaculate Heart. And now emphasis is on the First Saturday Communions of Reparation.

Think Of It!

In closing we recall the following words from the very first chapter of this book: I was tempted to call this book *Fatima And Nuclear War,* but greater than the terrible prophecy of "annihilation of several entire nations" is the secret's fantastic promise: If men listen to this message from Heaven, not only would the atheist leadership in Russia *be converted,* but there would be *"an era of peace."*

Think of it! Depending on the world's response to this message, the nuclear age could be one of destruction in which "the living will envy the dead," or of that peace of which the angels sang over Bethlehem.

✝✝✝

[1.] Historia C.P.G., by Ventimiglia, Naples, 1773, cf. Sign of Her Heart by Haffert, AMI Press, pp. 217-219.

Chapter XXX.

Comments On

H E R   F I N A L   W O R D S

In the beginning of this book, we stressed the importance of Lucia's own words relaying to us Our Lady's own words. *We pray that the final words of Lucia we are about to quote in this last chapter will resound around the world like rolling thunder.*[1]

After Stalin initiated a five year plan to eradicate the church in Russia, at least 80,000 clerics, monks and nuns were killed. Only about 300 churches remained open.[2] But following the collegial consecration of Russia in 1984, within 6 months more than 5,000 churches were reopened in the Soviet Union (106 in Moscow alone!). Baptisms tripled. Marriages increased ninefold. The number of monasteries went up from 18 to 121.[3]

As things were going in Russia and in the world in the early eighties, *who would have thought this possible?* Patriarch Aleksy II of Moscow, head of the Orthodox Church in all Russia, said:

"I never thought this moment would come."[4]

Simultaneously in Fatima and in Russia

On October 13, 1991, an amazing event took place simultaneously in Fatima and Russia. Archbishop Tadeusz Kondrusiewicz, Apostolic Administrator of Moscow, went to Fatima and preceded the statue of Our Lady from the chapel of the apparitions to the

Basilica through a handkerchief-waving crowd of hundreds of thousands *while the event was televised live, by satellite, to Russia.*

In Moscow a giant television screen had been set up for crowds to see Fatima in Russia for the first time. Persons from the crowd were invited, by the wonder of radio and TV, *to speak to a panel of experts at Fatima* including a Bishop who had once been hunted behind the Iron Curtain, the Rector of the Fatima Shrine, the Russian Orthodox writer Vladimir Zelinsky, and others, both Orthodox and Catholic.

It was the 74th anniversary of the miracle of Fatima, the miracle given so that "all might believe" that if the requests of Our Lady of Fatima were heard, *"Russia will be converted."* This happened just one year after the "conversion of Russia" *in the sense Our Lady of Fatima is thought to have used those words.*

Cardinal Tisserant, head of the Oriental Congregation, had said many years before that *we would know* that the "conversion of Russia," as Our Lady meant it, would have arrived when a law would be passed in Russia granting true religious liberty.[5]

That happened on October 1, 1990.

Greatest Day at Fatima

When I had met with Sister Lucia in 1946 I was surprised to learn how little was requested by Our Lady for the conversion of Russia: *the sacrifice demanded by fulfillment of our daily duties.* Our Lady indicated two simple gifts to aid us in this: The Rosary with its guiding mysteries, and the Scapular as a sign of consecration to Her Immaculate Heart.

Our Lady also asked for the First Saturday devotion so that once a month (through confession, Communion, Rosary and Rosary meditation) we would renew our purpose and make reparation to Her Immaculate Heart.

In the ensuing forty-five years (almost half a century!) I saw 25 million throughout the world respond by pledging to fulfill these conditions for the conversion of Russia and world peace.[6]

But year had followed year. And even though many responded, *the majority did not.* So when suddenly the Iron Curtain fell... it seemed to take not only the Patriarch of Moscow but the entire world by surprise.

Seemed Almost Impossible

Just six months before the Archbishop of Moscow came to Fatima to celebrate October 13, Pope John Paul II had come to Fatima to thank Our Lady for sparing his life ten years before. It is believed the KGB of Russia had masterminded the attempt to kill the Pope.

Hundreds of thousands came to Fatima to be with the Holy Father on this occasion when His Holiness presented to Our Lady the bullet which struck him but mysteriously diverted to avoid vital organs. (It was placed in Our Lady's crown.)

Six months later the crowd drawn to Fatima for the Mass celebrated by the Archbishop of Moscow *seemed as great as when the Pope was there.* Some say a million attended. Certainly there were hundreds of thousands.

It seemed as though the whole Portuguese Nation, which only a few years before was almost in the grip of Communism, seemed to sense that this event at Fatima, televised to Russia, was a sign of at least the beginning of Our Lady's triumph. Yes... but only the beginning.

The Final Words

On the day after Pope John Paul II made the Act of Consecration at Fatima on May 13, 1982, Lucia said:

"The Consecration will have its effect" but to obtain the era of peace *"the Blue Army* (i.e., the World Apostolate of Fatima) *will have much to do."* This startling statement was made in a triple context:

1) It was made at Fatima on May 14, 1982, when she was asked if the Consecration made by the Pope the previous day at Fatima fulfilled the necessary conditions for the conversion of Russia. (It did not. But Sister Lucia had spoken at length with the Holy Father who would fulfill all the conditions in 1984.)

2) Specifically she was asked if this meant that the *annihilation of several entire nations* threatened by Our Lady in 1917 *would now be averted.* And it was to this that she answered: Although the Consecration will have its effect, the Blue Army will have much to do.

3) The statement was made to a lawyer who was the President of the Blue Army in Brazil and a member of the International Council (which governs the Apostolate throughout the world). She was speaking, in a sense, specifically to the Blue Army.[7]

In this complete context it is apparent that *this statement is applicable to each one of us* whether specifically members of the World Apostolate of Fatima or not. Each of us still has MUCH TO DO... and as we have said previously, that "much" concerns especially the First Saturday reparation.

Example in Philippines

In 1987 a small group in Manila, which had felt the urgency of these words of Sister Lucia, wanted to make a special effort to get Blue Army pledges but ran into obstacles within the Blue Army.[8] Therefore, they printed hundreds of thousands of pledges under a different name (Two Hearts Apostolate). Within one year they obtained a million pledges.

Not being satisfied with this, they held an enormous rally in Manila (the Pope sent Cardinal O'Connor of New York as his personal legate) and they called upon all these new members to say an EXTRA Rosary each day "for a fellow Filipino who is a Communist."

Padre Pio had said "Russia will be converted when there is a Blue Army member for every Communist."[9] Could it be that those one million "Two Hearts" pledges in 1987 tipped the balance? *Almost immediately restoration of the churches began in Russia* (5,000 restored to worship in just the two years from 1988-1990).

In a book I wrote the following year (1989) I suggested that Our Lady accepted this vast commitment from the devout Philippine people to help save all the world.[10] Suffering at the hands of Communist guerrillas and from one almost overwhelming natural disaster after another, the people seemed to be saying: "Here I am Lord!"

Not the Name but the Commitment

The name is not important. The commitment is. The substance of the "Blue Army" is the *pledge* formulated with Sister Lucia in 1946: Morning Offering, Scapular, Rosary. The pledge made by the Associates of Akita is almost the same.

This is Our Lady's formula for conversion and holiness. She needs no more to lead us to the Sacraments. She needs no more that sufficient First Saturdays of reparation to save the world! As Bishop Venancio used to say:

"She needs so little to do so much!"

Now we see a similar response developing in Eastern Europe. Tomorrow it may be with you, reading these lines, suddenly *knowing* that despite obstacles within or without, you can make the difference.

The fact that Our Lady either willed or permitted these important words of Lucia to be addressed specifically to the Blue Army seems to impose a special obligation on its leaders. The crumbling of the Iron Curtain and the opening of 5,000 churches in Russia is a beginning. But before the final triumph of the Immaculate Heart of Mary, those words of Sister Lucia spoken at Fatima on May 14, 1982, must be heard over the world:

"The Consecration will have its effect... but the Blue Army will have much to do."

Back from the Brink

By reading Lucia's memoirs we have come to know the Fatima message more profoundly. We begin to see that *God in His Mercy has now decided to help man draw back from the brink* of what happened to Sodom. In another chapter we referred briefly to Fatima in the light of history, and especially of current history. But *all the history of man's relation to God highlights the apocalyptic events of Fatima.*

To Moses God revealed Himself in a burning bush. To the children of Fatima He revealed himself *in a Bleeding Host in the hands of an adoring angel and in light...* brighter and more wonderful than the light of a burning bush... *shining from the Immaculate Heart of Mary.*

On Sinai, God reminded mankind of the law He had written in men's hearts but which had become obscured by sin. On the mount of Fatima, *by a miracle unprecedented in all history,* He reaffirmed major truths taught by His Incarnate Word and by His Church.

It is no wonder John Paul II called Fatima "the Marian Capitol of the world." Perhaps even more it is the new Mount Carmel, where by a miracle of fire Elias showed that God is God and delivered His people from idolatry... or it is like Sinai for a world which had lost its sense of sin.

Now it not a Moses, an Elias, or a Jonah whom God sends, but the Woman who stood beneath the Cross, the new Eve. In His Mercy He had now entrusted the peace of the world *to a Mother* who comes to say that "men must stop offending God, already so much offended," while at the same time offering Her helping gifts of Scapular and Rosary... signs of affiliation and prayer and pleading for First Saturday Communions of reparation.

The Great Challenge

We have had a sufficient response to obtain changes in Russia. Will we now obtain a sufficient response for the triumph, for the *"era of peace for mankind?"*

Since the crumbling of the Iron Curtain it has become apparent that the Soviet Union was a conglomerate of diverse ethnic and religious groups. While 5,000 churches were reopened after 1988, so were 5,000 Mosques for Russia's millions of Muslims. *The era of peace promised at Fatima requires harmony among all these diverse groups,* not only in Russia but in the entire world. The very name "Fatima" gives a special aura to this promise.[11]

These are some of the reasons *to hope that the "final words" we quote from Sister Lucia may roll across the world like thunder.* The final triumph of the Heart of mankind's Mother requires that much, very much still be done. Even now it may be too late to avoid correction by fire if the world continues to refuse correction by Grace.

Either way, *the era of peace is promised.* And this peace will be that of which the angels sang over Bethlehem. It will be a glorious era in which men, finally recognizing the "formula of holiness" given by a loving Mother at Fatima, will come to live in an atmosphere of Grace instead of sin. It will be a triumph of the love of the Hearts of Jesus and Mary in each of us as it was in St. Joseph.

Blessed are those who, like the children of Fatima, look to their Heavenly Mother and say: *"Use me to-day"*... because yesterday is gone and tomorrow is not yet here.

††††

1. By "final words" of Lucia we do not mean that these are the last she has spoken or will speak. They are the final words we shall quote from her in this book.

2. New York Times, November 9, 1991, p. 2, col. 1.

3. Ibidem, quoted by Patriarch Aleksy II.

4. Ibidem.

5. Eugene Cardinal Tisserant was a member of the French Academy, Dean of the Sacred College of Cardinals (therefore second to the Pope in the hierarchy of the Church) and Prefect of the Oriental Congregation. His Eminence spoke 18 languages, including Russian and four other Eastern languages. He was knowledgeable about Fatima and even more especially about Russia. Because of his eminent position and access to facts unknown to many (such as the 1960 secret) I myself asked him what he thought Our Lady meant by "conversion of Russia" and *when we might know it had taken place.* It is interesting that when he gave this answer just four months before his death the Cardinal expressed the thought that due to the poor response of the world to the message of Fatima he did not think it would happen "without the world first suffering a great chastisement."

6. Within one year after the pledge was formulated with Lucia's help in 1946, by actual count over one million pledges were signed in the U.S. The Apostolate at first was known simply as the "March of Pledges" (instead of the march of an army). Shortly afterwards it came to be known as "the Blue Army" (reference to the blue of Our Lady). Later count, especially from nations outside the U.S., was not always reported. In a meeting of leaders

from all over the world at Fatima in 1972 it was determined that the total membership at that time had reached 25 million. Many more were added later but since there is no record of attrition, no larger figure has been subsequently quoted.

[7.] The lawyer in question is Dr. Jose Lucio de Araujo Correia of Sao Paolo, Brazil. He spoke with Lucia in the Carmel at Fatima the very day after her meeting with the Holy Father. At the same time Lucia conveyed to me personally the message that *no further petitions were needed* for the collegial Consecration. (She herself and her entire community had previously signed such a petition circulated by the Blue Army. The original, with her signature, is to be seen at the Blue Army Shrine in Washington, N.J., U.S.A.) After speaking with the Holy Father she was apparently satisfied that the Consecration would be completed in the manner required by Our Lord as indeed happened on March 25, 1984.

[8.] A self-perpetuating national president, who had begun the Blue Army many years before in one of the Provinces, refused to cooperate. When asked by the President of the Episcopal Conference to step down so that the committee in Manila could take over, she refused because she was afraid of city folk." Such problems are rarely black and white. Much prayer is needed for cooperation and unity in the Apostolate where Satan must be sending legions to sow suspicion and dissension.

[9.] Padre Pio made this statement in the presence of myself and Msgr. Colgan and six other priests of the Blue Army together with Cardinal Stitch of Chicago. See my book *Dear Bishop!*.

[10.] The title of the book is *The Meaning of Akita*, of which 100,000 copies were printed and distributed in the Philippines alone. The remark was inspired by the words of Our Lady at Akita that one reason She had so far been able to hold back a terrible chastisement was because of the response of a generous few.

[11.] See booklet *The Hand of Fatima* by John Haffert, 40 pages, AMI Press 1984. Archbishop Sheen expressed the opinion that Our Lady appeared at Fatima (the only town in all Europe to bear this name) because She came not only for the conversion of Russia but also of Islam. The name is that of the daughter of Mohammed and mother of all his descendants. The word "conversion" might be misleading because many Christians are more in need of real conversion than many Moslems. The immediate goal is for Islam and Christianity togetherness.

Appendix:

An Important Interview with Sister Lucia

On October 11, 1992, a Cardinal and Bishop from India, accompanied by a priest from brazil with a Portuguese layman as interpreter, asked Sister Lucia about the consecration of Russia, the 1960 secret, the memoirs, and other important matters. This interview is noteworthy not only because of the importance of the questions but because all four present confirmed the accuracy of the transcript, a complete copy of which may be obtained from Carlos Evaristo, P. O. Box 133, 2496 Fatima. Sister Lucia made at least 18 unequivocally clear statements:

1)   The collegial consecration made on March 25, 1992, in St. Peter's Square in Rome, was accepted by God and Our Lady.

2)   If some Bishops did not participate one cannot say that they committed a sin or a fault. What is of importance is the fact that the MAJORITY of Bishops participated.

3)   The Bishops were asked to make this consecration in union with the Pope each in his own diocese because it was intended to be a consecration made by the People of God.

4)   "Russia" did not have to be mentioned by name. The well known intention of the Pope and the Bishops was sufficient.

5)   No further consecration of Russia is needed, but "each Bishop can consecrate his own Diocese to

the Immaculate Heart of Mary." (Note: Renewal of such a consecration is mandated in the encyclical Ad Coeli Reginam to take place annually on the Feast of the Queenship of Mary, August 22.)

6)   The conversion of Russia has taken place. Sister Lucia explained:

7)   Our Lady never said Russia would be converted to Catholicism. "The fact is that in Russia the Communist, atheist power prevented the people from carrying out their faith. People now have an individual choice..."

8)   The 1960 Secret was intended "only for the Pope and the immediate Church hierarchy."

9)   Our Lady never said that the secret should be made public.

10)   The Pope can reveal the secret, but in Sister Lucia's opinion it would not be prudent for the Pope to do so.

11)   While repeatedly trying to evade the question Sister Lucia seemed to admit that Our Lady continues to appear to her.

12)   At Fatima Our Lady never mentioned Garabandal.

13)   Sister Lucia did type letters to her niece and other letters which some have said were forgeries. She answers all her own mail. Her mail is not intercepted or censored in any way. (She was obviously refuting the false allegation that she was in any way "silenced.")

14)   Asked which books on Fatima were best Sister Lucia said the Memoirs are the most authentic. She could not speak for the translations but she said "the Portuguese is accurate." (Note: The author of this book, who knows Portuguese, has accurately followed the original handwritten pages of Sr. Lucia.)

15)   Sr. Lucia's formal education went only as far as the fourth grade. It was suggested that therefore she must have been enlightened by the Holy Spirit when writing. She answered: "Yes, I believe so."

16)   Asked about a priest who had been insisting that the collegial consecration had not been made and that the Pope should reveal the 1960 secret Sister Lucia said that he should "humble himself to accept that the Consecration was made." and that if he changed "his apostolate could become a great means of spreading the message of Fatima."

17)   Hell is a reality. We should continue to speak of hell as Jesus did. People condemn themselves to hell.

18)   Asked what advice she would like to give today, Sister Lucia said: "Pray, pray, pray, and follow the Holy Father."

†††

*Above: John Haffert with Tatiana Goritcheva at
Peace Congress in Fatima, May 10-13, 1991,
75th anniversary of the apparitions.*

In 1948, two years after his first interview with Lucia,
Haffert wrote a book titled, Russia Will Be Converted.

Tatiana, member of the Soviet intelligentsia and once
head of the Komsomol in Leningrad (now St. Petersburg),
is author of an internationally known book on the religious
changes in Russia. She said that this promise, of which
Haffert wrote 44 years previously, is now being realized.

Even though persecution of religion has ceased in
Russia as promised by Our Lady of Fatima, Her message
appears to be ever more urgent in the light of dispersion of
nuclear weapons and unresloved regional conflicts.

"We have part of the promise," says Haffert. "Now let us
strive for the ultimate part: Our Lady's triumph with an era
of peace for mankind. *Fatima proves that what seems
impossible to man is possible to God."*

About The Author:

John Haffert was born in 1915, son of a newspaper publisher. Almost all his youth was spent in private school and seminary. At the age of 25, while teaching at a Carmelite minor seminary, he published his first book titled *Sign of Her Heart.*

Archbishop Fulton J. Sheen, who wrote the preface, called it "masterly." It set the tone of twenty books which followed, several of which have had printings of over 100,000.

In his second book titled *The Brother and I,* Mr. Haffert told the amazing story of a vision to a Carmelite lay brother in 1933, in which the Brother was instructed to entrust a message to Mr. Haffert to be made known to the whole world.

In 1946 in an interview with Sister Lucia, visionary of Fatima, Mr. Haffert was surprised to find that the message entrusted to him in 1933 was the message of Fatima contained in a "pledge" formulated in that meeting with Sister Lucia. He at once started a "March of Pledges." By 1948 hundreds of thousands of signatures had been obtained. On the inspiration of a pious pastor, Msgr. Harold Colgan, the apostolate was renamed "the Blue Army" and spread throughout the entire world. It is now known also as "The World Apostolate of Fatima."

For this worldwide apostolate the second Bishop of Fatima, the Most Rev. John Venancio became its elected President, on the condition that Mr. Haffert "Be at my right hand."

Lasting memorials to Mr. Haffert and Msgr. Colgan are the international center of the apostolate behind the Basilica at Fatima and a national U.S. Center with Shrine in Washington, N.J. Among Mr. Haffert's more important books, in addition to *Sign of Her Heart,* are a book on the Rosary titled *Sex and the Mysteries,* and one on the Eucharist: *The World's Greatest Secret.* Of the latter Padre Pio said: "It will have success during his lifetime, but especially after his death." It has already become a Catholic "best-seller."

At the request of the Bishop of Akita, Mr. Haffert translated the work of Father Yasuda on the *Tears and Messages of Our Lady of Akita* and wrote a small book titled *The Meaning of Akita.* Perhaps his most important work after *Sign of Her Heart* is *Her Own Words,* a commentary on the Memoirs of Sister Lucia.

It was out of the fullness of his knowledge of the events of Fatima and Akita that Mr. Haffert produced one of his most recent books: *To Prevent This!,* in which he suggests that the warning of Akita is similar to the third secret of Fatima and describes the response necessary now to prevent that "several entire nations will be annihilated" (words of Our Lady of Fatima).

John M. Haffert
(Picture taken in 1992)

Books by John M. Haffert:

Russia Will Be Converted
Mary In Her Scapular Promise (Sign of Her Heart)
Meet the Witnesses
From A Morning Prayer (The Brother and I)
The Peacemaker Who Went to War
A Letter from Lisieux
Queen's Promise
Night of Love
The World's Greatest Secret
Sex and the Mysteries
Explosion of the Supernatural
Dear Bishop!
Who is the Woman of the Apocalypse?
The Hand of Fatima
Go! Your Mother is Calling
The Meaning of Akita
Her Own Words
To Prevent This!
Finally Russia!
Her Glorious Title
You, Too.! Go Into the Vineyard

Book by Fr. Teiji Yasuda translated by Mr. Haffert:
Akita — The Tears and Message of Mary

Contact the 101 Foundation
for information about obtaining these books.

UNUS IN
SUI AMORE

JMJ

Fatima Prayer

By the infinite merits of the Sacred Heart of Jesus and the Immaculate Heart of Mary, I beg the conversion of poor sinners.

Like St. Joseph , I plunge my heart into the Flames of Their Love in the mysteries of the Rosary and wearing the Scapular, constant sign of my consecration.

Come Creator Spirit! Make me one in Their Love so that every act of my day, every beat of my heart, may hasten the coming of God's Kingdom in the world.

I shall renew this prayer, especially on the first Friday and Saturday in a Communion of reparation, for my own sins and the sins of all mankind. Amen.